Cult Film as a Guide to Life

CULT FILM AS A GUIDE TO LIFE

Fandom, Adaptation and Identity

I.Q. Hunter

Bloomsbury Academic
An imprint of Bloomsbury Publishing Inc

B L O O M S B U R Y
NEW YORK · LONDON · OXFORD · NEW DELHI · SYDNEY

Bloomsbury Academic

An imprint of Bloomsbury Publishing Inc

1385 Broadway	50 Bedford Square
New York	London
NY 10018	WC1B 3DP
USA	UK

www.bloomsbury.com

BLOOMSBURY and the Diana logo are trademarks of Bloomsbury Publishing Plc

First published 2016

© I.Q. Hunter, 2016

Library of Congress Cataloging-in-Publication Data
Names: Hunter, I. Q., 1964- author.
Title: Cult film as a guide to life: fandom, adaptation and identity/I.Q.Hunter.
Description: New York: Bloomsbury Academic, 2016. | Includes index.
Identifiers: LCCN 2016005634 (print) | LCCN 2016009446 (ebook) |
ISBN9781623568979 (hardback) | ISBN 9781623565022 (ePDF) |
ISBN 9781623563813 (ePub) Subjects: LCSH: Cult films--History and criticism. | Motion
pictures--Social aspects. | Cults. | BISAC: PERFORMING ARTS / Film & Video / History
& Criticism. Classification: LCC PN1995.9.C84 H86 2016 (print) | LCC PN1995.9.C84
(ebook) | DDC 791.43/653--dc23 LC record available at http://lccn.loc.gov/2016005634

ISBN: HB: 978-1-6235-6897-9
PB: 978-1-6235-6510-7
ePDF: 978-1-6235-6502-2
ePub: 978-1-6235-6381-3

Cover design by rawshock design
Cover image: Scene from 'Polyester' (1981)© NEW LINE /THE KOBAL COLLECTION

Typeset by Deanta Global Publishing Services, Chennai, India
Printed and bound in the United States of America

For my sons, Tom and Will

CONTENTS

ILLUSTRATIONS

PREFACE

Ask for my life story and you'll get a list of films.

Cinephilia began for me around lunchtime on Boxing Day 1975 when I was eleven and Steven Spielberg's *Jaws* opened across England. We – my father, a school friend and I – were in the front circle of the ABC cinema in Plymouth. In the 1970s, so far as I recall, there wasn't much for kids to look forward to at the pictures, aside from the Roger Moore Bonds and the odd second-rate Disney. The biggest new films like *The Exorcist* (1973) and *The Godfather Part II* (1974) were typically 'X'-rated and out of bounds to us under eighteens, and the only 'A'-rated ones that aroused serious enthusiasm were disaster movies like *The Poseidon Adventure* (1972), *The Towering Inferno* (1974) and *Earthquake* (1974). *Jaws*, though also a species of disaster film, was thrillingly unprecedented, a massive hit not only 'A'-rated but with proper grown-up scares and gore.

Back then it could take months for films to cross the Atlantic. *Jaws* had been released in the United States on the 20th of June, and during the summer-long build-up of shark-fever, I bought all the poster magazines and cut-out reports in *The Daily Mirror* about its blockbusting success. Finally, after hours of excited queuing outside the ABC, I saw Ben Gardner's wormy head lurch out of a hole in his boat, and as we recoiled in our seats with shock and delight my little world changed forever.

Before long I had dragged the rest of my family to the ABC and was developing into a *Jaws*-crazy pest. On holiday during the legendary hot summer of 1976, I hustled my father off the beach for a matinee at some second-tier picture house in Charmouth, arriving halfway through as the *Orca* set out to sea. Then, once *Jaws* disappeared from even third-run cinemas, I trotted off to see *King Kong* (1976), '*Jaws*ploitation' rip-offs such as *Grizzly* (1976), *Tentacles* (1977), *The Swarm* (1978) and, of course, *Jaws 2* (1978), and eagerly read their paperback novelizations in an effort to relive my first encounter with a picture that really mattered to me. *The Swarm*, I pompously announced to my long-suffering father, was definitely worth ***1/2, for by then Maltin's and Scheuer's film guides, with their reliably middlebrow star ratings, had replaced *Film Review* as my gateway to the film canon.

Jaws would become a lifelong obsession and, though I didn't know the concept at the time, a *cult*. Blockbusters like *Jaws* are not usually classed as cult films, which tend to be obscure, overlooked and quirky movies with a passionate and sometimes contrarian fan base. But no other word than 'cult' will do for my personal investment in *Jaws*, which quickly advanced to collecting – or rather the

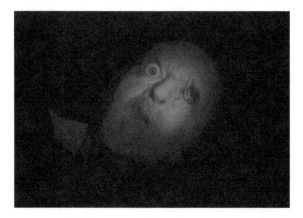

Figure 1 Ben Gardner shakes my world.

disorganized accumulation of – *Jaws* jigsaws, soundtrack LPs, 'Making of' books like *The* Jaws *Log*, and licensed spin-offs like the 'Game of *Jaws*' where you had to pluck wheels, fish bones and similar junk out of a plastic shark's maw before elastic bands snapped it shut. Forty years on, I am still hooked on all things *Jaws*, even if that obliges me to suffer through *Mega Piranha* (2010) on SyFy with its weightless CGI sharks and D-list cast of 1980s pop stars. In 2012 I rushed to the multiplex for *Jaws*'s digital rerelease and pre-ordered the lush Blu-Ray Steelbook, at last count my seventh copy of the film across various formats. A pilgrimage to the Martha's Vineyard locations is only a matter of time.

I'm still not entirely sure *why* the film swallowed me whole. Fascination with *Jaws* possibly had unconscious aspects that my eleven-year-old self, so jung and easily freudened, could not comprehend. Maybe there was an erotic component, precociously stirred by skinny-dipping Chrissie Watkins, the huge phallic shark-cum-vagina dentata, and the rest of the film's dollar book Freud. But that had more to do, I think, with encountering the sex scene in Peter Benchley's novel between Ellen Brody and Matt Hooper, whose eyes bulged memorably (as mine did when I read it) while he pumped towards orgasm on well-thumbed page 161. It was probably the first sex scene I had ever read, having sneaked the forbidden novel home from the local library and gulped it down in secret and in one sitting.[1] Larger, ideological messages in the film may have gently introduced me to life beyond adolescence. What better film than *Jaws* to instil, early in absorbent youth, the lesson that ordinary men have a duty to overcome their phobias and confront threats to family and community? At any rate, my obsession with *Jaws*, which at first seemed so random and personal, was evidently shared by countless other pleasurably traumatized youngsters, and *Jaws* swam deep into the collective unconscious of my generation. Spielberg's grip tightened further on our imaginations with *Close Encounters of the Third Kind* (1977), which I saw, on my own this time, in the cavernous Odeon on Plymouth's Union Street. These films, and then of course *Star Wars* (1977), were cultural watersheds for those of us at the tail end of the Baby Boom, as Spielberg and George Lucas achieved what you might call generational capture through exciting family-friendly summer blockbusters.

So that's how I became a cultist, albeit a cultist of a film that was not exactly cult. My love of *Jaws* remains – and this isn't too strong – part of who I am, my celluloid Rosebud or madeleine. *Jaws* was an education in film, an inspiration to teach and write about cinema (and to run a fortieth anniversary symposium in June 2015), and, with the passing of time, an object of complex nostalgia for a happy childhood, for the 1970s, and for film as a social experience in cinemas that had balconies, single screens, Pearl & Dean advertising, and designated no smoking areas on the right-hand side of the auditorium.

The year 1975 – August the 14th to be precise – was also when *The Rocky Horror Picture Show* was released and slowly became the key film of the 'midnight movie' cycle. Outrageous movies like *Rocky Horror*, with its sweet transvestites, raucous sex, and camp violence, are what we usually think of as cult films. *Jaws* and *Star Wars* were in many ways everything their cult was pitted against – mass entertainment for kids, great white heroes (Brody (Roy Scheider) was a police chief after all, the embodiment of the Man) and reassuring happy endings at least till the sequels came around. Cult meant oddball films watched by oddballs at ungodly hours in dingy cinemas; it meant, in England, enthusing about obscure films noirs at the National Film Theatre on London's Southbank and haring off to see a John Waters triple bill under club conditions at the Scala in King's Cross. As a teenager stuck in a provincial extremity of Britain, I could unfortunately do none of these things.

Then video came along and cult changed for good. For me, as a film-struck student in the 1980s, exploring the cult canon beyond *Jaws* – those films often poorly rated in Maltin and Scheuer or left out altogether – became a possibility for the first time. Thanks to books like Danny Peary's *Cult Movies*, I now had a checklist of films to catch not only at rep cinemas, but also, miraculously, on VHS, and later still in bespoke cult film seasons on TV, such as the BBC's *Moviedrome* hosted by Alex Cox. Cult fandom required commitment and effort in censor-plagued England, for as well as habituating midnight screenings it now involved tracking down bootleg videos of *A Clockwork Orange* (1971), *The Texas Chain Saw Massacre* (1974) and *The New York Ripper* (1982). The early 1980s was, of course, the period of the 'video nasties' panic in the UK which turned so many of us into amateur experts on Nazisploitation, Italian zombie films and whatever else the British Board of Film Censors (BBFC) was busy snatching from the local video store shelf. Watching frantically accumulated tapes underpinned a new kind of cult lifestyle centred, in my case, on rare and banned movies obtained under the counter or ordered from the back pages of the horror magazine *Samhain*. There were still cinema clubs, such as the Scala and, my own haunt, the Penultimate Picture Palace off the Cowley Road in Oxford, where I saw *Rocky Horror*, double and triple bills of art-house classics like *Last Tango in Paris* (1972) and *In the Realm of the Senses* (1976), midnight movies like *Pink Flamingos* (1972), and second-wave cult films like *Blade Runner* (1982), *Liquid Sky* (1983), and Cox's own *Repo Man* (1984). But cult film as a way of life became more about domestic consumption on VHS, and, as my cultism took hold, piles of videos rose around me like tiles in a hypocaust.

And now, thirty years after the video revolution, I find that cult is everywhere. It's a brand, a label, a category on Netflix. I've a four disc set of exploitation films from the 1920s to 1950s that the DVD box claims to be cult movies, but strictly they're not. Titles like *Slaves in Bondage* (1937) and *Delinquent Daughters* (1944) are simply the kind of thing that today's cult 'paracinemaniacs' might be tempted to buy from amazon.com – obscure, trashy, and requiring a certain sensibility and, frankly, an effort to sit through and appreciate. They are as far removed from the entertainment values of the multiplex as the vanished world of the subsidized avant-garde. In fact, no one is quite sure what cult means any more. Cult movies undoubtedly still exist, from Hollywood misfires like *The Big Lebowski* (1998) and *Fight Club* (1999) to incompetent mind-warping oddities like *The Room* (2003), but no real aura of exclusivity clings to them, however expensively they are repackaged on Blu-Ray (in a bowling ball shaped box, in *Lebowski*'s case). It is true that cult as immersive social event has revived at festivals such as Lebowski Fest, where fans of The Dude celebrate the slacker life with White Russians and bowling tournaments, and at Secret Cinema screenings, where you can experience *Alien* (1979) in a creepy warehouse and *Back to the Future* (1985) in a recreation of 1950s Hill Valley. But for cultists pining for the lost authenticity of midnight at the Elgin and the Scala, that requires a recalibration of what counts as a cult movie. *The Big Lebowski* and *Fight Club* are cultish enough in their respectively dishevelled and brutal ways, and *The Room* slots into a tradition of cult enthusiasm for amateurish bad movies, but genre hits like *Alien* and amiable, unadventurous Hollywood products like *Back to Future* were no more seen as potentially cult on first release than *Jaws* was when I first saw it at the ABC. Cultists have traditionally been written up as a harder core contingent than mere fans, travellers rather than tourists, whose arcane interests differ from fans' typical investment in the popular, accessible and mainstream. This distinction is increasingly hard to make. Cult is now as much about Gen X nostalgia for mainstream films seen on video in childhood, such as *The Goonies* (1985), *Labyrinth* (1986), and *Ferris Bueller's Day Off* (1987), as it is about rummaging through the dustbins of cinema for trash like *Slaves in Bondage* and searching for intense transformative experiences shared with only a select few devotees. TV series such as *Doctor Who* (since 1963, on and off), *Breaking Bad* (2008–13) and *Game of Thrones* (since 2011) are no less cultish and adored, their fans tracking rumours and trivia online, and celebrating episode premieres, overnight DVD binges and just-one-more-episode blowouts on the SkyBox with rapturous tweets and hashtags. Cult, in short, has merged with popular media fandom.

To some extent, then, cult is a historical category, with a prehistory in the 1920s, stirrings in the 1950s, a Golden Age in the 1970s and a long withdrawing reorientation towards new practices of fandom and new definitions of cult films. Even as cult rarities like 1970s martial arts flicks and 42nd Street grindhouse porn are gussied up for Blu-Ray release and available at 'one click', the collecting fetishism satisfied by video and DVD is giving way to online streaming. Blogs, tweets, Instagram and chatrooms are the new rep theatres. Cult is no longer the province of countercultural Baby Boomers and Reagan-era videohounds but of wider 'communities', much more female and otherwise culturally diverse (cult with its obsession with lists, collecting, esoteric information, taboo-breaking and obscurity always smacked of stereotypical masculinity – white men in black T-shirts obsessing about horror and sex films and the minutiae of censor cuts). Indeed a good deal of writing in my own manor, academia, is increasingly driven by fan interests, for what better ambition could there be for a cultist than to make a career out of what you love?

*

Cult Film as a Guide to Life explores cult as a phenomenon and as lived experience. This is a highly personal, even autobiographical book, not only because it loosely bundles together, along with new material, some of the pieces on cult I've published over the last fifteen years or so, but because it reflects my abiding obsessions (*Jaws*, *Showgirls*, Kubrick, sleaze of all kinds) and is unapologetically grounded in private pleasure. As Maude says in *Harold and Maude* (1971), 'It's all memorabilia, but incidental and not integral, if you know what I mean.'

Chapter 1 is a beginner's guide to the history of cult film, taking in some of the key movies such as *Casablanca* (1942), *Rocky Horror* and *Mean Girls* (2004) on a brisk tour of the basic themes of the newish field of 'cult studies'. It is followed by the first piece I ever published on cult, a defence of Paul Verhoeven's lap dance epic *Showgirls* (1995). I initially served this up to a small, unimpressed audience at a conference in 1997, when *Showgirls* was still a byword for a bad film, indeed regarded as *the* supremely bad film of contemporary Hollywood. My argument that it was nothing of the kind was thought eccentric and even sinister. In the piece I took issue not only with *Showgirls*'s critical reception but with its first and most visible cultists, who, mostly gay, celebrated it as a camp disaster. My defence of the film was met as a tiresome *de*-queering of its cult status as well as an unseemly encomium to political incorrectness and my own poor taste. 'Beaver Las Vegas!' (Chapter 2) is published here unchanged as a time capsule of laddish film criticism, with an afterword – cagey but not especially shamefaced – explaining how its programme for cult-influenced academic film writing underscores what follows.

Chapter 3 explores how film interpretation edges into cultish over-interpretation and conspiratorial craziness. Latching on to Stanley Kubrick's

The Shining (1980) and *Eyes Wide Shut* (1999), the chapter raises questions such as: How do you conceptualize engagements with films that are private and idiosyncratic rather than socially orientated or politically engaged? What are the uses of film beyond making sense of them correctly? And how can you both appropriate a film for your own purposes and yet be sufficiently open to and respectful towards it that it might renovate your sense of the world and yourself? The chapter, taking its cue from Ernest Mathijs, rethinks cult and cult interpretation as strategic and pleasurable means of wasting time.

Chapter 4 looks at the relationship between cult and adaptation. In part this involves examining how far the 'cultness' of a cult book can be preserved in the transfer to film, which may or may not itself turn out to be cult. Cult books make up an unstable grouping consisting of youth favourites (*The Catcher in the Rye*), Beat novels (*Naked Lunch*, *On the Road*), and underground classics (*Against Nature*), and while they have been occasionally adapted, only a handful (*The Princess Bride* (1987), *Naked Lunch* (1991), *Trainspotting* (1996)) have entered the cult film canon. Cult film and adaptation may seem awkward bedfellows but not if we attend to the question of emotional investment.

Adaptation studies has recently turned its attention to spin-offs, both commercial and fan-produced. One example is the exploitation film, which Chapter 5 discusses in relation to the '*Jaws*ploitation' movie. Here I argue that adaptation can be fruitfully conceptualized as a form of exploitation, and showcase my indulgence and passion for obscure rip-offs of Spielberg's master-text from *Grizzly* to *Sharknado 2: The Second One* (2014). The subsequent chapters, 6 and 7, explore erotic adaptations, in other words, sex films that parody and imitate mainstream hits and take liberties with their sexual subtexts and possibilities. Chapter 6 charts and describes attempts by British cinema in the 1970s to imitate and compete with continental European erotic films, either by producing home-grown takes on the softcore glossiness of *Emmanuelle* (1974); or by adapting classic erotic literature such as *Justine*, *Lady Chatterley's Lover* and *Fanny Hill*; or, in a twist on British cinema's expertise in heritage adaptations, by concocting bawdy exploitation versions of canonical eighteenth-century novels such as *Pamela*, *Tom Jones* and *Joseph Andrews*. Chapter 7 turns to contemporary softcore parodies and rip-offs of Peter Jackson's *The Lord of the Rings* trilogy (2001–3), which adapt blockbuster fantasy into cult trash with some parallels with 'slash fiction' (erotic fan fiction that often queers mainstream texts). The chapter concludes with a discussion of *This Ain't Jaws XXX* (2012), a hardcore pornographic 'adaptation' of *Jaws*, and tries to unpick the resistance of the seemingly boring and anti-aesthetic genre of pornography to interpretation and evaluation.

The book ends by looking at the intersection of real life and cult films. Chapter 8 considers the parallel adaptations of *2001: A Space Odyssey* (1968) – Kubrick's film and Arthur C. Clarke's novelization – and investigates further how adaptation might overlap with cinephilia. Chapter 9, the final chapter – which, like Lebowski's rug, really ties the book together (or attempts to) – directly addresses the promised theme of cult film as a guide to life. By this I mean the utility of cult film as therapy, self-medication, means of private escape and pragmatic material for furnishing a meaningful existence. With reference to fan-favourites like *Bloodsucking Freaks* (1976) and *The Shawshank Redemption* (1994), I explore how cult films offer opportunities for self-realization through private cinephile connoisseurship.

Cult films may not always be good films; they may not always be films that are good for you. But if you give yourself up to the absolute pleasure of cult movies, they may just save your life.

Acknowledgement is due to many friends, colleagues and students who have supported the book through its ludicrously extended gestation. I especially thank Katie Gallof, the most sensitive and patient of editors, and those who provided invaluable feedback on some chapters: Nathan Abrams, Kate Egan, Ernest Mathijs, Laura Mee, Jamie Sexton, Justin Smith and Ellen Wright. The book's mistakes and errors of judgement are, of course, entirely my own fault.

Cult Film as a Guide to Life is dedicated to my sons, Tom and Will, and to the memory of John Hunter, my much missed late father, who started it all by taking me to see *Jaws*. I would not have finished the book without the love and encouragement of Elaine Hunter, who, basically, put up with me while I wrote it.

Four chapters have been previously published. Chapter 2, 'Beaver Las Vegas!: A Fan-boy's Defence of *Showgirls*', is from *Unruly Pleasures: The Cult Film and Its Critics*, ed. Xavier Mendik and Graeme Harper (Guildford: FAB Press, 2000). Reprinted with permission. Chapter 5, 'Exploitation as Adaptation', is from *Scope: An Online Journal of Film & TV Studies*, 15 (November 2009) and eBook *Cultural Borrowings: Appropriation, Reworking, Transformation*, ed. Iain Robert Smith. *Copyright © 2009 Iain Robert Smith and Scope. Reprinted with permission.* Chapter 7, 'Tolkien Dirty', is from *Lord of the Rings: Popular Culture in Global Context*, ed. Ernest Mathijs (London and New York: Wallflower Press, 2006). Copyright © 2006 Ernest Mathijs. Reprinted with permission of Columbia University Press. Chapter 8, 'From Adaptation to Cinephilia: An Intertextual Odyssey', is from *Science Fiction Across Media: Science Fiction Across Media: Adaptation/Novelization*, ed. Thomas Van Parys and I. Q. Hunter (Canterbury: Glyphi, 2013).

With the exception of 'Beaver Las Vegas' the versions presented in this book have been revised, updated and extended. To avoid undue repetition and self-plagiarism, some material has been cut or transposed between chapters.

Chapter 1

For Virgins Only: A Brief Introduction to Cult Film

> I would like, if I may, to take you on a strange journey.
>
> *The Rocky Horror Picture Show*

In the 1980s, to see Kubrick's *A Clockwork Orange*, which he had withdrawn from British distribution, I had to make do with a bootleg video picked up in a market. To see Pasolini's emetic masterpiece *Salò, or The 120 Days of Sodom* (1975) in a print unmolested by the BBFC required a trip to Paris, where it was screened once a week at midnight in a cinema opposite the Pompidou Centre. I now have both movies uncut on Blu-Ray and over the last couple of months have purchased online or streamed from YouTube many randomly discovered cult films I never thought I'd see without some effort or expenditure – *The Beast of Yucca Flats* (1961), *Deported Women of the SS Special Section* (1976), *Andy Warhol's Bad* (1977). As for reading material, Peary's *Cult Movies* trilogy, *The Psychotronic Encyclopedia of Film*, *Incredibly Strange Films* and other staples of cultists' shelves in the VHS era are now supplemented by a bewildering plethora of *Rough Guides*, websites and listicles about cult film.[1] There are, for random example, no less than two full-length books on John Carpenter's anti-Reaganite retread of *Invasion of the Body Snatchers* (1956), *They Live* (1988).[2] Cult studies has meanwhile become a well-trodden, academically respectable field, with textbooks, undergraduate modules and numerous PhDs on the most esoteric cult-related topics.[3] Instead of scarcity, which seems the natural state of cult, there is glut. This is truly, you might think, springtime for cultists.

In spite of such consumer plenty and the predictably extensive Wikipedia entry on cult film, it is nevertheless worth my returning to and expanding on the themes of the Preface in order to introduce the topic in more detail for the benefit of any cult 'virgins' out there (as *Rocky Horror* fans call newbies experiencing the film for the first time). There will be some slippage between a history of cult movies and a précis of academic writing on what is variously defined as a 'genre', mode or discursive category (though of course academics, like professional critics, can also be cultists and increasingly the two identities are irreversibly spliced like the BrundleFly in Cronenberg's *The Fly* (1986)).

Although this chapter will focus on cult *films*, bear in mind that it may not be the film itself that is the centre of the cult. There are numerous cult directors such as Oscar Micheaux, Sam Fuller, Dorothy Arzner, Ida Lupino, Ed Wood Jr., Doris Wishman, Russ Meyer, Werner Herzog, David Lynch, Lucio Fulci, Stanley Kubrick, Tim Burton, Guy Maddin and the 'Pope of Trash', John Waters. In the auteurist perspective of much cult, they are often mysterious like Kubrick, tortured and visionary like talentless 'Badfilm' maestro Wood and British horror director, Michael Reeves, or outright bug-eyed crazy, like Fernando Arrabal, the Spanish surrealist director, who is interviewed on a DVD extra for *Viva La Muerte* (1971) winsomely peeking out from behind a chair he's holding up in front of his face. There are also cult stars, starlets and character actors (Bruce Lee, Divine, Harry Dean Stanton, Dorothy Stratten, Judy Garland, Claudia Jennings, Dick Miller, Bruce Campbell), and cult performances, riveting in their charismatic strangeness, excess and tantalizing overlap with the actor's off-screen persona (Crispin Glover, for example, who, in life as well as in *Back to the Future* and *Willard* (2003), seems as mad as a box of frogs). Stars' cult may be distinct from the films to which they contributed, and linked, for example, to their continuing potency as cultural symbols after death. As Mikita Brottman says, 'The deaths of Montgomery Clift, James Dean, Marilyn Monroe, Judy Garland, Bruce and Brandon Lee ... were far more significant, culturally and ideologically, than the films they made.'[4] Then again there are cult soundtracks (*Vampyros Lesbos* (1971), *The Wicker Man* (1973)), cult studios (Hammer, Amicus), and a fair few cult special effects maestros (Tom Savini, Rick Baker) and stop-motion animators (Ray Harryhausen, Phil Tippett).

But for now, to keep things manageable, we'll stick to just the films.

What is – or was – a Cult Film?

To start with the simplest definition: *a cult film is a film with a devoted following or subcultural community of admirers.*

The word 'is' should be regarded with caution in that sentence, given the hazy status of 'cult film' these days. It is, was, usually (but certainly not always) a film without broad audience appeal, such as a rediscovered classic; a 'midnight movie'; or a marginal, trashy, bad or exploitation film. Typically, a cult film is 'transgressive' – a word that will come up a lot in this book – in matters of representation, taste or technical competence. Cult films are frequently associated with genres such as exploitation, crime, science fiction, anime (Japanese cartoons) and horror that are acquired tastes and seem in some way oppositional, though there are also numerous art movies (*Persona* (1966)), documentaries (*Grey Gardens* (1975)), underground films (*Chelsea Girls* (1966)), musicals (*The Wizard of Oz*), and Westerns (*Johnny Guitar* (1954), *The Searchers* (1956), even, God help us, *Heaven's Gate* (1980)) that make the final cut. Such films are generally either mainstream ones revived years later by dedicated fans in a spirit of nostalgia or revisionism, or commercially unsuccessful films appropriated soon after release by an enthusiastic and usually subcultural audience (countercultural, gay, punk (*The Great Rock 'n' Roll Swindle* (1980)), pagan (*The Wicker Man*), Mod (*Quadrophenia* (1979)). Having discovered that the films speak to them, cultists celebrate either privately through repeated viewings or socially by, for example, dressing up at screenings. Cult films, which may have crashed at the box office, typically find an audience by word of mouth or on video and DVD or online. *Harold and Maude, Blade Runner* and *Streets of Fire* (1984), for instance, were commercial and critical failures on first release and only later became 'cult classics', eventually repackaged as such on video and DVD, classed as cult on Netflix, or rereleased to cinemas on the basis of their acquired cult reputation. In other words, films become rather than are born cult. As John Waters once said, nobody *wants* to direct a cult film because that invariably means birthing a failure. Cult films are adopted orphans and what defines them is the intensity of their fandom 'beyond all reason', as J. P. Telotte, quoting Andrew Sarris, put it in one of the first academic collections on the phenomenon.[5]

Cult films are not defined by their textual qualities so much as by wider criteria such as those outlined below in a representative online guide to cult in *Bright Lights Film Journal*, which lists the distinguishing marks of this 'super class' of movie.[6] Like any genre or retrospectively defined class of film, such as film noir or the 'mindfuck' puzzle movie (*The Sixth Sense* (1999), *Inception* (2010)), the cult film is a discursive formation, in other words, a term of art constructed by rough agreement by audiences, distributors, critics and so on as it circulates through culture[7]:

1. Marginality   Content falls outside general cultural norms
2. Suppression   Subject to censor, ridicule, lawsuit, or exclusion
3. Economics   Box office flop upon release but eventually profitable
4. Transgression   Content breaks social, moral, or legal rules
5. Cult following   Generates devoted minority audience
6. Community   Audience is or becomes self-identified group
7. Quotation   Lines of dialog become common language
8. Iconography   Establishes or revives cult icon.[8]

That is a pretty fair summary of how 'cult film' is currently understood and mobilized in talk about movies. You'll notice that the content of a cult film is left vague beyond its being somehow transgressive or outside the mainstream, though even that is questionable if we invite *The Princess Bride* and *Dirty Dancing* through the portals of cultdom. The tension between 'cult film' implying, on the one hand, a certain *kind* of film (offbeat, under the radar, and possibly offensive) which is loved by a self-selecting audience of outsiders and, on the other, *any* film which has acquired and sustained a fan following well beyond its initial release is an issue we'll return to throughout the book.

The prehistory of cult can be traced back to the early days of cinema and, for example, the cult of Rudolph Valentino, and the Surrealists' delight in *photogenie* and sexual subtexts that made *King Kong* (1933) such a favourite of theirs.[9] Ernest Mathijs and Jamie Sexton point to the tradition of cinephile criticism, such as MacMahonism in France, named after the Le MacMahon theatre in Paris, which lauded maverick B-movies and directors through its magazine *Présence du Cinema*, and the ongoing tradition of cult criticism or at any rate cultish approaches to watching films.[10] Cult is related to cinephilia more generally, which is a personal love of cinema itself rather than a specific film or kind of film, and typically fixes on what Paul Willemen described as 'the cinephiliac moment': 'the fetishizing of fragments of a film, either individual shots or marginal (often unintentional) details in the image, especially those that appear only for a moment'.[11] Cult films might well be defined as those films that allow for the maximum number of cinephiliac moments. For the cinephile, the cinema is a holy place with unique emotional and physical satisfactions. While this often implies a distinctly elite, intellectualized attitude to watching movies, it shares with cult an obsessive belief in cinema and its powers of transformation. Sexton has explored the little discussed early uses of cult and associated terms in film culture, and shows that cult originally had a largely negative meaning, implying an irrational attachment to the worthless products of the cultural machine, and only acquired its current more positive use from the 1960s.[12] You could certainly argue that film criticism has always involved a degree of cultism, in the sense of ornery cinephile attachments to the culturally devalued. *Auteur* critics such as Andrew Sarris (who collected his reviews in *Confessions of a Cultist*) were cultists by any definition, with their 'bromantic' devotion to directors like Fuller and Orson Welles and championing of what Manny Farber called 'termite art' against the mainstream.[13] Parker Tyler, who wrote about Orson Welles 'as big cult hero', helped divert cinephile criticism into a new and camp tradition.[14] Even *Cahiers du Cinéma*'s 'category E', denoting films that only seemed under the sway of the dominant ideology but whose contradictions split apart under the pressure of appropriately applied analysis, was arguably a cult category. It legitimized an elite audience of insiders reading films like John Ford's *Young Mr Lincoln* (1939) and directors like Douglas Sirk in satisfyingly special and bizarre ways inaccessible to his films' intended mass audience or indeed to virtually anyone else. Cult requires a sense of difference from this imagined Other of clueless consumers of mainstream Hollywood. The development of cinephile enthusiasm for film involved the strenuous recuperation of popular genre cinema, on the assumption not only that it was a serious art form in need of boosting by committed intellectual effort but also that mass audiences were dupes oblivious to its ideological machinations. This kind of cult criticism goes back to the 1940s and what Greg Taylor calls vanguard elite film criticism in the United States, which reacted against whose 'hope for cultural restoration lies in the artistic critic's freelance aestheticizing of everyday life'.[15] As Taylor says, 'Cult criticism places a high value on connoisseurship; it glorifies the critic-spectator's heightened ability to select appropriately and tastefully'.[16] This 'art of seized spectatorship' (148) has since colonized highbrow academic writing on film, with artistic appreciation and the autonomy of the artist downgraded in place of 'the relocation of the site of aesthetic production to the mind of the critical spectator' (150), on the one hand, by judging films by their suitability for illustrating esoteric theories within a progressive framework and, on the other, by focusing on 'microlevel resistance to perceived high and middlebrow hegemony' in fan studies and other displays of popular empowerment (153). There continues an important interrelation between cult recuperation of films and their critical revival, with the cult of films like *2001: A Space Odyssey* (1968) and *Blade Runner* reinforced by the critical work devoted to them and their utility in theorizing and teaching. In the case of *Blade Runner* its status as a paradigmatic 'postmodern' film established it, like *Blue Velvet* (1986), as a staple of university modules on and textbook primers to postmodernism back in the 1990s.

Casablanca

The phenomenon of cult film as we now understand it is generally reckoned to have begun in the 1950s and to have matured, as it were, in the 1960s along with concepts such as camp. Its arrival is firmly linked to the midnight movie phenomenon of the 1970s and to the evolving tastes of Baby Boomers, the bulge in the American population that occurred from 1946 to 1964 and transformed popular culture.

Casablanca (1942) is generally cited as one of the first Boomer cult films, watched repeatedly by audiences who knew it off by heart and recited lines along with the actors. Telotte classes it as a 'classical cult film', by which he means a Hollywood film from the 'Golden Age' of the 1930s to 1950s that is rediscovered and adored by a new audience, often a specific one (gay 'friends of Dorothy' who revered *The Wizard of Oz*) or one smitten by camp quirkiness (Sternberg's lavishly bizarre *The Scarlet Empress* (1934), Huston's offbeat spoof *Beat the Devil* (1953)).[17]

Casablanca was, of course, a very successful product of conventional Hollywood filmmaking, which won Oscars for Best Film, screenplay and direction. Released in November 1942 to coincide with an Allied landing and summit conference in Casablanca, it was made as propaganda for United States' participation in the war, so that Rick's shift from cynical neutrality and isolationism to committed action could be read as a stirring allegory of the United States'. *Casablanca* was rediscovered as a cult film in the late 1950s, by which time its original reception context has passed into history and it had become an object of nostalgia. Bogart's Rick seemed to anticipate the modern ironist existential heroes that would populate French New Wave movies like Godard's *Breathless* (1960). According to Danny Peary:

> The *Casablanca* – Humphrey Bogart cult really took root in the early sixties in Cambridge, Massachusetts, when the Brattle Theatre started

running the picture three weeks a year, year after year. It was there ... that Bogart addicts came back repeatedly and joined their idol as he spoke ... classic lines.[18]

Casablanca first played at the Brattle, an art cinema across from Harvard University, on 21 April 1957, was held over for a second week and then became the final film in the cinema's subsequent Bogart festivals; the cult inspired a Casablanca Club instituted in the theatre's basement.[19] In classical cult films like *Casablanca*, *The Wizard of Oz* and *The Big Sleep* (1946) the audience, Telotte writes, is 'united by a certain fondness for the conventions and appeals of classical narrative, and by an almost worshipful ... attitude towards particular figures from Hollywood's so-called "golden age" '.[20] The cult experience of a classical cult film like *Casablanca* is one of release from the unsatisfactory realities of today because it projects 'appealing images that speak to the contradictions in our present lives'.[21] Hence some of the reasons for *Casablanca*'s cult appeal as time went by are: nostalgia for the certainties of the 1940s; awed reverence for Bogart's iconic masculinity and imperturbable cool; and delight in the film's endless quotability, which allows you not only to start beautiful friendships by swapping lines with other fans but also to adapt them for deployment in real life. In *Play It Again, Sam* (1972), for example, Allan Felix (Woody Allen)'s nervous, castrated 1970s masculinity is put straight by Bogart (Jerry Lacy), who appears either as a ghost or, more likely, an imaginary friend. Bogart drills Allan in seduction technique, reassuring him that contemporary women still respond to the unreconstructed directness of an old-fashioned man's man. *Play It Again, Sam* ends with Allan inserted into a reworking of the end of *Casablanca*, consummating the cultist's fantasy that life will finally converge miraculously with the movies.

Figure 2 Lessons in love from Bogart in *Play It Again, Sam*.

Umberto Eco, in a much-quoted essay, one of the first on cult films, analysed the appeal of *Casablanca* in detail. For Eco, *Casablanca* became cult because it is both incoherent and archetypal. Easily deconstructed into memorable lines and imitable fragments, *Casablanca* is a film of portable quotations, yet it also provides 'a completely furnished world so that its fans can quote characters and episodes'.[22] According to Eco, *Casablanca* is so relentlessly, if unconsciously and naively, intertextual that it is 'not just one film, it is many films, an anthology'.[23] The film, as James Card says, seems to have arrived by lucky accident: 'an almost magical coalescence of elements, a nearly *accidental* creation of something wonderful'.[24] Hence the stories that the film was written on the fly, that the ending was not decided till the last minute, and that Ronald Reagan was going to play Rick. The film consequently appears somehow adrift from authorship, art and intention as if it were made up as it went along. Its casual intertextuality recommended it to what Eco calls the 'instinctive semioticians' of 1960s audiences, which revelled in the clichés as fragments of a lost and more confident culture; postmodern films by contrast, such as *Raiders of the Lost Ark* (1981), signal their quotations deliberately to appeal to modern cine-literate audiences.[25] More importantly, *Casablanca* also rounds up all the clichés of Hollywood cinema and indeed narrative itself – it, Eco says, is a tangle of Eternal Stereotypes: 'Two clichés make us laugh but a hundred clichés move us.'[26] Because *Casablanca* is sublimely typical of Hollywood, it seems in retrospect, as Robert Ray puts it, 'classic Hollywood's most representative film'.[27] To love it is to love Hollywood itself. Peary too notes that *Casablanca* contains all the key elements of Hollywood entertainment:

> [It] is maybe the *only* picture which succeeded in [containing] almost every element that would appear on an audience checklist: action, adventure, bravery, danger, espionage, humor, intrigue, a love triangle, a masculine hero, a mysterious heroine, patriotism, politics (without being *too* political), romance, sentimentality, a theme song, a time factor, a venomous villain, and war … . [It] is that rare *lucky* film where everything came together, clicked, and there was perfection.[28]

Casablanca's clichés added up to a complex mythic structure that helps account for its longevity and aptness for rediscovery by new generations. On the one hand, it is a heroic quest narrative – the hero, not wanting to, gets involved in the wider world and discovers his true self. This underlying 'myth' is reproduced in many later films, such as *Star Wars*, which burnish their mythic potential more completely to speak to wide audiences in universal terms. But it also has particular American resonances, especially from the Western, whose hero initially resists involvement but must ultimately commit himself. *Casablanca* mediates between two aspects of American mythology; on the one hand, there is the appeal of isolationism and individualism and, on the other, idealism and group action. This is resolved only when Rick ultimately realizes that neutrality is not an option.[29] The film is, therefore, deeply romantic in its seemingly outmoded insistence that heroism, sacrifice and commitment are meaningful and worthwhile. And as *Play It Again, Sam* suggests, this message of everyday heroism can be adapted to social use, even in the seemingly unheroic business of chatting up women.

Casablanca is no longer a cult film, not really. The film's artistic merit has always been debated, but it is now cinematic folklore. Its cult status can perhaps be revived in one-off screenings by fans donning trilbies and trench coats, and many aficionados no doubt enjoy evenings in front of the TV imagining themselves, for the hundredth time, in 'a whole beautiful world full of knowledge and thoughts and ideals'. But like other classical cult films, *Casablanca* has passed through the awkward phase of cult and become simply a classic, like *King Kong*, *Citizen Kane* (1941) and especially *Vertigo* (1958), whose cult grew in the years when Hitchcock had withdrawn it from circulation till, in 2012, it was voted the greatest film of all time in the latest *Sight and Sound* poll.[30] Films dip in and out of cult status depending on their availability or have parallel lives as cult movies and classics or 'ordinary' schedule fodder.

Midnight Movies

Midnight movies, the crucible of cult in the 1970s, were marginal films, new or revived, which catered to young hip repeat audiences and were shown at unusual times in rep cinemas and on college campuses. The films of this period, roughly 1970–82, had weird, offbeat or transgressive material (*Night of the Living Dead* (1968), *El topo*, *Pink Flamingos* (1972), *Eraserhead* (1976)), or could be read ironically by young audiences (for example, the anti-drug exploitation film, *Reefer Madness* (1936), which, in a haze of dope, they ridiculed for its straightness and naivety).

Midnight movies had been a feature of movie exhibition in the United States since the 1920s, and were especially popular in the 1950s when horror marathons would run all night.[31] Although experimental films such as *Flaming Creatures* (1963) were programmed by underground theatres and avant-garde theatres in the late 1960s, midnight movies as a cult phenomenon are usually dated from the first screening on 17 December 1970 of Alejandro Jodorowsky's 'spaghetti Eastern' *El topo* at the Elgin Theatre, Greenwich Village in New York, where it ran for six months, seven nights a week, at midnight and 1.00 am on Fridays and Saturdays.[32] *El topo* was a 'head' film, a term referring to mind-expanding films, sometimes drug-influenced or imitative of drug effects, which are especially appreciated when stoned or tripping (this included Disney's *Fantasia* (1940)). *El topo* was taken up by the counterculture, which responded to its alternative style, messages, heavy symbolism and druggy logic. Viewers could lose themselves in its somewhat narcissistic and naive symbolic drama, as they could in the convoluted mythically charged worlds of John Fowles's cult novel *The Magus* or J. R. R. Tolkien's *The Lord of the Rings. El topo* is both quasi-religious and implicitly political. On the one hand, it is a Christ story, albeit interwoven with Zen, Buddhist and other mythic elements; on the other, it is anti-authoritarian (the plot recounts the hero killing various 'masters') and anti-capitalist (the town, which El Topo and his freakish horde, representing the alienated young, invade in the final section, is a parody of corrupt American consumerism), and shot through with topical references (the self-immolation at the end evokes that of Buddhist monks protesting against the Vietnam War). *El topo* found its place (as did many cult films of the period) as art-house exploitation, with its eye-popping scenes of violence, lesbianism, and perversion ripe for allegorical interpretation and lent an additional aura by its director's wild-eyed crazy persona as a psychedelic guru. Audiences receptive to allegory might conclude that it was about the counterculture being overtaken by violence (the Manson murders, the Rolling Stones' Altamont concert) and turning from politics to the quiescent cultivation of the inner self.[33] To judge from contemporary accounts of screenings at the Elgin, they were the occasion for 'midnight mass', with viewers returning numerous times to steep themselves afresh in the film's bizarre imagery and hidden meanings and consulting the published screenplay of *El topo* to make sense of Jodorowsky's otherwise inscrutable private symbolism. There is, incidentally, a long-standing association of cult film with religious cults. The films are holy texts, a religious living theatre of cruelty, with the screenings as masses (or satanic rites), the stars as objects of devotion, and the audience as bacchants retrieving in their frenzied fanaticism and disordering of the senses some of theatre's origins as a Dionysian ritual, offering sanctuary from everyday life and glimpses of the transcendent.

Other repertory theatres started to show similarly unusual films at midnight screenings in urban centres and college towns across the United States, mostly to counterculture audiences. George Romero's zombie movie *Night of the Living Dead*, for example, having gained a critical following and commercial success in Europe, was rereleased on New York's 42nd Street in 1969 as the bottom half of a grindhouse double bill.[34] Midnight screenings started in 1971, when it ran at the Waverly Theatre on Sixth Avenue every Friday and Saturday night, and then spread across the United States. It ran for two years from May 1971 to July 1973 continuously in New York on the midnight movie circuit.

A hardcore mini-canon was memorialized in Stuart Samuels's *Midnight Movies* book, which he adapted much later as a documentary, *Midnight Movies: From the Margin to the Mainstream* (2005). The other films in Samuels's canon, *Pink Flamingos, Eraserhead, The Harder They Come* (1972) and *The Rocky Horror Picture Show*, all had long running engagements at theatres which became ritualized social occasions complete with audience participation. Midnight screenings gave the perfect out-of-hours performance space for these taboo-breaking films whose themes were so closely intertwined with the counterculture's journey from optimism to pessimism. In fact, these films' violence, political allegory, sexual complexity, and yearning for both escape and apocalypse were shared by many of the male-orientated youth films of the period, notably road movies like *Easy Rider* (1969), *Five Easy Pieces* (1970), *Two Lane Blacktop* (1971), and *Zabriskie Point* (1970). Although the canonical cult films seem distinct, their characteristics overlapped with those of the New Hollywood (the wave of radical auteurist American films from around 1967 to 1980). The same is true of the interpretative strategies required to go along for the ride and make sense of them, which required a tolerance for hair-trigger shifts in tone, irony towards genre conventions and alertness to intertextuality. Midnight movies were New Hollywood films *in extremis*, if you like, with a comparable triangulation of exploitation, genre and art or underground cinema. Younger directors of the 'Hollywood Renaissance', especially 'the Movie Brats' of the film school generation, were themselves cultists in their reverence for and imitation of heroes such as Godard and Hitchcock. Brian De Palma's early career is evidence of his wholly cultist immersion in Hitchcock in films like *Obsession* (1976), which reworked *Vertigo*, and *Dressed to Kill* (1980), which reworked *Psycho* (1960). It is worth noting that British cult movies, similarly, came out of the social and sexual upheavals of the late 1960s, a period when the industry, struggling with the withdrawal of American finance, drew on diverse sources of funding and experimented with new combinations of art, genre and exploitation to reach out to declining audiences. Art-exploitation crossovers like *Witchfinder General* (1968) and *Performance* (1970) spoke to a generation of confused radical politics and changing sexual mores, so that, as Justin Smith says, '*Witchfinder General*'s accomplished and disturbing concoction of sexual violence and profoundly ambivalent gender and generational relationships attempts to articulate a response to the cultural politics of a complex historical moment.'[35]

The midnight movie phenomenon was tied into a 'trash' or 'camp' aesthetic which relished not only films that cut across generic boundaries but ones that were so-bad-they're-good, an aesthetic arguably unformulated before the 1960s. The cult of the Z-movie director, Edward D. Wood, Jr., is a case in point. His exceptionally low-budget exploitation films such as *Glen or Glenda* (1953) and *Plan Nine from Outer Space* (1959) achieved notoriety for their idiosyncratic incompetence, especially after being featured in the Medveds' *The Golden Turkey Awards*.[36] Scrapheap films like Wood's and Doris Wishman's, another excitingly awful exploitation director, can be bunched together as 'paracinema', to use the coinage popularized by Jeffrey Sconce:

> seemingly disparate subgenres such as 'bad film', splatterpunk, 'mondo' films, sword and sandal epics, Elvis flicks, governmental hygiene films, Japanese monster movies, beach party musicals and just about every other historical manifestation of exploitation cinema from juvenile delinquency documentaries to soft core pornography.[37]

In other words, cult was and is not only a kind of movie but a taste for, and way of looking at, all sorts of bizarre, disregarded and unrespectable alternatives to 'the mainstream'. The cult of paracinema assumes receptiveness to camp, badness, transgression, certain kinds of difficulty ('appreciating' the scrambled aesthetic procedures of *Glen or Glenda* requires much the same patient forbearance towards uncompromising textual deviance as avant-garde classics like *Berlin Horse* (1970) and *Room Film 1973* (1973)), as well as delight in finding oneself among others of the elect who share such derided preferences. What especially attracts cult interest in trash is the aggressively lowbrow, which is so lowbrow as to be effectively oppositional.

The definitive cult film remains *The Rocky Horror Picture Show*, which began as a British stage show in 1973 during the period of 'gender-bending' glam rock. Released in 1975, it was initially a flop before hitting the midnight movie circuit, where it started to build a hardcore audience and became one of the decade's highest grossing films. In April 1976 the Waverly Theatre, which had recently turned to running cheap movies to a mostly gay audience, was persuaded by Tim Deegan, a Fox executive who saw the film's cult potential, to replace *Night of the Living Dead* with it as the midnight screening.[38] Audiences started to call back – one Louis Farese is credited with the first call back, shouting out to Janet as she shelters under a newspaper, 'Buy an umbrella, ya cheap bitch!' – and an alternative script was incrementally pieced together.[39] People started turning up in costume; engaging in scripted participation (the call backs would have local variations and change over time), such as throwing toast and shooting water pistols at the screens; and by taking over screenings created a uniquely comprehensive and organized cult following. Fox capitalized on this unexpected success and over the next couple of years two hundred theatres across the United States screened *Rocky Horror* at midnight. A fan club, with Sal Piro as its president, gained around 10,000 members and produced a newsletter, *The Transylvanian*. *Rocky Horror* is still shown at cinemas worldwide and has a significant internet fan presence (last time I looked, there were over 50,000 people in the fan club).

The audience was, as you might expect, at first chiefly gay, responding to the film's camp excess and the screenings' safe spaces for outrageous self-expression. Bruce Austin, a sociologist, studied the audience at Rochester, New York in 1979 and found that it was largely men aged seventeen to twenty-two, white, mainstream and middle class, who went for the experience rather than for the film itself.[40] (Later audiences, in so far as they were subcultural at all, were punk rather than gay, and Janet Staiger reports that homophobic and misogynist remarks became more common.[41]) *Rocky Horror* corresponds to Eco's definition of a cult film in its makeshift genre hybridity. A ramshackle pastiche and nostalgic compilation of horror, SF and the musical, the film embodies nostalgia for classical Hollywood as well as for the British horror film currently on its uppers through lack of American funding (*Rocky Horror* was filmed at Bray Studios and Oakley Court, the locations for most of the Hammer movies). *Rocky Horror* was also nostalgic for, even as it celebrated, the moment

Figure 3 Frank N. Furter (Tim Curry) giving himself up to absolute pleasure in *The Rocky Horror Picture Show*.

when the innocence of the 1950s was debauched by the counterculture. The movie itself is an awkward combination of film and theatre and never quite loses its staginess, as when Frank N. Furter (Tim Curry) throws water at the screen and gurns at the audience, and when The Criminologist (Charles Gray) presents dance steps for 'The Time Warp' and invites the audience to join the Transylvanians' revels. The cult audience, responding to the film's residual theatricality, breaks down the fourth wall and essentially completes the film. In fact, the film is unimaginable without the audience, which *becomes* the show.

As with *El topo* and other midnight movies like *Harold and Maude*, *Rocky Horror* is about liberation, however brief and doomed, and its takeaway message is, as Frank put it, 'There's no crime in giving yourself over to pleasure.' 'Don't dream it, be it,' the film urges, as its insipid repressed heroes, Brad (Barry Bostwick) and Janet (Susan Sarandon), are seduced by Frank N. Furter's bisexuality and the sexual free-for-all of the 1970s. This liberation is reproduced in the audience, so that the screening becomes a celebration of polymorphous sexuality and a performance stage for outcasts (at least initially, when the audience seemed mostly to consist of sexual minorities):

> *Rocky Horror* ... is a *cause célèbre* for any disenfranchised member of society. It offers a pessimistic world view that appeals to postmodern sensibilities in the nuclear age. Its vilification of institutions, degradation of heterosexual romance and its reflexive critique of its own production (in which the audience participates) make *Rocky Horror* a unique document. It criticizes and parodies both other films and itself. It is thus a stable culture document in the 'late postmodern' age of deep anxieties, insecurities, violent reactions, and cynical world views.[42]

The film's subversiveness was dramatized in Alan Parker's *Fame* (1980), in which a young woman, a *Rocky Horror* virgin, attends a screening compèred by Sal Piro and loses her inhibitions, smoking a joint and high-kicking along to 'The Time Warp' on stage.

Cult as Lived Experience

Rocky Horror emphasizes that understanding a cult film simply by analysing it as a text misses the fact that cult films, regardless of authorial intention, are valued for the live, even carnal experience they offer, even if, as with *Plan Nine from Outer Space*, the experience is one of unrelieved badness made palatable only by shared laughter.

> As devoted as the cult fan may be, he recognises that the film promises only temporary transcendence. Indeed, this is the initial attraction of the film: the moments of intense pleasure it offers comes at little cost, and at whatever level of commitment one chooses. Unlike mainstream film fanatics, whose devotion to certain films is akin to an earnest and steadfast romance, the cult film fan's relationship the film is largely fetishistic. The film is imbued with value directly proportional to the pleasure it brings.[43]

Cult films respond to audience needs – 'our own sense of difference and alienation', as Telotte says – and, like being a David Bowie fan, allow an opportunity to belong to an inclusive audience of similarly different people.[44] Gregory Waller studied midnight movies in one US town, Lexington, Kentucky, for over six years in the early 1980s, when the films, such as *Monty Python's Holy Grail* (1975), tended to be comedy, rock movies and horror or, like *Rocky Horror*, recombinant versions of all three. Their aesthetic of excess and anti-authoritarian attitudes, Waller argues, offered some respite from the conformism of the Reagan period.[45] As well as escape, cult texts are anchors for meaning, which is why, later on in this book, I'll explore their utility as 'guides to life' and the feeling as you watch them sometimes that, to quote Frank again, 'Suddenly ... you get a break! All of the pieces seem to fit into place. ... That elusive ingredient, that spark ... that is the breath of life. Yes, I have that knowledge! I hold the key to life ... itself!' Cult films provide alternative family units and emotional attachments, on screen and off. Objects of fan desire, the films may even be, as Justin Smith has argued of British cult films, explicable in psychoanalytic terms as 'transitional objects':

> Fans use these films as resources through which to rehearse subjective identities and demonstrate cultural competence. The strategies and processes involved are various, just as individual needs must be diverse. Yet if cultural texts can be viewed, like religious icons, as objects through which we

structure our desires in the constitution of our own subjective identities, then cult films are the repositories of fears and longings in the negotiation of sexual difference and subjectivity. ... Such texts endorse cultural marginality, reassuring their devotees that not 'fitting-in' is fine, maybe even heroic. They offer alternative systems of order, symbolic rituals and rites of passage. They provide frameworks for alternative forms of belief.[46]

More straightforwardly, cult films may also provide 'subcultural capital' (impressive knowledge of popular culture, mostly) as well as the cachet of negotiating the film's ambiguities and range of references[47]: As Nathan Hunt deftly puts it,

> Through their use of trivia fans lay claim to having special access to, and hence, dominion over, specific texts owing to their supposedly superior knowledge of them. ... Trivia are used to establish who is an insider and to declare others to be outsiders who do not have the right to participate in fandom.[48]

The extension of the film into life is important because the cultist's life may thereby become one of profound aesthetic exploration and production, especially if you are inspired, for example, to write fan fiction, make films, become a film scholar, critic, blogger or programmer, be creative with your identity, or in some way contrive to inhabit the film completely, like Woody Allen in *Play It Again, Sam* and the character in *Diner* (1982) who speaks nothing but lines from *The Sweet Smell of Success* (1957). For the director Steven Soderbergh *Jaws* was a revelatory and life-changing experience:

> I remember the summer of '75, and having my head taken off. I was 12, and I went to see *Jaws*. I was so affected that I really thought to myself, for the first time: 'How did this happen to me? Who did this?' It was the first time I became conscious that someone actually made movies ... Seeing *Jaws*, finding out who Spielberg was and what he did was very formative for me.[49]

An obvious way in which cult films take over not only your lives but also your valuable personal space is collecting, to which my tottering piles of *Jaws*-related DVDs, videos and novelizations attest.[50] But as well as promoting things to buy, collect and do, ways to dress, smart lines to repeat, characters to imitate and material to inspire a sense of community, cult films may engage the intellect, as when cultists pursue references in *The Holy Mountain* (1973), Jodorowsky's surpassingly arcane follow-up to *El topo*, or spend hours figuring out what the black monolith represents in Kubrick's *2001: A Space Odyssey*. This is what you might call the scholarly aspect of cult. Cultists often share esoteric ideas and conspiratorial theories about what films mean, responding to the fact that many cult films are dense with textual ambiguities that demand interpretation and committed re-viewing.

On a less intellectual level, cult films such as *Withnail & I* acquired viewing rituals like drinking games once they'd landed on video (the idea is to drink whatever Withnail does on screen till you drift into a similar arena of the unwell, which is manageable till he starts on the lighter fluid). You can even take your cinephile body on tour, exploring cult landscapes and expanding love of a film into 'real life' through imaginative re-mappings and pilgrimages of fantasy. For example, just to mention British movies, devotees of *Withnail & I* may head off, clad in replicas of Withnail's ankle-flapping coat, to the wilds of the Lake District in search of the cottage where Withnail and Marwood go on holiday by accident. And if you and your droogs want to trace Alex DeLarge (Malcolm McDowell)'s steps in *A Clockwork Orange*, you can location-scout Brunel University in Uxbridge, London, where he underwent the Ludovico treatment, and *dérive* around the connecting walkways of the concrete prefab development of Thamesmead in SE28, perhaps taking a selfie on Binsey Walk in Thamesmead South where the fight on the edge of the Flatblock Marina was filmed. Admittedly I've engaged in such *flaneurie* only via Google Earth, but there are online location guides to *A Clockwork Orange* should I ever risk an actual visit to one of London's most extreme postcodes.

The most significant sites of British cult tourism are probably connected to *The Wicker Man*'s various locations around Scotland, which were sutured together to create the island where Sergeant Howie (Edward Woodward) met his fiery doom. The true cross of the Wicker Man itself has long disappeared, but I know at least one pilgrim who returned with a sliver of wood that he claims to be a relic of the iconic prop and stores in the wooden box of the original Region One collector's edition of the DVD. The film has inspired considerable such cult tourism or psychogeography, by which fans invoke the ghostly historical valences of the film, perhaps celebrating, in a mood of elevated intellectualism, its counter-hegemonic landscapes of resistant Scottish paganism.[51] Fans of *Get Carter*, meanwhile, can bid online for bricks from the now demolished car park from which big man Carter (Michael Caine) throws the out-of-shape Cliff Brumby (Bryan Mosley).

Nostalgia – another word that, like transgression, will echo repeatedly throughout this book – is folded into these cultish behaviours insofar as experience of the cult film has its own momentum, played out in one's personal history. Re-watching the film is a re-encounter with memories of both the film and one's life when it first entered the imagination. As Lincoln Geraghty remarks in relation to collecting, 'Fans create a sense of identity through the association of personal memories and nostalgia with particular objects they collect. Nostalgia ... is a transformative process rather than an inhibiting and conservative emotion.'[52] This sense of nostalgia is built into many of the films themselves, which look back on the past and resurrect styles at their moment of obsolescence. Thus, *Withnail* looks back to the dog days of the 1960s from the disillusioned 1980s, encapsulating a sense of loss and sell out that mourns for the 'greatest decade in the history of mankind'. *Streets of Fire* revivifies the 1950s through film and music references, creating a timeless postmodern simulacrum that cancels distance between the present and the sacred past. *Dirty Dancing*, itself nostalgic for the early 1960s, may inspire nostalgia in viewers for their first youthful experience of the film on video in the 1980s. As Hadley Freeman says:

> *Dirty Dancing* taught my generation of women, and continues to teach generations of younger women, about their moral compass. We came for the sex, but we have stayed because it shows us something even more real and scary. It teaches us something about ourselves and the world.[53]

Cult Now

The Golden Age of the midnight movie carried on into the 1980s till video arrived and many repertory theatres closed. Video created entirely new canons of cult films as well as new forms of collecting, consumption and mutual exchange of cult enthusiasms. Films became cult because they found an audience on video: *Scarface* (1982) (a hip-hop favourite; Tony Montana (Al Pacino) was a role model for upwardly mobile gangsta rappers), *Dirty Dancing* (the first film to sell a million copies on video tape in the UK), *Blade Runner*, *This is Spinal Tap* (a cult among rock bands, naturally), *The Princess Bride*, and, of course, the numerous video nasties, such as *Cannibal Holocaust* (1980) and *Zombie Flesh Eaters* (1979), that achieved a continuing afterlife as cult items in Britain because the BBFC banned them. Above all, video made films available for intense scrutiny, which encouraged new cult viewing strategies of interrogative rewind and pause to isolate cinephiliac moments. *Blade Runner*'s textual errors, inconsistencies and ambiguities (How many replicants are there? Is Deckard (Harrison Ford) one himself?) only revealed themselves when viewers, like Deckard scanning the photograph of a replicant's room into a 3D rendering machine and exploring it minutely for clues, had watched it numerous times and immersed themselves in the film's dense and allusive hyperdiegesis. With the realization that cult can be an imitable sort of genre, directors produced films with the oxymoronic aim of being instantly cult. Horror and trash films programmatically opposed to the mainstream – *Attack of the Killer Tomatoes!* (1978), *Repo Man*, *Basket Case* (1982) and *Evil Dead II* (1987), – were made for (and often by) a new generation of cult fans, who were enthusiastic repeat consumers of ironic exploitation. By the 1990s, directors like Quentin Tarantino, in films like *Pulp Fiction* (1994), had developed an intensive postmodern aesthetic that was utterly cultist in its appropriations, allusiveness and indifference towards categories of cinema beyond the immanently cool. As Tarantino said at the Cannes screening of *Pulp Fiction*, with a nod to T. S. Eliot's dictum that great artists don't borrow but steal:

> I steal from every single movie ever made … I love it – if my work has anything it's that I'm taking this from this and that from that and mixing

them together. If people don't like that, then tough titty, don't go and see it, all right? I steal from everything. Great artists steal, they don't do homages.[54]

Cult is now a much sought-after and commercialized market. In fact, it is difficult to think of any kind of exploitation film, from Japanese pink films (softcore pornography) to blaxploitation and Nazisploitation cinema, which has not acquired its cultists and amateur historians, while earlier cult films have re-entered the market in newly collectable forms. There are multi-disc releases of *Blade Runner* in its seven versions, fortieth anniversary Blu-Rays of *Rocky Horror*, collectable limited editions of arty trash such as *Nekromantik* (1987), and Criterion Editions of *Two Lane Blacktop*. The number of cult films that are truly unavailable or accessible only through shared torrents and momentarily posted videos is relatively small. *Superstar: The Karen Carpenter Story* (1987), Todd Haynes's short film about the singer's final years in which all the roles are performed with Barbie and Ken dolls, was pulled after a copyright infringement suit, but pops up irregularly on YouTube. The unreleased Rolling Stones documentary, *Cocksucker Blues* (1972), which the Stones allow to be shown a few times a year with its director Robert Frank in attendance, similarly plays online hide and seek. It is true that Dennis Hopper's *The Last Movie* (1971), his disastrous follow-up to *Easy Rider*, languishes on video with no DVD in sight, and Jerry Lewis's unreleased Holocaust comedy, *The Day the Clown Cried* (1972), remains stashed in his vault, but otherwise seeing cult films is determined more by one's budget and dexterity at online ripping than by proximity to rep theatres.

As my inclusion of *Dirty Dancing* in the roster of cult films implies, the definition of cult films has unquestionably become rather vague and contested since the days of the midnight movie. Even *Jaws* has been inducted into cult in the Frenchs' book, *Cult Movies*, now that it is no longer a contemporary blockbuster but an icon of 1970s cinema and fixed point in childhood memory.[55] So far as American and European cult films go, bona fide ones are still out there. *Fight Club* (one of the top-ranked films on IMDb), *Donnie Darko* (2001) and *The Big Lebowski* have all followed the traditional cult trajectory from box-office failure to classic – *Donnie Darko* was a rare midnight movie success and played in one cinema in Manhattan for twenty-eight months.[56] *The Big Lebowski* plays like a homage to the New Hollywood style of cult film in the 1970s with its loose, Altman-like plotting, ramped up intertextuality and constant bad language. Hyperbolically bad films like *The Room*, *Birdemic: Shock and Terror* (2010) and *Troll 2* (1990) have also found enthusiastic ironic audiences, who share clips on YouTube of favourite moments of idiot savant *photogenie* (such as, from *The Room*, 'I did not hit her, I did not. Oh, hi Mark,' 'You're tearing me apart, Lisa'). Yet, if you trust books like *The Rough Guide to Cult Film*, few films considered even marginally cool, which have niche appeal, or are capable of counter-intuitive appraisal and interpretation are potentially outside the cult canon. Google 'cult film' or consult Wikipedia and you'll find the list of candidates gets ever longer and more unwieldy – *Office Space* (1999) (loved for its cynicism about white collar life), *Labyrinth* (1986), *The Goonies* (1984) (I don't get the appeal of this one at all), *Clue* (1985) (ditto, as Patrick Swayze says in *Ghost* (1990), which was a sleeper hit but *possibly not cult*), *Mean Girls*, *9 ½ Weeks* (1986), *Point Break* (1991), *Pulp Fiction* ... and that is only to mention American movies since the 1980s. Forty-five years after *El topo*, the term 'cult film' as traditionally defined, therefore, seems itself a little rackety and old-fashioned, a harking back to the days memorialized, in this book's Preface, of midnight movies, ratty rep cinemas, mimeographed fanzines, banned films on dubbed videos, and subcultural enthusiasm about the 'transgressive'. Justin Smith has suggested that, with the eclipse of the midnight movie, cult had had its classic moment, and that in the current phase of 'post-cult' 'subcultural distinction has been elided through hegemonic processes to the point that the cult is almost totally recuperated ideologically and reproduced commercially to feed the personalised media culture'.[57] Consequently, as Jamie Sexton has pointed out, cult is becoming an object of nostalgia for those of us (including, admittedly, me sometimes) who associate it with hunting rare films and who snobbishly decry its popularization as a commercial category.[58] For some cinephiles it is further infused with melancholic yearning for a lost world of serious cinema, represented by the art films of the 1950s to 1970s or perhaps by the New Hollywood 'before *Star Wars*', when convention insists it all started to go wrong.

By midnight movie standards *Mean Girls*, for example, is as inconceivable a cult film as *The Princess Bride*. A high school comedy *Mean Girls* is the uplifting tale of a girl, Cady Heron (Lindsay Lohan), who is absorbed into and then revenges herself on the Plastics, a clique of queen bees. It wasn't a failure but received generally positive reviews and was a box-office success, earning $24.4 million over its opening weekend and converting its $17 million budget into a $129 million take. Acquiring a passionate following on DVD, *Mean Girls* seems to owe its legs in part to its irresistible quotability ('Boo, you whore', 'On Wednesdays we wear pink', 'Stop trying to make fetch happen'), which could now be shared online in Tumblr posts (more than 10,000 posts and 477,000 notes in one month alone) and in *Mean Girls* themed gifs.[59] There is even a '*Mean Girls* Day', commemorating the start of Cady's romance with Aaron Samuels (Jonathan Bennett) (he asks her what day it is, and she replies 'It's October 3rd'.) Online articles on the film's tenth anniversary, when it was rereleased on DVD in an anniversary edition, highlighted the appeal of its female-centric plot, relatability, and explicitly stated message:

> It's the rarest of rare things, a female-centric film that operates as a traditional male-escapist film yet tells its hero's journey without resorting to giving the female lead a weapon and screaming 'Empowerment!'. Lohan's lead grows up just a little, sacrifices just a little, and becomes a better person while also snagging the token hot guy at the end. It's a female centric film that operates

on the rules of male-escapist fantasy. It is an empowering film not because the female lead kills people, is in an arbitrary position of authority or even stands up to men in authority, but because it is a female comedy about women and about issues arguably specific to young women as they grow up in the educational system.[60]

Mean Girls fandom entails dressing up (in pink on Wednesdays, naturally), sympathizing with self-perceived outsiders (homeschooled white girls from Africa, guys too gay to function, women with wide vaginas and heavy flows), and perhaps taking to heart its point about empowerment and inclusivity. As Barbara Klinger says,

> Repeated experiences with the same film can operate normatively, continually reaffirming appropriate gender identities, for example. By the same token, favorite texts can continue to inspire feelings of liberation in women looking for strong role models (even in what appears to be a compromised genre such as the chick flick).[61]

Mean Girls is not a cult film in the mould of *Rocky Horror* (or even *Heathers* (1988), the obvious, much darker and 'cultier' point of comparison). Its inclusion in virtually every roll call of contemporary cult films, however, suggests that cult today is not only chiefly in the domestic sphere (the primal scene of cult may well be sleepovers), but also increasingly reflects the tastes of young women; this at a time when female fandom has become a commercial force to be reckoned with and once obscure female-led fan practices like slash fiction are disseminated more widely than ever. In short, *Mean Girls* makes us rethink some of the standard definitions of cult and ask why committed viewers of female-centred movies have traditionally been regarded as 'merely' fans rather than cultists.[62]

   Cult film being a discursive category, its definition is liable anyway to change with use over time. Key questions are raised, however, by this apparent and confusing expansion of the category to embrace films as various as *Birdemic* and *Mean Girls*. Are we perhaps simply confusing 'cult' with sustained popularity? For that matter, how many people make for a cult? Does a cult film require a gang of enthusiasts or is just one lonely acolyte enough? Can a blockbuster (*The Lord of the Rings*, the James Bond films, superhero franchises, *Titanic* (1997)) be cult, or does that require its fandom to be especially intense, wayward or somehow radically different? Blockbusters like *Inception* and 'world-building' epics like *Avatar* (2009) certainly cultivate the kind of repeat viewing and long-term investment that was once the speciality of diehard cultists. It takes, for example, nine hours to work through all the extras on the three Blu-Rays (five DVDs) of the extended version of *The Hobbit: The Battle of the Nine Armies* (2014). My sense, to judge from the use of 'cult film' in books that keep the term alive in popular discourse, like *100 Cult Movies You Must See Before*

Figure 4 Romance blossoms on 3rd October in *Mean Girls*.

You Die, is that cult films are still mostly unconventional small-scale, often independent movies that were overlooked or undervalued on initial release and built up a long-term, and somewhat exclusive, following through word of mouth. Mainstream or blockbuster movies only re-emerge as cult because of their continued popularity years after they should have passed into the limbo of the back catalogue that invariably awaits even the most expensive, acclaimed and profitable films. Their fans keep them alive with what might seem excessive investment, disproportionate to the films' status as throwaway products of popular culture.

At any rate, cult abides.[63] That said, the cult *experience* of cult films perhaps, for those invested in certain kinds of authenticity and sceptical that *Mean Girls* is a proper cult film, remains arguably more elusive than in the days of either midnight movies or fourth-generation dubs of *Cannibal Holocaust*. It is true that the exclusivity, communal excitement and aura of liveness of the midnight movie have revived with the *Mamma Mia!* singalongs, LebowskiFest, one-off marathons of *The Hobbit* trilogy, 'Schwing-alongs' with *Wayne's World* (1992) and other audience participation events at the Prince Charles Cinema in London, and pop up Secret Cinema screenings (a UK one for *Back to the Future* in 2014 sold 60,000 tickets, while in 2015 Secret Cinema's *The Empire Strikes Back* (1980) sold 100,000 tickets and grossed £6 million at the box office).[64] 'Live' events are programmed into the distribution of new blockbusters like *Star Wars: The Force Awakens* (2015) as well as screenings of old fan-favourites, with the film itself 'augmented by synchronous live performance, site-specific locations, technological interventions, social media engagement, and all manner of simultaneous interaction including singing, dancing, eating, drinking, even smelling'.[65] Screenings of 35mm prints have become a new kind of cult event, promoting a sugar rush of authenticity in the presence of the seemingly obsolete format, much like the limited 'roadshow version' on 70mm Ultra Panavision of

Tarantino's *The Hateful Eight* (2015), complete with overture and intermission. Is this merely a manufactured simulacrum of cult, a kitsch retro revival of the midnight movie phenomenon but without the countercultural politics that energized it? Well, perhaps. But let's not forget the commercial opportunism behind the midnight success of *El topo* and especially *Rocky Horror*. Away from the distribution circuit, other new forms of cult practice flourish, such as box set blowouts and witty bantering commentaries during screenings via tweet-alongs. These new kinds of glocalised experiences on social media combine intimate liveness and extended sociability and have changed the temporality of cult.[66] There are now 'pre-cults' such as *Snakes on a Plane* (2006), whose cult was exhausted before the film had even been released, while the cult of *Sharknado* in 2012 barely outlasted the Twitterstorm of mocking comments during its premiere on SyFy.[67] Cultism as lived experience still happens, therefore, but in ways more engaged with wider modes of contemporary film viewership, and this again makes previous understandings of cult seem narrow. As Klinger says, with reference to her notion of 'replay culture':

> Certain species of cult cinema are not discontinuous from dominant industry or social practices; instead they represent continuity with, even a shining realization of, the dynamics of media circulation today. In this sense, cult is a logical extension of replay culture: it achieves the kind of penetration into viewers' 'hearts and minds' that media convergence and multi-windowed distribution promote; cultish viewing, in turn, represents a particularly dedicated and insistent pursuit of media inspired by replay. At the same time, cult helps to drive replay culture, motivating both media industries to rerelease films and fans to generate events, testimonials and DIY productions that visibly enter into and influence the mix. Reflecting the complex dynamics of today's mediascape, cult is both a product and an engine of replay.[68]

The global reach of cult also makes earlier narratives of cult history seem insular. I don't mean looking at films and directors from other, foreign language cinemas. Though I haven't discussed it much here, seizing on foreign films for their otherness and exoticism has always been an aspect of cult in Britain and the United States, from *El topo*, *Aguirre, The Wrath of God* (1972) and martial art films in the 1970s to 'Asian extreme' horror and crime films (*Battle Royale* (2000), *Ichi the Killer* (2001)), which were marketed as cult in Britain for their flamboyant violence, to Turkish remakes of American blockbusters, like *Turkish Superman* (1979), that cult audiences in the West love for their paracinematic weirdness.[69] Cult has often involved dislocating film from the cultures that produced them by such strategies as reframing 'video nasties' as auteurist personal cinema, which made cult icons of Italian and French horror directors such as Dario Argento, Ruggero Deodato, Jean Rollin, Joe D'Amato and Lucio Fulci. The prized difference of cult films, however, sometimes evaporates when they are slotted back into their original contexts. Trash exploitation films, for example, which seem so deliciously 'unhinged' in isolation, seem more like highly conventionalized products of ruinous production circumstances once you've seen a few dozen of them. *Reefer Madness* is in many ways a fairly standard 'classical exploitation' film of the 1930s, while even the eye-popping excess of *Zombie Flesh Eaters* doesn't seem quite so *outré* once cut adrift from the video nasties panic and restored to the *filone* (sub-generic cycles) of 1970s Italian exploitation. Moreover, what 'ordinary' or 'natural' audiences made of, say, *Plan Nine from Outer Space, Faster Pussycat! Kill! Kill!* (1965), or *Zombie Flesh Eaters* on their original theatrical release (or when they showed up in double bills on 42nd Street grindhouses) is a good deal harder to pin down than what cultists, who were invariably not their first or intended audience, subsequently made of them.[70] Knowing as much as we do, and probably rather more than we need, about the cult preferences since the 1970s of young white progressive middle-class American ironists, it is perhaps more interesting to wonder about audiences beyond the usual demographics of cult reception. What is cult in Poland, Ghana, Vietnam, and among the global audiences for Nollywood (Nigerian popular cinema), for instance? What is cult among children and old people? And, on a different tack, what about audiences who enjoy cult films but wouldn't necessarily identify themselves as cultists and who don't, for example, watch 'bad films' in the prescribed ironic fashion? After all, not everyone who likes *Rocky Horror* and turns up to the odd revivalist screening might be considered a cultist. Most products of 'the deliberately engineered ephemerality of cinema', as Richard Maltby remarks,

> do not seek out landmark status for themselves, but are designed to fade back into the overall field of our cultural experiences.... Like individual dreams that may be vivid and impressive at the time and briefly on waking, most individual movies receive little subsequent support from the processes of long-term recall and re-narration that characterise the building of our memories of significant life events.[71]

In fact, even those fans who hold on to their dreams and turn films into cult landmarks don't always do very much. Few cultists are likely to watch *Rocky Horror* five hundred times, as Sal Piro reportedly had by the early 1980s, or construct wonderfully detailed sites about *The Shining* like *The Overlook Hotel*, curated by Lee Unkrich, the director of *Toy Story 3* (2010).[72]

Making sense of these changing definitions of cult prompted my first effort to write about the phenomenon in a chapter on *Showgirls*, which I saw and fell for, in every sense, back in 1995.

Chapter 2

BEAVER LAS VEGAS! A FANBOY'S DEFENCE OF *SHOWGIRLS*

Andrew Sarris once began an interview with a sustained defence in intellectual depth of his *auteur* theory, and concluded by confessing that what really kept him coming to the cinema was its girls. Here is the beginning of wisdom.

Raymond Durgnat[1]

The only thing I could imagine with regard to *Showgirls* is that part of the audience will go home in a state of excitement and, thinking of the film, make love or masturbate. That's not so bad.

Paul Verhoeven[2]

'The Worst Hollywood Film Ever Made'

Showgirls (1995), Paul Verhoeven's lap-dance musical, is that rare object in cultural life – a film universally derided as 'bad'. *No one* seems to like it. At a time of alleged cultural relativism and collapsing standards of aesthetic judgement *Showgirls* has emerged as a welcome gold standard of poor taste and world-class incompetence.

From the start critical reaction to the film was numbingly hostile. According to *Halliwell's*, only one of the fourteen leading British critics and two out of thirty-four critics in Chicago, New York and Los Angeles ventured so much as a good word for it.[3] The rest teetered on hysterical loathing. Mocking the film's brashness, overblown dialogue and the acting deficiencies of its young star, Elizabeth Berkley, critics deplored above all Verhoeven's hypocrisy in exploiting the very sleaze and voyeurism that his film purported to expose. Gina Gershon alone escaped general censure, if only because her arch performance as Cristal, an omnisexual dancer, appeared to send up everything around her. Not surprisingly, despite being the most hyped film of the year, *Showgirls* was a commercial disaster. Costing $40 million it took no more than $25 million in domestic theatres, and although video sales and overseas revenue meant that it eventually turned a profit, it was still the second most costly write-off of 1995.[4]

With startling rapidity *Showgirls* became a byword for Hollywood at its most embarrassing. The 1996 Golden Raspberry Awards, anti-Oscars for the turkeys of the year, conferred on it an unprecedented seven 'Razzies', including worst film and worst director. Verhoeven, who gamely turned up to accept his trophy in person, declared, 'The worst thing has happened to me today. … Yet I am very happy, because it was much more fun than reading the reviews!'[5] Since the film was released few, even among hard-core aficionados of trash, have bothered to come to its defence. An exception was the director Quentin Tarantino. 'The thing that's great about *Showgirls*,' he enthused, 'and I mean great with a capital great, is that only one other time in the last twenty years has a major studio made a full-on, gigantic, big-budget exploitation movie [*Mandingo* (1975)]. *Showgirls* is the *Mandingo* of the '90s.'[6] He sensibly implied that, like ballet and fetish porn, the film was an acquired taste whose low pleasures were never meant to appeal to mainstream critics.

But even as an exploitation film *Showgirls* came dreadfully unstuck, for it not only missed but alienated its core audience of overheated heterosexual males. Seeming to address only straight men probably didn't help its chances. (That *Showgirls* is a campy musical suggests that an address to gay audiences, or at least a space for gay appropriation, was built into it as a possibility. This ambiguity wasn't stressed in the promotional material.) Other single-mindedly male-orientated films of the period such as *Striptease* (1996) and *Barb Wire* (1996), whose appeal rested on the exposure of celebrity silicone, also flopped badly in spite of aggressive publicity campaigns. Like *Showgirls* they were too tame to attract the porn trade, but neither romantic nor arty enough to break into the couples market for erotica.

As the first widely distributed blockbuster with an NC-17 rating, *Showgirls* was unwisely promoted as a groundbreaking sex film. Its salacious peek-a-boo trailer, imploring viewers to leave their inhibitions at the door, raised hopes not only of forbidden material 'beyond your wildest fantasies' but also of a new rapport between Hollywood and sexploitation. In fact, *Showgirls* is no more explicit and creatively perverse than most straight-to-video erotic thrillers, with which it shares a conventional *Playboy*-derived aesthetic of nipped, tucked and air-brushed female beauty. As the title insinuates, it mostly 'shows girls' in various states of arousal and undress – usually in the context of stage performances. Indeed, many critics attacked the film for not being explicit enough.[7] Several also compared it unfavourably to Atom Egoyan's *Exotica* (1994), also set in a strip club, but which, in the standard, critically approved manner of art films, 'problematizes' both the depiction of sexuality and the voyeuristic pleasure of the audience.

Showgirls did, however, very briefly attract a cult following. In 1996 gays in New York and LA set up special *Rocky Horror*-style screenings to celebrate it as 'the camp classic of the decade'.[8] Emboldened by this 'resurrection', as Verhoeven called it, and eager to re-launch the film by any means, MGM/UA rereleased it to emphasize what the reviewers had managed to overlook – the deliberate tone of mocking self-parody inspired by the tastelessness of its setting. As such *Showgirls* was redesignated as a prefabricated cult film, an exercise in heterosexual camp like *Repo Man* and *Mars Attacks!* (1996), whose in-jokes, rarefied irony and fondling delight in kitsch nourish cult viewing. What is so unsettling about *Showgirls* is that lines like 'I've a problem with pussy', 'It must be strange not to have people come on you' and 'The show goes on' are not bracketed off as inappropriate or deliberately funny comic effects. As with *Blue Velvet* (1986) the audience doesn't immediately know whether to laugh at or with the film. Should we, as most people ended up doing, regard its zingy clichés as evidence of naivety and bad writing or should we give Verhoeven the benefit of the doubt and conclude that they are integral to a meticulous spoof? Either way, the original negative critical judgement has become the definitive one, which the ironic 'so bad it's good' interpretation confirms rather than subverts. When Randy, the film geek in *Scream 2* (1998), is asked to name his favourite scary movie and smugly replies '*Showgirls*. Absolutely frightening', he acknowledges not only industry lore but a truth universally recognized. *Showgirls* is *Plan Nine from Las Vegas*. Case closed.

So why do I like the film? How could I be so wrong? Four years after it slunked off the screen (this chapter was written in 1999), trying to defend *Showgirls* might seem either perverse or uninterestingly weird. Who decides what counts as a cult film? Is cultism a personal or shared experience? Here I want to describe the viewing practices of one fan of *Showgirls*, a fan (myself) who also happens to be an academic. Whereas most cult films are marginal or overlooked movies with vociferous support from devotees of the different and transgressive, *Showgirls* largely attracted either disdain or camp appreciation as a pathetically 'bad' celluloid atrocity. It became a modest cult hit a few years ago among gay American audiences, who lovingly mocked its clichés and bizarre excesses, but no community of admirers has ever emerged to celebrate the film's merits. That I actually like *Showgirls*, then, to the point of being a one-person non-ironic cult audience, raises some interesting questions: Is my fandom a sad example of misplaced enthusiasm and poor interpretative skills? How does such active and perverse reading reflect the fan's needs and fantasies? Who, in a period of cultural relativism, has the authority to decide whether a fan's taste for and interpretation of a film are 'wrong'? And how many people do you need to make a cult?

A good deal of recent academic film criticism endorses a 'hermeneutic of suspicion', reading movies to find in them evidence of bad faith and ideological complicity. But film studies, for some of us, is mostly a continuation of fandom rather than of politics by other means. This chapter therefore muddles any distinction between fan and academic, enthusiastic partisan and severe enforcer of political rectitude. I define the film cultist as a sort of consumer-age aesthete, who insistently asks, as Walter Pater did, 'What is this song or picture, this engaging personality presented in life or in a book, to *me*?' As a cultist, therefore, I am less concerned with whether my interpretation of *Showgirls* is 'right' than with the solipsistic pleasures of being fascinated, aroused and uncritically 'interpellated' by a remarkable trash film. Still, film criticism has always 'advanced' by the aggressive re-evaluation of 'bad' movies, and what passes for a canon in film studies is little more than a quirky makeshift record of the enthusiasms of cultists, auteurist romantics and off-duty academics (categories at best blurred and overlapping). In this spirit, through an account of one fan's subjective discursive practices, I offer an interpretative defence of *Showgirls*, vaguely hoping thereby to re-appropriate a much-loved film from its camp detractors. At the very least here's a chance for scornful readers to find out what it's like passionately to admire the worst Hollywood film ever made.

A Sort of Interpretation

Briefly, my defence of the film goes something like this: *Showgirls* is a coherent, self-reflexive and stylistically dynamic send up of consumerism, Hollywood and the mechanics of the star system. Incidentally, I don't mean that the film is just 'interestingly' symptomatic of its period, whose discourses it happens to articulate more openly than most other texts. Nor am I making out that it is politically transgressive (the standard line nowadays for revisionist appropriations). *Showgirls* strikes me as being very far from progressive. It is an anti-humanist, even dehumanizing, film and like all exploitation movies entirely in love with its debased subject matter.

What I have to say about the film is necessarily very partial, leaving out much that many critics would regard as central to it. More could be said about its sardonic plagiarism of other movies – Busby Berkeley musicals, *All About Eve* (1950), *The Lonely Lady*, Verhoeven's own *Keetje Tippel* (1975) – and the contribution of the screenwriter Joe Eszterhas, who seems to have taken the film more seriously than Verhoeven ever did. One might also explore how *Showgirls* represents Las Vegas in comparison with the numerous other recent films set there – *Bugsy* (1991), *Casino* (1995), *Leaving Las Vegas* (1995), *Mars Attacks!*. Two key aspects of the film, its relation to erotic thrillers and its depiction of predatory lesbians, are covered elsewhere in excellent discussions by Linda Ruth Williams and Yvonne Tasker.[9] But I'll restrict myself, then, to a couple of ideas and move swiftly on to the main theme of this chapter, which is how the film works as the object of private cult fandom.

What is striking about *Showgirls* is not so much its sexual content as the possibilities for sexual display that it does *not* exploit. There are no romantic sex scenes – soft lights, soft focus and jazz music – no extraneous sequences in showers, no female masturbation or lesbian scenes; in short none of the staple turn-ons of softcore porn. The film records public performances with sexual content (lap dances, the stage show) rather than a succession of private sexual encounters. The forceful sweeping Steadicam presents sharp-edged action movie images of bodies in movement and hard at work. Besides a rape, the

Figure 5 A tender moment between Nomi (Elizabeth Berkley) and Zack (Kyle MacLachan) in *Showgirls*.

only sex scene, between Nomi (Elizabeth Berkley) and her boss Zack (Kyle MacLachan), is presented as a very obviously simulated performance, with much flailing about in a swimming pool. There are no intimate close-ups of the female body like the conversation piece pussy-shot of Sharon Stone in Verhoeven's *Basic Instinct* (1992); the emphasis is strictly on breasts, augmented or otherwise. The emotional implications of sex and the subtleties of sexual pleasure are unimportant; what matters is sex as performance, sex as work, sex as commodity and commercial transaction. Instead of adventurous, intimate explorations of 'sexuality', the film distributes quantities of choreographed flesh, nude 'stuff', across the widescreen.

This matter-of-fact crudeness of exposure – landscaping by nudity, if you like – is matched by the dialogue's hyperbolic obscenity. From mere exclamations ('Fuck! Fuck! Fuck!') to scatological jokes ('What do you call the useless piece of skin around a twat? A woman!'), the film boorishly insists on a vulgar anti-romantic 'realism' that identifies sex with the body. Yet for all its shamelessness, the film frustratingly declines to offer any release into authentic inner emotions. Far from being distinctive to character, sex in the film is a means by which bodies manipulate other bodies on their way to meeting career goals. As Claire Monk remarks – as a criticism of the film – 'The message we gain [is that] valuing the authentic self over the commodified self and of erotic self-expression over commodified sexual display is to be despised.'[10]

Nomi, with her multiply punning name ('No me', 'No! *Me!*'), highlights the film's existential ethic in her solitary (she's an orphan) and narcissistic trajectory towards gleeful self-abasement. The film suggests that under consumerism there are no authentic identities but merely a series of performances. Throughout the film names are exchanged (at the Cheetah lap dancing club everyone has a fantasy pseudonym); bodies – shaped to conform to standardized ideals – matter more than do any real selves. At the Stardust club the performers are interchangeable, functions of the corporate necessity to keep the show going – anyone could be the next 'Goddess'. The film deliberately eliminates psychological depth by reliance on stereotypes and by ambiguity of motivation. Who is exploiting whom when Nomi performs sex with Zack? Who knows whether her orgasm is real or cunningly faked? The acting is so exaggerated and histrionic that we get little sense of true emotion or uncalculated response. In keeping with this functional thinness of characterization, the film outrageously foregrounds its own glaring artificiality, from the numerous absurd coincidences (Nomi meets the same guy when she arrives in and leaves the city: she's Marilyn, he's Elvis) to the joltingly crude dialogue. Above all, it revels in Las Vegas's abolition of nature, the perfect setting in which to define the self as an empty denatured signifier.

The overriding theme of the film is sex as the performance of power, sex as a route to advancement within a corporate system founded on exploitation. Buying and selling are the business of Las Vegas, and no relationship in the film is uncontaminated by commerce. Nomi moves from prostitute to lap dancer to showgirl not to exorcise personal trauma or as means to self-expression but in order to more perfectly achieve independence through self-commodification – to become a complete material girl. Although she resists actual prostitution in the course of the film (in the backstory she is a crack-addicted call girl in New York), it is made clear that little real difference exists between the apparently discrete 'levels' of her career.

So far, so conventional, perhaps. What matters, however, is the relentlessness with which the film works through its metaphor of capitalism as prostitution. This motif, familiar from *Vivre Sa Vie* (1963), *American Gigolo* (1980) and even *Pretty Woman* (1990), which normalized prostitution as a career move, is used systematically to emphasize that, as one character says, 'someday you're going to have to sell it'. People are just exploitable flesh, whores in all but name. No less than *Casino*, in which Las Vegas symbolizes America's economic history from gangsterism to Disneyfication, no less even than Pasolini's *Salò*, *Showgirls* is about how a totalizing system of exploitation can be made to work. The exploitation in the film is of course inescapably gendered, so the film awkwardly does its best to universalize from the specific oppression of woman. The aim, however, is free-wheeling misanthropy rather than narrow misogyny: as one critic said, 'Reality, for Verhoeven, is that most people are nasty shits.'[11] The men are entirely unsympathetic, their expressions of power ranging from harassment at auditions to its logical conclusion in rape. The women, who are marginally less vile, have power so long as they are willing to be objects of consumption. Their complicity in exploitation is not only useful to them but also essential to their fantasies of self-creation – complicity alone enables them to maximize consumption. One hint of escape from *huis clos* is the friendship between Nomi and her housemate Molly. But even this transcendent interracial sisterhood is ambiguous; at best it is a means of sticking together to work the system more effectively.

The metaphor of prostitution is brash and cartoonish, as befits the reductive cynicism of an exploitation film. Far from stirring itself to denounce capitalist consumerism, the film merely lays bare how it functions in a 'life-mostly-sucks, people-are-mostly-shitheads' kinds of way.[12] That America, let alone

Las Vegas, is about consumerism; that sex is power; that we all commodified now – these gems of T-shirt philosophy do not require scandalized exposure. They are merely common knowledge, as obvious to us in life as they are to the showgirls (Cristal, for example, doesn't resent Nomi sabotaging her career – it's the way of things). Hard-bitten Gumpisms of postmodern cynical reason are spat out all through the film: 'Life sucks', 'Shit happens'. But the revelation of basic economic instincts can offer nothing new about human nature and social reality. The naked truth is on the surface – the system has nothing to hide because it is complete, perfect and impregnable.[13]

Nomi's experiences are therefore a fable of that most open of secrets – the dark side of the American Dream. She leaves Las Vegas at the end of the film, disgusted by the city's values and having, she says, gambled and won herself. But she is heading off for Los Angeles – in other words, for Hollywood – where the same system of exploitation is played out on a larger budget. *Showgirls* itself – and this is the film's sickest joke – only proves the point. Remorselessly exposing its actresses' bodies, it blurs the distinction between sexual performance in sleazy strip clubs and bidding for stardom in Hollywood movies. Berkley, churning eagerly over MacLachan's crotch, is just one more hungry wannabe lap dancing her way to the big time.

Showgirls mocks distinctions between good/bad, art/trash, authentic/ inauthentic, the aesthetic and ethical ideals trashed by the logic of consumption. Although judgements about aesthetics and talent are made throughout the film, it is unclear how seriously we should take them. Nomi's skill as a dancer is much discussed, but she employs it in an apparently worthless context. At the sex club James's dance routine, which is meant to be arty self-expression but looks suspiciously like pretentious nonsense, is booed offstage. Should we applaud the audience's good taste or condemn it as stifling 'genuine' artistry? Nomi is commended for her own good taste when she buys a Versace dress (she pronounces it 'Ver-saze') – yet Versace is the Verhoeven of high-fashion, an ironic pasticheur of trash for whom unembarrassed *bad* taste is a mark of true style. In *Showgirls* trash is indistinguishable from art; stripping from dancing; self-expression from pretentiousness; low-budget filth from expensive porn; Vegas from Hollywood; Hollywood from America. It's all grist for the mill of exploitation, the closed unbeatable system of consumer capitalism.

Memo from Boysville

To me as a fan of *Showgirls*, for whom it is *the* key cult film, this kind of legitimate, correct and persuasive interpretation of its meaning is not especially important. I can imagine that people might be cautiously intrigued by my brief interpretation of the film without caring to revise their appalled opinion of it. 'OK', they might respond, 'the film is a satire, but it's not a very good one. You're right about its intentions – but it botched them.' Still, why I like the film has little bearing on whether I get the meaning of it right *in public*, although as an academic I am obliged – that is, paid – to pretend that this matters very much indeed.

So what does it mean to be a fan or cultist of *Showgirls*? Being a fan of a canonical cult text like *Star Trek* seems relatively straightforward, at least if fannishness is identified with its more spectacular and productive manifestations. Trekkers watch *Star Trek* 'obsessively' – fandom is still widely perceived as 'sad' and inappropriate enthusiasm – turn up at SF Cons with phasers and pointy ears, and identify with a supportive community of like-minded enthusiasts who also 'get' the point of their beloved programme. Trekkers, though, are an unusually active and self-conscious species of fan. Most cult viewing is considerably less public, organized and socially useful. For many of us it is a private, even hermetic, activity enjoyed at home in front of the video recorder. As Steve Chibnall notes, 'Video transformed films from collective experiences to privatised commodities which may be used (like any others) in the process of individual identity formation and communication.'[14] By Trekkers' standards I'm not a proper fan at all; at any rate not an especially flamboyant, productive or sociable one. A description of what I actually do as a cult viewer would, I suspect, bore ethnographers of oddball tastes in movies. They'd be more interested in the dissident gay cultists at midnight screenings who performed along with the film, called out favourite lines ('You *are* a whore, darlin'!') and imitated the Busby Berkeley dance routines. Unfortunately, I can't claim to appropriate the film on behalf of subversive reading practices. Indeed by trying to reclaim *Showgirls* for myself, in the po-faced belief that it is really a good film, I risk seeming to want to 'straighten out' the camp interpretation and dismiss gay fans as delinquent misreaders.

What I do as a cult fan is this. I watch *Showgirls* on video, mostly by myself, and remind myself why I like it. Every time I see the film my interpretation is mysteriously reaffirmed. Fast-forwarding to keynote scenes – the 'Goddess' number, sex in the pool, the 'Ver-saze' dress – I am diverted, amused and interpellated by the tone of heterosexual camp. Today as I write, the clippings file on my desk bulges inches thick with newspaper and internet reports, press packs, interviews with the cast (Berkely gauche and nervous, Gershon breezily unembarrassed) and off-prints on Verhoeven. Beside the file, under two coffee cups the screenplay waits to be thumbed through once more. The soundtrack album whirs on the CD-ROM. A British quad (£10: predictably cheap) looms on the study wall as, more in hope than expectation, I trawl the Net again for 'showgirls' links. (The official and fan sites closed years ago; now you mostly get Las Vegas porn – 'the hottest sexiest nude showgirls, via live, real time video! Click here!' An advanced search finally comes up with blurred stills and orange-hued video-captures of the relevant celebrity nudes. Happily, I also come across some fan reviews on IMDb that echo my own evaluation of the film: I am, it seems, *not* alone.) Lurking in public I talk about the film, bore my friends with opinions about it, use it as a sign (or warning) of my unreliability in matters of aesthetic value. Now and then I lecture on its merits to disbelieving students (an activity which, if critical orthodoxy is any guide, uniquely couples sexual harassment with time-wasting). And, of course, vacillating between fandom and academia, I turn out articles like this.

In other words, my sedentary behaviour as a cultist isn't that much different from my usual life of academic research. I watch the film, drone on about it, collect secondary material and now and then jot down a few ideas. The only significant difference between *Showgirls* and the other films I research is that I rarely come across anyone who agrees with me about it – which only spurs on my mission to explain. In fact, the distinction between being a fan – an idiosyncratic partisan of texts and readings – and being a 'serious' academic is not always very clear. Joli Jensen has pointed out that academic research has much in common with fandom – *we* produce articles and attend conferences, *they* write slash fiction and go to conventions – but a 'system of bias ... debases fans and elevates scholars even though they engage in virtually the same kinds of activities'.[15] That's why it's hard for me to distinguish between the cultural production of this chapter on *Showgirls* and the sort of thing I might write for a fanzine. At most, they're just two kinds of rhetorical performance, which seek access to nominally different but equally valid interpretative communities.

Since I'm interested in Verhoeven generally – 'he has his followers, alas', David Thomson remarked[16] – liking *Showgirls* gears smoothly into an overall fondness for the director's work. What I like most about his films is that their facetious sarcasm and excess seem to speak directly to me. The elitist thrill of secretly shared irony, of exclusive access to double coding, encourages my belief that, like Sirk's admirers in the 1970s, I comprehend his films in ways unavailable to ordinary punters.[17] This empowers me to construct around Verhoeven a personalized but sociologically explicable cult as 'my favourite director'. For this fan, therefore, the point of identification in *Showgirls* was not with any of the characters but rather with the director himself – the unapologetic 'bad-boy' of flash-trash cinema, the intellectual Dutchman who frolics among the clichés of Hollywood blockbusters. A bewitched tourist in American excess, Verhoeven embodies an ideal of aroused, vicarious but wholly optional cultural slumming. Since I am captivated not only by Hollywood movies but also by the easy cultural capital I can make by 'seeing through' them, I recognize in Verhoeven my own (European?) ambivalence towards disreputable material which I both love and am culturally obliged to rise above.

This kind of postmodern irony can be seen as the 'habitus', the last refuge, of middle-class white male intellectuals.[18] It helps to explain why I might invest so heavily in – and be so wrong about – a 'bad' film like *Showgirls*. For as Chibnall writes, 'Paracinema ['bad' cinema] has provided opportunities for (predominantly) young straight white male academics to reclaim marginalised areas of cinema's history and to resist the dominant paradigms of film theory which have tended to problematise and pathologise male heterosexual pleasure in the text.'[19] A perverse liking for an 'obviously' bad film is a strategy for carving out some interpretative space and ensuring distanciation from an earlier generation of academics. Liking *Showgirls* is a special kind of cultural capital by which I signify both an independence of taste ('It's *my* film. No one else understands it') and my identification with the growing number of academic connoisseurs of trash cinema. Although few of them have much time for *Showgirls*, they certainly understand the sensibility that led to my over-investment in the film. Furthermore, my liking for the film can be understood – which is to say written off, symptomatized – in standard psychoanalytic terms as a fetishistic substitution, a screen memory, for some forgotten hurt (the marginalization of men within academic discourse? The trauma of separation from my mother? Who knows.) As Laura Mulvey says, the fetishist is disingenuous in pretending that the fetish ('preferably glittering, dazzling, attracting and holding the eye') has objective value.[20] 'Out of [his] perverse refusal of socially accepted value, a worthless object is elevated to the status of cult.'[21] Since I've little interest in psychoanalysis– science for people who don't know anything about science – I am unmoved by the possibility that I am in more need of therapy than an education in good taste. But I must admit that for many, more worldly critics my liking for *Showgirls* is easily explicable as a symptom of arrested development, and my preference for fan criticism as a childish recoil from the disenchanted world of adult film criticism.

Of course, describing the sociocultural background of my taste for *Showgirls*, proving the overdetermination of my failed taste, neither undercuts nor legitimizes my opinion of the film nor of the meanings I have discovered in it. To know *why* I read it in certain ways is not a prescription for how anyone, including myself, *should* read or judge it. Naturally, it dismays me to think that my interpretation of *Showgirls* is merely symptomatic of my position in the academic field. Rather than being an engaged, active and freethinking cultist, I am cruelly redescribed as a case study in cultural negotiation – Exhibit One: the postmodern white male academic. On the other hand, if movies really are nothing else than discourses knitted together by history, and if my skills of understanding and evaluation are merely functions of my social position and store of cultural capital, then I might as well relax into being a fanboy and a one-man cult audience. What else can I do? Society, history and habitus have rigidly shaped my tastes and sensibility, even down to my fondness for a trashy sex film. Liking *Showgirls* is the pathological response of a dubious social type. Sure, I could become more self-conscious and guilty about my tastes and interpretations – 'Omigod, I'm a middle-class white fanboy! Help!' – but that is scarcely grounds for dismissing them entirely. Why should I renounce what feels so right for me? And in any case who has got the cultural authority these days to write people off as bad readers?

The philosopher Richard Rorty offers an account of interpretation that I find relevant here in two important ways. First, he suggests how we can get beyond the 'genetic fallacy': confusing the merits of an interpretation or value judgement with the psychological or social factors that gave rise to it. Second, his pragmatist take on interpretation enables us to resolve a few of the tensions between academic work and cult fandom, between reading as a contribution to knowledge and reading as a private act of self-creation.

Rorty invites us to give up trying to discover the right as opposed to the most useful personal framework for interpreting texts. We should forget about processing texts through the grid of theory in the belief that we will uncover its true objective meaning: 'One learns to "deconstruct texts" in the same way in which one learns to detect sexual imagery, or bourgeois ideology, or seven types of ambiguity in texts; it is like learning how to ride a bicycle or play the flute. Some people have a knack for it, and others will always be rather clumsy at it.'[22] Proving that a text is merely a disguised ideological formation is a trick, a nifty party-piece, simply another way of putting it to work. Rorty wants to blur the difference between interpreting a text (i.e. like an academic) and playfully using it (i.e. like a cult fan) as a resource for idiosyncratic negotiations of cultural space. We should 'just distinguish between uses by different people for different purposes'.[23] In consequence he has a thoroughly laid-back approach to interpretation:

> I should think that a text just has whatever coherence it happened to acquire during the last roll of the hermeneutic wheel, just as a lump of clay only has whatever coherence it happened to pick up at the last turn of the potter's wheel. ... Its coherence is no more than the fact that somebody has found something interesting to say about a group of marks or noises which relates them to some of the other things we are interested in talking about. ... As we move from relatively uncontroversial literary history and literary criticism, what we say must have some reasonably systematic inferential connections with what we or others have previously said – with previous descriptions of these same marks. But there is no point at which we can draw a line between what we are talking about and what we are saying about it, except by reference to some particular purpose, some particular *intentio* which *we* happen, at the moment, to have.[24]

What is appealing about this is the element of romantic voluntarism – the assumption that we choose to read texts in whatever ways suit our own purpose. Rorty takes the standard post-structuralist notion of the open text and pushes it towards an irresponsible free-for-all aestheticism. Critics otherwise sympathetic to talk of open texts and active readers might still prefer to cling on to some notion of interpretative authority. Rather than privileging specific hermeneutic strategies they may wish to invest authority in the discourse of certain types of readers – expert and productive fans, for example, or those who speak from the experience of oppression. Rorty, however, recommends only that we strive for and value criticism that is 'the result of an encounter with an author, character, plot, stanza, line or archaic torso which has made a difference to the critic's conception of who she is, what she is good for, what she wants to do with herself: an encounter which has rearranged her priorities and purposes'.[25] That critics' (or fans') vivid description of such an encounter may in turn inspire other readers (or fans) to yet more vivid descriptions of their encounters with beloved and life-changing texts.

There are, needless to say, problems with Rorty's highly attractive anti-theory of interpretation. If you read with the narcissistic monomania he describes, then it is hard to see how any text could ever succeed in challenging you and altering your self-image. An honest encounter with texts and authors whose purposes are radically, incommensurably different from your own would become impossible by definition. Rather, as paranoid leftist critics somehow manage to find traces of ideology in every text they read, so too free-wheeling Rortyians find yet another excuse to ventilate their private obsessions, and the result is potentially as boring as other people's recounted dreams. Nevertheless, it is not hard to see in Rorty's defence of 'unmethodical interpretation of the sort that one occasionally wants to call "inspired"' an aestheticist manifesto for cult reading, which discards for good the line between academic interpretation and the unruly pleasures of fan activity.[26] Interpretation under this description is a series of quirky, unpredictable, self-pleasuring experiments in disguised autobiography. *Legitimate* interpretation is simply what you can get away with in public: the rare experiments for which other fans and critics happen to find a use.

For me, as an unmethodical if not very inspired fan, *Showgirls* has been an invaluable cultural resource. As I thought, talked and wrote about the film I worked through whatever obsessed me at the time – the double life of the academic fan; the sexual thrills of consumer culture; the inevitable triumph of capitalism; the agreeable way that irony legitimizes an addiction to trash culture; and so on. It was a means of revising what Rorty calls one's 'final vocabulary': 'the words in which we tell, sometimes prospectively and sometimes retrospectively, the story of our lives'.[27] Verhoeven's bitter, sexy, uncaring, stupidly ambiguous film lent itself perfectly to my intellectual fantasies and aesthetic needs. Now that this article is done and *Showgirls* is finally out of my system, I hope other fans and critics will be able to salvage something useful from my strange interlude in Vegas. Above all, I hope they'll be inspired to look again at *Showgirls* and then, goaded by the error of my interpretation, start beavering away on their own.

Afterword: My Bad (2016)

'*No one* seems to like it,' I wrote in 1999. Well, that wasn't entirely true. Tarantino liked *Showgirls* and so, it turned out, did many others, not all of them fanboys.

I just didn't know that at the time, not having the access I do now to the internet. The *Salon* critic Charles Taylor subsequently came out as a fan:

> *Showgirls* throws critics because it refuses to hold itself as superior to its subject, to deny the fascination and attractiveness of the flashy, trashy world it shows us even as it acknowledges its ruthlessness. ... Verhoeven and Eszterhas tapped right into the trash energy that powers American popular culture and understood how much that culture powers our fantasies of success.[28]

And so, more surprisingly, did the great New Wave director Jacques Rivette, who called *Showgirls*

> one of the great American films of the last few years. It's Verhoeven's best American film and his most personal. In *Starship Troopers*, he uses various effects to help everything go down smoothly, but he's totally exposed in *Showgirls*. It's the American film that's closest to his Dutch work. It has great sincerity, and the script is very honest, guileless. It's so obvious that it was written by Verhoeven himself rather than Mr. Eszterhas, who is nothing. And that actress [Elizabeth Berkley] is amazing! Like every Verhoeven film, it's very unpleasant: it's about surviving in a world populated by assholes, and that's his philosophy. Of all the recent American films that were set in Las Vegas, *Showgirls* was the only one that was real – take my word for it. I who have never set foot in the place![29]

In a 2003 roundtable on the film in *Film Quarterly*, Noël Burch argued that *Showgirls* 'takes mass culture seriously, as a site of both fascination and struggle. And it takes despised melodrama seriously too, as indeed an excellent vehicle for social criticism.'[30] The British Film Institute guide, *100 Cult Films* calls it 'extremely smart cinema: a passionate critique of the performance and exploitation of labour in the entertainment industry'.[31] In 2014 Adam Nayman's short book, *It Doesn't Suck: Showgirls*, echoed my revisionist argument at greater length and in persuasive detail.[32] He too highlights the film's irony, satire of America, and Verhoeven's and Eszterhas's use of exploitation to excoriate the vulgarity of contemporary culture by 'integrating grindhouse or rape-revenge-cinema tropes into their topless MGM musical'.[33]

Showgirls has continued flouncing towards cultdom, though still mostly in the guise of a now canonical bad film. When MGM/UA released the DVD in a VIP Limited Edition collector's box set with shot glasses and nipple pasties, the commentaries led by David Schamer, at MGM's insistence, mocked the film to seal its newfound commercial value as a camp classic.[34] Although, as Verhoeven has noted, Hollywood has gone in for few such sextravaganzas since, *Showgirls* prompted a sequel. *Showgirls 2: Penny's from Heaven* (2012).[35] A camp parody, if such a thing were needed, *Showgirls 2*, like *Basic Instinct 2* (2006), was

Figure 6 Penny (Rena Riffel) and friend in *Showgirls 2*.

deliberately rather than ambiguously naive camp.[36] A labour of love filmed for $30,000 via a Kickstarter campaign, *Showgirls 2* starred starred Rena Riffel, who produced and directed it (after Verhoeven declined), and who'd played Penny, a minor character in the original. Featuring cameos by a number of the cast, *Showgirls 2* reprised *Showgirls*'s plot over two and half hours that parodied many of the original's scenes and displayed its own line in quotable surrealism: 'Women are like bananas. They're sweetest when they're ripe. Right before they shrivel. But you, you are a banana split. With a cherry on top. And nuts.' Nayman and at least one other reviewer likened it to David Lynch's *Mulholland Drive* (2001), in which Riffel also appeared, but it is closer to the programmatic amateurism of John Waters or Troma.[37] The most interesting aspect of *Showgirls 2* is that it was a kind of female appropriation of the material and confirmation of the original's campness, made strictly for its fans: 'At its most basic,' as one online reviewer wrote, 'this is a movie about how much fun it is to obsess and quote and remember *Showgirls*, or any enormously ridiculous movie, for that matter. It's commentary under the guise of babble.'[38]

'Beaver Las Vegas!' was originally published as a chapter in Graham Harper and Xavier Mendik's collection, *Unruly Pleasures*, three years after I'd given it as a paper, to general disbelief, on a poorly attended panel at a Birmingham University conference on American studies.[39] Although hardly well known, the chapter nevertheless ended up as the piece of work with which I am still identified, not always for welcome reasons, and what minor impact it had was less than wholly positive. I originally and naively planned to publish it in *Sisterhoods*, a book on feminism and adaptation that I was co-editing, but the other editors, distinguished feminist scholars who perhaps wisely took a dim view of the idea, spiked it.[40] Some readers, as I anticipated, found the chapter a jejune and solipsistic inquiry into the problematic status of the postmodern white male academic fan, which is a social fraction from which, you might think, more than enough had already been heard. The chapter was specifically castigated at one of the first major conferences on cult film, which I couldn't attend because I was in, of all dubious places, Amsterdam (an excuse that caused some amusement), and subsequently in the book that collected papers from it, *Defining Cult Movies*, a foundational text for the subsequent development of academic cult studies. Jacinda Read held it up as an example of a kind of 'new laddism' in film studies, in which male cult enthusiasm legitimated 'othering' female tastes and derived its energy from countering the spectre of 'political correctness'.[41] Though much of the impetus of cult came from gay fans, the contemporary cult of trash can indeed be seen by its detractors as a straight male space of nostalgia, a zone of fantasy for those in full-on Oedipal revolt against the (feminized) mainstream. It was, again, a perfectly fair point, albeit one I thought I'd acknowledged by ironizing (*the* reflex defence mechanism of the time) the figure of the male cult fan. Read highlighted the shift taking place from cult being the preserve of soi-disant transgressive male fans of paracinema (gay as well as straight men) to its being more about fandom in the 'feminized' domestic space, where films like *Dirty Dancing* and *Titanic* deserved recognition as meaningful objects of female devotion and nostalgia rather than symbols of everything wrong with mainstream Hollywood. In fact, I'd argue that the main, albeit wholly unintended, usefulness of my chapter was in helping in some small way to generate Read's and Joanne Hollow's chapters, which are cited far more often in cult textbooks than 'Beaver Las Vegas!', whose main use to other scholars seems to be as a self-contained symptomatic case study. Read's and Hollow's criticisms of the masculinity of cult have proved highly influential. I pay appropriate homage to it myself by including a little section on *Mean Girls* in the previous chapter.

What is very apparent to me now is how much I *needed* to believe what I wrote in 'Beaver Las Vegas!'. Liking Verhoeven, for the first few years of my academic career, was part of how I projected myself, my schtick, and 'Beaver Las Vegas!' was, as it admitted, a deliberately provocative calling card from someone at a 'new university'. Being slightly at the margins of academia and not caring too much about respectability, I felt a sense of solidarity with other, mostly male, aca-fans carving out a space for cult and legitimating their passions in paid work. As an academic, I especially felt that I should disassociate what I then called my fanboy enthusiasm for Verhoeven from the task of coolly analysing his films, but it pained me to submit them to the rote symptomatic interpretation required by the then dominant critical discourse. What I did in the essay to reframe the film amounted to standard cultist ploys – reinscribing authorship and intention, so that what seemed bad turned out to be deliberately so or a means of Brechtian distanciation (the Sirkian move, you might say) and the film's flaws thereby reimagined as modernist renderings of kitsch; reading the film within the wider perspective of Verhoeven's films and neglecting Ezsterhas to some extent (a major flaw); blurring outside and inside the text; and suggesting the whole movie was ironic, setting up a satisfying distance between those in on the joke and the putative mainstream audience who took it as face value. I also read the film allegorically, which, like auteurism, is a standard cult strategy for both appropriating a movie and making it legible to a wider audience. For cultists of bad films these are powerful and satisfying methods of aggressive re-evaluation, a fact we'll return to when looking at Badfilm in Chapter 4. In fact, the piece did attempt to make my efforts seem respectable. Even though the essay's final section on Rorty was an aestheticist defence of, basically, saying what the hell you liked about movies if it worked for you, it was nevertheless a sop to the requirement to bung in some theory and sound vaguely progressive even as it cut the branch from under me.[42] The chapter, as it freely admits and like all my writing since, is torn between, and perhaps fatally compromised by, the desire to write as a freelance cinephile and the careerist need, even in a fan-press book, to talk the academic talk 'rigorously' enough to get entered into the research assessment exercises that justify our existence and social usefulness, encourage feverish overproduction of articles, and intermittently blight our professional lives.[43] Rorty's private-public distinction spoke to me because it summed up the disconnection I struggled with between how I wanted to write and the discourses, which I still tend to incorporate by over-quoting authoritative-sounding theorists, that made my writing acceptable within the field.[44] Although the chapter's somewhat passive-aggressive tone, moments of contrarian trolling and 'Het-camp' self-indulgence now grate even on me, I still pursue its argument of emphasizing cinephilia as a private project of self-fulfilment and identity formation, even if that does risk sounding like elite connoisseurship and an excuse for not doing proper research.

The context of 'Beaver Las Vegas!', the pre-9/11 tail end of relaxed postmodern celebration of different tastes, private pleasures and consumerism, therefore now seems remarkably distant. The chapter is complacently inside the whale of consumerism with little sense that very much is at stake in film interpretation beyond shopping around for readings that hang nicely together and, to put it pretentiously, stake out a distinctive position within the cultural field. The moment of the film and the chapter, in Britain that of *Loaded* and New Laddism, was soon overtaken by the feminization of fandom and the current integration of cult into academia within pretty strictly defined parameters – as transgressive texts to be understood in relation to subcultural fans, within a certain obligatory left-wing political framework, and against a background construed in stark apocalyptic terms as a war in endtimes against patriarchy, racism and 'neo-liberalism'. It was a moment too when grand theory was lapsing and more formalist and historical approaches (valuable but often dull and unambitious) were coming on the scene, and the field seemed up for grabs. The chapter yearned for a more relaxed style of cinephile writing that combined fan ardour with playful aestheticism.

'Beaver Las Vegas' is therefore something of a period piece, rather like the film itself; more Lad Vegas than Las Vegas. Being right about the film, as opposed to using it as a temporary sanctuary and excuse, was never the whole object of the exercise; indeed for a long while I didn't rewatch it, fearing I'd find it was actually as bad as everyone thought and that my defence was entirely a convenient post hoc fabrication. Twenty years after I first saw *Showgirls* I don't, however, disagree with what I wrote about it. If I *was* wrong about the film I was at least wrong productively and on my own terms. Writing about *Showgirls* did, however, alert me to those problems with fandom and in particular with writing about fans and cultists. Obviously I did identify then, in the blithe 1990s, as an enthusiastic fanboy on top of my day job as an academic. This caused no end of trouble because it so blatantly gendered my fandom. It would be embarrassing to identify as a fanboy nearly twenty years later, not only because I am middle-aged and hopelessly adrift from millennials' tastes in popular culture but because the credentials for serious fandom, at any rate as they are written up in academic research, have changed – from liking a film (a lot) to being considerably more active and productive. (In recent years I have often shied away from identifying *too much* as a fan, not because I think other people aren't 'proper' fans but because compared with many fans I hardly seem a fan at all; I feel more like an ageing dabbler who finds it hard to keep up. My identity may be professionally defined by fandom (I happen to write about things fans like) but not my private life, where I am merely someone who watches, owns and nowadays streams too many films). Fan studies, like fandom, has flourished since the 1990s, but it is still unclear what the pay-off has been. Although cult is obviously a species of fandom, I have to admit that I am not wholeheartedly pro-fan. Indeed my scepticism about the value of researching fandom has strengthened, even as my enthusiasm for cinephilia and cinephiliac writing has grown. My interest, I suspect, was always in the films themselves rather than, sociologically, in their fans. I am increasingly cautious about the emphasis, especially among 'aca-fans', on researching *only* fans, which as often as not means researching oneself and those among whom one feels comfortable in the safe spaces of the social network bubble – progressive 'us', in other words, rather than problematic 'them'. This academic investment in fandom can, at worst, lead to romanticizing fans (and aca-fans) as especially astute and authoritative viewers with ownership of films' meanings and significance. There is, admittedly, some truth in this view of the fan as super-viewer. After all, if you are receptive to a film, know a lot about it and have watched it countless times, you have earned the right to be taken seriously (the same is true of that other niche audience of attentive obsessives, film scholars). Even so, in the desire to vindicate fans and their awesomeness, fan studies arguably risks becoming unbalanced in its approach to audiences and their investment in films. Crucially, as I suggested at the end of the last chapter, it downplays the investment of other kinds of audiences in films that mean a good deal to them without its resulting in, for example, spectacular and easily researched online productivity. For one thing not all fans are, as it happens, particularly fannish. There are many 'fans who merely love a show, watch it religiously, talk about it, and yet engage in no other fan practices or activities'.[45] For another, studying fans doesn't necessarily tell you much about audiences in general or even much about the films. *There is nothing necessarily very interesting about liking something, even liking it a lot.* Fans are outliers, whether they are vocal enthusiasts or 'anti-fans' whose identity is configured around hating certain films. The pre-teenage boy who loves *Jurassic World* (2015) and the licensed Lego kits but cares nothing about what the film means, and the middle-aged woman with vague but fond memories of replaying *Dirty Dancing* on video – their emotions and interpretations are equally valid and revealing, as work on audiences and audience memory (fields I really ought to move into, if I can acquire the skills) is making clear.[46] With *Showgirls* the fans were a problem to me; their ironic appreciation short-circuited, however legitimate their uses of the film were to them, what I thought of as a more correct reading of the film – a paradoxical desire to be right about *Showgirls* while also appropriating, regardless of whether my reading held up, it for personal use. True, this could be framed as a debate within fandom, but it confirmed that fans needed also to be challenged, ignored or corrected, and that fan interpretations and uses of films could be no less incurious, limited and conformist than anyone else's. Hence, to be consistent, I feel now, more than I did when I wrote 'Beaver Las Vegas!', that taking cultists as a guide to how audiences relate (or should relate) to texts is potentially as misleading as taking fans as 'ideal readers' with greater authority than other anyone else. Fans and cultists may have the skills to enter into a film's zone of play but the fact they may also have too much investment in it can be a problem. In any case, though much less often discussed, love and hate (the two poles of fandom) are extremes even among 'committed audiences'.[47] Indifferent and bored audiences, rather than cultist audiences of passionately engaged fans, may be closer to the norm, and a good deal of viewing is distracted, semi-engaged and casual, and interpretations and meanings are elicited haphazardly if at all. If I were to write on *Showgirls* again, I suspect I'd be more interested in patterns of reception among viewers who didn't identify as fans, such as those who made it a hit on video or caught it offhandedly late night on TV, or those for whom it is an oddity or a guilty pleasure, or who simply, without any great fuss, really don't think it is *that* bad.[48] That shift (which, unlike textual analysis, needs 'external funding') towards looking at audiences and memories would certainly be a salutary jolt to the chapter's self-regarding assumption that, however idiosyncratic my response to *Showgirls*, I had nevertheless 'got' it in ways most people didn't or couldn't.

The problems I battled with in the chapter were the role of interpretation and the value of private readings of a film, while being aware that interpreting a film is a narrow and specialized approach to understanding it. Cultism isn't necessarily about reading movies and figuring out what they mean: that is a bloodless understanding of what undoubtedly can be the Dionysian, visceral, erotic, experiential aspect of watching, remembering and re-watching cult movies as divisive and flamboyant as *Showgirls*. Nevertheless, interpreting films and taking pleasure in getting them right – or rather right for you – can be important to cult practices. What fascinates me is the question, when does interpretation, insofar as that is a useful activity at all, slide into paranoia and conspiracy theory? That is the topic of the next chapter.

Chapter 3

Wasting Time in the Stanley Hotel

There is a thin line between clever and stupid.

This is Spinal Tap

The trick is not to care.

Fight Club[1]

Arguing that *Showgirls* was a coherent satire and not an aesthetic car crash necessarily involved me in the dark arts of film interpretation. And that's fine. It's my job and I get paid to do that stuff. I have, shall we say, a very particular set of skills, skills I have acquired during a very long career, skills that make me capable, within the limits of my small ability, of interpreting movies in print. But as a rule, I don't worry too much about what films actually mean unless I have to, which is rarely and frequently under protest – when I've been chivvied into it in a seminar, perhaps, or during a pub conversation where I'm the tame film guy who amusingly 'reads too much into things' for a living; the jargon of my profession then rises to the lips easily enough. On the other hand, I've admittedly spent hours of leisure time mansplaining to appalled loved ones why *The Wolf of Wall Street* (2014) is one of the greatest movies ever made, and doing that certainly required countering their objections with my own florid, parti pris interpretation of its purposefully satanic amorality (admittedly to no effect whatsoever). Generally, though, what a film 'means' bothers me only professionally or if I find myself in a fandom that involves debating meaning – as, to be honest, most of the ones I am familiar with tend to be. After all, it's hard to be a Verhoeven fan without having an angle on whether his films' trashiness and ambiguity are intentional, or a Kubrick fan without the perseverance to untangle the symbolism of *2001* and *Eyes Wide Shut*. But, while searching for deeper meanings is an intrinsically human activity, it is optional, insofar as there are numerous uses of films that are not curtailed by getting them right or coming up with a publishable interpretation. That is one thing fan studies has, to its immense credit, drilled into us.

Let's consider further the tensions explored in the last chapter between interpreting a film and what I've been calling, for want of a better term, personal use. I don't just mean welcome spin-offs like making fan fiction, a fan film or a comprehensive homage website. There are existential enhancements such as the film inspiring you, sharpening an emotional response or leading to conversations about life generally, such as you might also get out of a Jane Austen novel in a reading group without that necessarily requiring genuflection to the history of Austen criticism. Among Austen fans, Deborah Yaffe notes, 'the enterprise of Austen interpretation involved us in the narration of our own lives. ... We all wanted a Jane Austen who would reflect back to us the best in ourselves.'[2] Cultists, like Janeites and everyone else, may not worry about a film's meaning or meanings. What they like or find significant about a film could equally well be the experience of seeing it in special circumstances, discrete cinephile moments that prick them (as Roland Barthes said of the *punctum* of a photograph), or simply the associations and memories it sparks that enables them to reflect on their own lives. Yet, along with collating facts and anecdotes about a film, interpretation, as we've seen, does sometimes rear up as an integral part of cult activity. This is especially so if the interpretation is backed up with esoteric squirrelled-away knowledge and is both radically different from what most people think a film means and also (a paradox here) likely, if you go public with it, to entertain and strike a chord with other cultists (whose responses are a kind of informal peer review, saving you from making a complete idiot of yourself). One of the best reasons for taking fandom seriously is that fans, like academics, may get so up close and personal with a movie as to see more in it than either ordinary audiences or inattentive critics. Would Carpenter's *The Thing* (1982), for example, have gained its current high reputation as a horror classic if fans hadn't, after its initial critical and box-office trouncing, made a case for it in fanzines, magazine reviews and online? Just as liking a film that other people don't is a marker of cult enthusiasm, so, as with *Showgirls*, coming up with a counter-intuitive interpretation is one of cult's signal contrarian and performative delights. This search for deeper, or secret, meanings is one of the compulsive pleasures of cultism and a point of significant intersection with everyday academic practice. Interpretation for cultists can be a significant emotional as well as intellectual journey, and makes the film available for new imaginative purposes regardless of whether it works for everyone. A film is (to borrow another sentence from Rorty, who is referring to Heidegger), 'one of the experiences with which we have to come to terms, to redescribe and make mesh with the rest of our experiences, in order to succeed in our own projects of self-creation'.[3] A fairly straightforward, tongue-in-cheek example is Danny Peary's reading of Ed Wood's *Plan Nine from Outer Space* as a subversive movie along the lines of *The Day the Earth Stood Still* (1951). According to him, the aliens, led by the apparently crazy Eros, are the voice of reason in warning that earthlings 'should get off their destructive course, which will lead them to blow up the universe'.[4] Wood, Peary concludes,

> is more critical of America's government and military strategy (that calls for an arms build-up and further nuclear experiments) than any other director

dared to be. (Better directors who made pictures that made sense couldn't get away with such pointed criticism of American institutions).[5]

Is it true? Does it matter?
Such interpretative zeal can sometimes, however, go too far.

Room 237

A deadpan satire of film interpretation seemingly driven off the rails by cinephile enthusiasm is Rodney Ascher's *Room 237* (2012). In this wily documentary about *The Shining*, the film is interpreted in an exasperating number of different ways, united in the belief that Kubrick's genius lay in devising puzzles. The interpretations range from the modestly explicatory – that the film is 'about' genocide – to the invigoratingly crackpot, that *The Shining* is Kubrick's coded admission to his wife, Christiane, of his involvement in *Capricorn One* (1977)-style faking of the Moon landings.

Room 237 conceives of the film as resembling the Da Vinci Code, the viewer as Alan Turing confronted with an Enigma machine, and Kubrick as like Walter Sickert supposedly confessing in one of his East End paintings that he was Jack the Ripper. The participants in *Room 237* are not characterized like the eccentrics, kippered in nostalgia, in the documentary *Cinemania* (2002), but kept as authoritative off-screen voices given enough rope to explicate their theories and illustrate them with fair use clips. *Room 237* doesn't challenge or judge their theories, but simply lays them out and allows viewers to make of them whatever they like. Geoffrey Cocks, an academic pursuing the line of his remarkable, indeed brilliant, book, *The Wolf at the Door*, reckons the film is an arcane treatment of the Holocaust, 'a culmination of Kubrick's lifelong approach-avoidance syndrome with regard to the Nazis and the Holocaust.'[6] His theory is based on such recondite or subliminal clues as references to the number 42 (1942 being the year the Holocaust was planned) and a German Adler ('Eagle') typewriter, and is augmented by biographical knowledge that Kubrick had planned a film about the Holocaust, *Aryan Papers*. ABC News correspondent Bill Blakemore argues, more conventionally, that it is an allegory of the genocide of Native Americans, citing the hotel's location on an Indian burial ground and prominently displayed tins of Calumet baking soda with an Indian on the label. Jay Weidner touts the faked Moon landings theory, which he had been pushing on his website www.sacredmysteries. com, offering as evidence the Apollo 11 jumper that Danny wears and the cans of Tang, one of the drinks sent into space with the astronauts, which are visible in several scenes.[7] This particular notion, finessing a long-standing conspiracy theory that NASA staged the landings, keeps resurfacing, much to the irritation of Kubrick's family and his producer, Jan Harlan, and inspired the film, *Moonwalkers* (2015).[8]

Figure 7 Danny's Apollo 11 jumper in *The Shining*: evidence of conspiracy?

The most striking readings, as opposed to fattened up internet memes, are from Juli Kearns, a playwright and novelist, and John Fell Ryan. Kearns, who, in line with critics who see the film as an 'impossible object' that deconstructs itself as it goes along, analyses the contradictory layout of the hotel and fixes on supposedly telling background details, like a poster of a skier whom she imaginatively re-describes as a minotaur to bolster her theory that the film reworks Greek myth.[9] Ryan, whose creative misreading is in equal measure avant-garde and populist in its diverting immediacy, screens *The Shining* simultaneously forwards and backwards, superimposing the two versions so that they occasionally synch and unlock more meanings. This Surrealist procedure, reminiscent of Douglas Gordon's installation piece *24 Hour Psycho*, which projects *Psycho* in extreme slow motion, would be at home in an art gallery or as an online video ripe for sharing on social media. Its method is familiar to anyone aware of the 'Paul is dead' theories that attended the release of the Beatles' *Abbey Road* or who has ever played Pink Floyd's *Dark Side of the Moon* as a soundtrack to *The Wizard of Oz*, or indeed spun Judas Priest and Led Zeppelin albums backwards in pursuit of satanic messages.

The readings in *Room 237* are not unrelievedly mad but on a continuum of plausible eccentricity. Some of the more 'reasonable' ones have, in fact, been around for a while. *The Shining* had a poor critical reception in 1980 and like a number of Kubrick's films it took time for its reputation to be revised.[10] In fact, Paul Mayersberg reported that it had the worst reception of any major film of the year.[11] Sympathetic articles in *Sight and Sound* by Mayersberg and P. L. Titterington helped turn the corner and anticipated the key ways in which the film was read with increasing enthusiasm and respect over the next thirty years.[12] Clusters of themes emerged in books and articles about Kubrick – what

Figure 8 An eerie superimposition in *Room 237*.

its fans thought, let alone 'ordinary' viewers that it had entertained, is, perhaps crucially, less well documented. The film was reconstructed as an allegory of genocide, drawing on, for example, the red, white and blue colour scheme based on the American flag and the significance of that Indian burial ground and other traces of Native American culture.[13] In an important essay, Fredric Jameson, being Fredric Jameson, argued that *The Shining* was consequently haunted by History rather than ghosts.[14] The Overlook Hotel, in Jameson's Marxist interpretation, is where repressed History returns, collects and vibrates, especially in the spectral form of nostalgia for the 1920s:

> It is by the twenties that the hero is haunted and possessed. The twenties were the last moment in which a genuine American leisure class led an aggressive and ostentatious public existence, in which an American ruling class projected a class-conscious and unapologetic image of itself and enjoyed its privileges without guilt, openly and armed with its emblems of top-hat and champagne glass, on the social stage in full view of the other classes. The nostalgia of *The Shining*, the longing for collectivity, takes the peculiar form of an obsession with the last period in which class consciousness is out in the open.[15]

The Shining was a pastiche of its genre and its lack of depth – as opposed to the semiotic overload that is winkled out in *Room 237* – was a mark of its symptomatic postmodernism. In short, it is a postmodern version of the modernist classic *Last Year at Marienbad* (1961), figuring the emptiness of what Jameson, in hope rather than expectation, calls 'Late Capitalism'. The other popular interpretation of the film in the 1980s read it as a reverse image of *Kramer v Kramer* (1979) (as Cronenberg also called *The Brood* (1980)): a film about white masculinity and child abuse.[16] Centring on Jack (Jack Nicholson) and his violence towards his wife and son, it became a 'family horror' film, which was a key critical framework for understanding 1980s horror films that paralleled the increasing attention paid to child abuse in real life. My own favoured interpretation, also widely disseminated, is that *The Shining* is about making sense of the film itself (it's a meta-horror film, as Jameson suggested) and its own production. The hotel is a film set (as indeed it was, in Elstree), Jack is a writer-director losing control of his cast (his family) while struggling to obey the overlooking ghosts (the producers, the money men). He is gradually driven mad as he writes the script (*The Shining* itself, perhaps) day by day. As my elder son likes to say: Whatever.

When I first taught *The Shining* as a postgraduate in the mid-1980s, these interpretative approaches, which were overturning the film's middling critical reputation, could be gathered together in a useful pedagogic framework, allowing for the film's recasting as a politically subversive or meta-horror film. An *auteur* approach, pretty much essential with a high-profile director like Kubrick, also aligned it with his other movies' themes of male violence, dehumanization, free will and control by higher powers, and with their open narratives, symmetrical compositions in single point perspective, overblown performances and baffling endings. The film's meanings have shifted since according to fashions in interpretation, and such has the literature on *The Shining* expanded that there are whole books devoted to this once dismissed failure.[17] On the whole, as a heavily authored and arty take on a popular genre, it has been seen as being *about* certain topics rather than passively symptomatic of them. Elaborating on that critical history, the various interpretations in *Room 237* are tied together by a belief that the film holds a secret message. As justification as well as convenient brake on completely free form interpretation, Kubrick is presented as controlling the text as keenly as the hotel controls its unfortunate caretaker.[18] While more conventional ideological interpretations, such as Marxist ones, assume that the hidden meanings of the films are authored by history, those in *Room 237* imply that Kubrick threaded them through the film's maze deliberately or unconsciously after years of meticulous planning and subterfuge. As Cocks puts it,

> And even if one or another, or several, of the symbols or signs were not intentional at any level of Kubrick's consciousness, the overall pattern of concerns and connections demonstrates a more general guiding intention in line with long-standing authorial concerns.[19]

Post-*Room 237* the theories continue to mount up. A deft, probably satirical one (it's hard to tell nowadays) is a webpost, widely covered by sites like AVClub and Buzzfeed, suggesting that *Frozen* (2013) is a covert remake of *The Shining*.[20] In this webpost, Fox News contributor Mary Katherine Ham, wanting to 'take my rightful place among the crazy people' in *Room 237*, demonstrates to her own amused satisfaction that both *The Shining* and *Frozen* are movies 'in which the menacing main character is a danger to family members, whose volatility increases after a long isolation inside a giant, ornate, high-ceilinged building in a cold, desolate landscape. Perhaps the acquisition of a brand new leadership position set off an unraveling this character cannot control.' A more serious, hermetic approach is taken meanwhile by Nathan Abrams, who explores *The Shining* via the Jewish reading strategy of Midrash, as 'a means of formal or informal elaboration on Jewish scripture, as a form of commentary, in order to elucidate or elaborate upon its deeper, hidden meanings'.[21] This enables him to 'read Jewish' so that *The Shining* becomes an occulted retelling of the binding of Isaac with Jack in the role of Abraham. Like Cocks, he enumerates the various ways in which Jack is coded as Jewish, from his association with the colour yellow to his left-footed limping, which conjures Jews as not just 'sinister' but satanically deformed by a cloven hoof.[22] This kind of Gnostic interpretation is often a feature of cult, as Mathijs and Sexton suggest, and promises 'an escape from the world through the acquisition of esoteric knowledge'.[23] Comparing such Gnostic traditions of reading with the hermetic interpretation that is still mainstream in academia, Rita Felski writes that 'Within such traditions, all valued knowledge is secret knowledge restricted to a circle of initiates, and truth is synonymous with what is not and cannot be said. ... And yet the mystery that is unveiled ... is usually some variation of the ever-same theme'.[24] The emphasis in *Room 237* on hidden messages cleaves, whether wittingly or not, to the chief work of much academic interpretation, which is to *unveil* what the film is really about or doing, even and especially when ordinary audiences don't notice it.

The trick in *Room 237*, and to some extent in these other examples, lies in refusing the distinction between the relevant and the accidental, and treating everything in *The Shining*, from wall decoration to fridge stickers and limps, as potential clues installed in plain site by The Master. Graham Allen comments on the links between the paranoid tactics displayed in *Room 237* and film interpretation itself, the blurring between what Freud called rational and paranoid interpretation, both of which necessarily suppress chance:

> Before we assume too wide and too comfortable a gulf between these two perceived interpretive trends, however, we should register the fact that they share a series of similar habits. The cool rational 'science' of academic criticism, for example, shares with its paranoiac doppelganger a tendency to assume almost god-like levels of control and intention in Kubrick's filmmaking.[25]

The film, he writes, is 'full of Kubrick's intentional "thought"; but we can also "look" at it as emptied of intention and buzzing with potential meaning not motivated by anything Kubrick had in mind or at the back of his unconscious'.[26] The blank, empty stare of the camera which indifferently records what is in front of it necessarily includes elements of chance, which is all the more disturbing in a ghost story where no distinction is made between the real and the unreal because both are uncannily visualized on screen. Nothing within the camera's vacant stare is potentially without significance. One might add that Kubrick's use of long-held shots encourages the viewer to explore visual space minutely in all his films, space that is often packed with extraneous interpretable information (the consoles in *2001*, the hotel lobby with its pictures in *The Shining*, the painterly landscapes of *Barry Lyndon* (1975)), though empty of obvious narrative or thematic weight. (Nobody, so far as I know, has made much of Stephen King's being inspired to write the novel by a stay at the Stanley Hotel.)

Although *Eyes Wide Shut* has attracted much 'conventional', peer-reviewed analysis, it too has fallen prey to immersive criticism that verges on cinephile paranoia. Or, more accurately, it has been inserted into existing conspiracy theories of which the analysts are true cultists, especially theories fixated with a secret elite group, the Illuminati and that confused, often anti-Semitic zone where the Far Right and Far Left meet and swap places.[27] Videos online and available to purchase subject *Eyes Wide Shut* to detailed explications in the spirit of 9/11 'truthers', which veer from quoting 'sanctioned' criticism like academic articles to wilder readings based on prior commitment to the existence of the Illuminati in real life.[28] This fine interpretative madness is, once again, a product of finding significance in any random element of the film – for example, set decoration (stars, pentangles) with Illuminati significance – and integrating it into a totalizing external theory that depends on counter-knowledge about the Illuminati's goddess worship or the hidden persuaders of MK Ultra mind control techniques. Cocks, who unlike the other chancers in *Room 237* had done significant archival research, finds ghostly echoes of actual history in *The Shining*, which lends his analysis some credibility because it presses the methods of Jameson one step further. Commentators like IlluminatiWatcher, however, whose mindset seems more influenced by *The X-Files*, follow Weidner in treating *Eyes Wide Shut* as a one-stop portal to alternative history, rather like *The Protocols of the Elders of Zion*. Not surprisingly some readings of *Eyes Wide Shut* link it with Scientology, the cult to which the film's star, Tom Cruise, belongs. In *Positif* Laurent Vachaud essays an elaborate decoding that depends on the film being about a cult, one of whose members is Alice (Nicole Kidman), the wife of Bill Harford (Cruise), which provides sex slaves to the elite. According to Vachaud this links, if not actually allegorizes, Kubrick's daughter, Vivian, joining Scientology around the time of the film's production. Vachaud claims that the final scene shows the couple's daughter being whisked away from the department store by some men seen earlier at a party, presumably to become a sex slave.[29] Vachaud recasts the narrative entirely as part of what Eve Kosofsky Sedgwick calls, in reference to New Historicism, 'a paranoid project of exposure', though he aims to unlock secrets in Kubrick's personal life rather than to claim it's a documentary style exposé of a real cabal.[30]

While this may simply testify to the popularity and reinvigoration of conspiracy theories in the age of the internet and their aptness to bounce around the sealed echo chambers of social media, there is a special relevance to *Eyes Wide Shut*. Partly this derives from the mystery around Kubrick (popularly imagined as a surly recluse) and partly from his Jewishness, which encourages anti-Semitic identification of the cabal, of which he is alleged to have inside knowledge, with the supposedly all-powerful wealthy Jewish family of the Rothschilds (in one of whose houses, Mentmore Towers, a sequence was filmed for *Eyes Wide Shut*), but above all because the film seems to be straightforwardly conspiratorial in its depiction of a secretive and powerful overclass of rich deviants to which our eyes are, presumably, wide shut. Abrams argues that it (one assumes deliberately) draws on anti-Semitic representations of rich decadent Jews, such as Ziegler (Sydney Pollack), a participant in an orgy, who is 'only concerned with protecting the identity and reputation of its guests, rather than the legality, morality, and ethics of the event itself'.[31] The film pastiches familiar imagery of conspiracy, especially in the central scenes of the cabal gathering at the secret orgy to which Harford gains temporary entrance during his symbolic wanderings through sexual temptation. It is important, however, that in a long expository scene of dubious believability (reminiscent of the psychiatrist's prosaic explanation of Norman Bates's madness in *Psycho*), Ziegler, the presumed pimp to the cabal, refutes Harford's own paranoid interpretation of events, in which the cabal murders a young woman. 'She had her brains fucked out. Period,' he explains. This leaves open the possibility that Harford has discovered not a conspiracy but a high-class swinging set and its damaged hangers-on. It is impossible to say which interpretation is true, not least because the film encourages awareness of so many uncanny repetitions, symbolism (loaded references to 'Under the Rainbow', Christmas trees, 'Fidelio'), and other intimations of a hidden order, which the audience, like a psychoanalyst unpicking a dream, is invited to construct into meaningful patterns. Ziegler, in the spirit of someone crudely dismissing fancy film interpretations, pours cold water on the enterprise with the authoritative finality of a professor slapping down a gullible student. The obvious meaning, the surface one, is all there is. If we take the auteurist line, this is Kubrick's cautionary reminder that, just as Harford was led astray by his fantasies, the viewer, all too eager to believe the worst, should think twice before reading too much into signs, portents and accidentals. Desire, indeed a masochistic desire, to see corruption and conspiracies of power everywhere blinds you to the banal paradise of ordinary bourgeois life, as Harford, after his nocturnal descent into the underworld of sexual opportunity, finds when he returns to his everyday world of monogamy, commitment and the dignified security of the marital bed. That the film, echoing *Rosemary's Baby* (1968) and 1970s conspiracy films like *The Parallax View* (1974), ambivalently draws on these fantasies suggests that images of sexual decadence are themselves expressions of a widespread fantasy relationship with power (as in *Society* (1989), *The Ninth Gate* (1999), *Hostel* (2005) and *Fifty Shades of Grey* (2015)), in which the ultra-rich are not only supremely powerful, but, rather more excitingly, sexually depraved.[32]

Figure 9 Bill Harford (Tom Cruise) out of his depth in *Eyes Wide Shut.*

No wonder the film, usefully bringing together these conspiratorial references, has energized cult interpretation of the wildest kind. The truth is out there, and *Eyes Wide Shut* is an insider's skeleton key to a monomaniacal wider framework, as the readings potentially link everything to anything – IlluminatiWatcher's marvellously swivel-eyed article ropes in *The Wizard of Oz*, Lady Gaga, the Windsors, Scientology and homosexual hazing rituals at Yale.

Yet even these seemingly abstruse and determinedly cultish interpretations have their uses – projecting fantasies onto the film is a means of reading the world within one of those capacious grand narratives that postmodernism once declared abolished. The world is thereby made a little less illegible if more alarming. It may even, as Justin Smith says of online cult interpretation, help rework the self:

> At the same time, internet identities allow for the orchestrated projection of a subjective self which cannot be exposed as incomplete, unfinished, or socially inept. They enable amateurism to be taken seriously. Newsgroup communications can be a way of producing a symbolic self that is a misrecognition of subjective identity – a mask of disavowal. Finally, the symbolic work which cult fandom enables allows for the fashioning of a text in one's own image. It also fosters the ability to confer order, significance and meaning, and ignore the established categories of critical value. One contextual reason for the cult fan's focus on textual marginalia is precisely its lack of critical provenance: it is neither highly acclaimed nor widely popular, but it is imaginatively accommodating.[33]

Conspiratorial thinking is for the most part pathological but it can also be a useful way of bypassing rationality, thinking about big issues and countering common sense with imaginative cherry-picking, making life as exciting as a blockbuster movie as well as seeing one's little self as an elite seer. (In fact, to be fair to conspiracists of Right and Left, to class something as a conspiracy theory is a good way of marginalizing its dissent from mainstream ways of thinking.[34]) One reason why Kubrick's films as a whole are so culty is that they are about making sense of the largest themes and historical events, but their protagonists, who, unlike the audience, are not in on the secret, are dupes, functionaries and fall-guys of higher powers. The films reveal conspiracies and the working of forces beyond our control, from the generals in *Paths of Glory* (1957) treating war as a chess game with living pieces; to the mad establishment of *Dr Strangelove, or: How I Learned to Stop Worrying and Love the Bomb* (1964) – 'Have you ever seen a Commie drink a glass of water?' which parodies the idea that fluoridation was a communist plot – to *2001*, which is suffused with conspiracy in depicting the suppression of evidence of alien life; to the political brainwashing in *A Clockwork Orange* and *Full Metal Jacket* (1987).[35] *2001* in particular insists on a complete rethinking of evolution and history; its mythopoeic *donnée* isn't that far off Erik von Daniken's contemporaneous tosh in *Chariots of the Gods* about aliens creating ancient civilizations. Moreover, as has often been noted – and will be again in Chapter 9 – Kubrick's films are organized so as to force the viewer to interpret them holistically and conspiratorially by slowing time to enable meticulous scanning of the mise-en-scène, insisting on textual gaps and cruxes, and thereby encouraging self-reflexivity and intertextual exploration.

Conspiracies and Crackpots

To some extent, what we find in *Room 237*, with the striking exception of Fell's video art, is conventional film interpretation – finding clues, patterns, inferences, drawing the film into preconceived world views with an emphasis on confirmation bias. This is in the tradition of sedentary close reading, making elegant patterns, finding figures in the hotel's carpet, and treating the film as a puzzle in need of a definitive solution, an aha! moment. As David Bordwell comments in a blog post on *Room 237*, the readings are at the very edges of professional criticism, though the academic credentials of the interpreters are, in a democratic and levelling spirit, not evident till the final credits:

> There are other arenas of film criticism, and there's no mandate that discussion in those realms adhere to the constraints urged by professional criticism. Some readers prefer to muse on barely perceptible patterns, incoherence, unlimited association, and relatively unrestrained speculations about Kubrick's mental processes. Fans like to think and talk about their love, and anything that gives them the occasion is welcome, no matter what any establishment thinks. To a considerable extent, Ascher's film documents the habits of folk interpretation.[36]

Donato Totaro has related the close readings in *Room 237* to what has been described as a new form of criticism, 'immersive criticism', a term he takes from Chuck Klosterman.[37] Klosterman defines it as follows:

> This is something I've decided to call 'Immersion Criticism', because it can't really be done unless you watch a movie 10 or 100 or 1,000 times. It's based on the belief that symbolic, ancillary details inside a film are infinitely more important than the surface dialogue or the superficial narrative. And it's not just a matter of noticing things other people miss, because that can be done by anyone who's perceptive; it's a matter of noticing things that the director included *to indicate his true, undisclosed intention*. In other words, it's not an interpretive reading – it's an inflexible, clandestine reality that matters way more than anything else. And it's usually insane.[38]

It's a style of criticism democratically available to anyone and enabled by DVD and Blu-Ray, which allow you to watch a film numerous times till background and foreground blur in significance and the difference between an accident of production and an intentional detail becomes altogether moot. As Klosterman says, it is not strictly speaking an interpretative reading, because it reads the film in relation to secret realities and intentions rather than teasing out its textual operations. Though Klosterman says it can only be done with *auteur* films, I don't see why. The trashiest-seeming movie can be unlocked if you subject it to sufficient interpretative pressure. Like Barthes in *S/Z* sushi-slicing 'Sarrasine' into countless mythemes, an immersive critic can, in theory anyway, take the most unpromising trash like *Glen or Glenda* and by fixating on every detail show that it is as dense with implication as *Finnegans Wake* or Mallarmé's '*Prose pour Des Esseintes*'. It takes a ridiculous expenditure of time and effort to read in such extravagantly cultist ways, but as Ernest Mathijs says, 'Films and shows are turned into cults by viewers who refuse, or cannot afford to use the ruling models of the progress, conduct and governance of spending time with media.'[39]

At the same time, while at once troubling and diverting, this makes interpretation seem a trivial practice. Conspiratorial thinking as a wider phenomenon certainly, in its anti-Semitic pomp, isn't trivial, but wayward film interpretation arguably is. Girish Shambu, for example, has sensibly complained that *Room 237* undermines, in fact libels, the whole idea of criticism and interpretation as a useful enterprise:

> There are at least two problems with *Room 237*'s depiction of criticism. First, it is an activity that often comes across as outré, freakish or crackpot. (Witness the range of theories proposed.) Second, and more important, film criticism here is a largely apolitical, hermetic activity that moves inwards, carving out a self-enclosed space, the space of a cognitive puzzle, a puzzle to be solved based on clues well hidden by a genius filmmaker. (Prominent mention is made of Kubrick's 200 IQ and his prowess at chess.)

He goes on to remark that this depoliticizes the act of interpretation as a socially engaged and accountable performance.

> Spotting hidden references to the Holocaust or to the genocide of Native Americans is not in itself a critically or politically reflective activity. *The Shining* (while being a wonderful film, for many reasons) simply does not engage with these weighty historical traumas. It is not 'about' them in any meaningful way. And neither does it have to be in order to be a great film. But when *Room 237* represents film analysis in a manner that treats it as little more than a clever puzzle-solving exercise, it gives no hint as to the social value and political/aesthetic worth of this public activity. It never intuits what is truly at stake in the activity of paying close, analytical attention to films.[40]

This is, so far as it goes, true. It is certainly tempting to write-off these interpretations of *The Shining* and *Eyes Wide Shut* as bearing the same relationship to scholarly film interpretation as conspiratorial pseudo-history like *The Holy Blood and the Holy Grail* and *Chariots of the Gods* does to peer-reviewed academic history. But I'm not sure this wholly grasps the issues. Interpretation and criticism are self-evidently not the monopoly only of the academy and professional exegetes; this is interpretation from below, Bordwell's 'folk interpretation', which resists as well as approximates 'proper' film analysis. Anyone with access to the internet can replicate and disseminate the esoteric methods of tenured interpreters, or repeat them as farce; fans do it all the time, partly out of enthusiastic wackiness (James Bond is a Time Lord, Jar Jar Binks is the real enemy in the *Star Wars* prequels, etc.) but also because films and TV programmes are sometimes calculated, as part of 'fan service', to generate fan theories (*Lost*, for example, and the later episodes of *Sherlock*).[41] These tend, however, to be restricted to analyses of the films themselves rather than spilling over into proof of real-life conspiracies. (Men's rights activists'(MRA) claims that the politically correct representations in films like *Mad Max: Fury Road* (2015) and *Star Wars: The Force Awakens* are part of a misandrist conspiracy to marginalize straight white men are perhaps an exception, though the overwrought MRA are merely, in envious parody, reversing feminists' claim that most films are, deep down, evidence of all-encompassing patriarchy.) Moreover, Shambu's phrase 'outré, freakish and crackpot' might equally apply to Marx, Freud, Jung, Lacan, Althusser, Foucault, Baudrillard, Deleuze, Butler, Žižek or whoever it is that film studies, springing – to adapt one of Wodehouse's gags – from theorist to theorist like the chamois of the Alps leaping from crag to crag, has decided to land on this time. If you find it difficult to take these theorists, their politics and the remorseless pursuit of theory-based evidence very seriously, you'll need to find other resources. Alternative readings to the canonical hermeneuticians of suspicion are essential if your politics are not left-wing, as they tend to be in academic film studies and certainly are not elsewhere. You may want – which is to say, *need* – to interpret films (*sotto voce* maybe) according to your own conservative, anti-feminist or libertarian lights, whether that entails reading *Eyes Wide Shut* as an exploration of the dangers of swerving from bourgeois values and doing bad, bad things, or plunging fearlessly into the abyss of tinfoil hat conspiracies about the Illuminati.[42]

At this point, the temptation is to throw up your hands in despair, drop film interpretation entirely as a lost cause, and tear the playhouse down. Films, you might conclude, can be tortured into yielding up any meanings or unveiling any deeper significance you like, especially if those interpretations are symptomatic ones and the results are, for the most part, preordained by the theories, political biases and bees-in-the-bonnets of whoever is performing an autopsy on the film. Agreement on facts about the film might be possible, but as the comedian Stewart Lee once said, supposedly quoting a taxi driver, 'Well, you can prove anything with facts, can't you?' The classic account of the hermeneutics of paranoia and its enervating repetition-compulsion is Sedgwick's essay on paranoid and reparative reading.[43] She writes that 'these infinitely doable and teachable protocols of unveiling have become the common currency of cultural and historicist studies'.[44] Here (choose any film you like) is *yet another* convenient, easily discovered proof of Zionist conspiracy, neoliberal machinations, Straussian neo-cons pulling strings, the New World Order or 'whatever'.[45] As Felski says, 'What is the use of demystifying ideology when many people no longer subscribe to coherent ideologies ... when "everyone knows" that hidden forces are at work making us think and behave in certain ways.'[46] Kubrick's films tell us as much. This is one very powerful reason why, fed up with such circularity, academic film criticism so often nowadays does choose to leave interpretation to amateurs and fans, and turns to the sturdier empirical realms of audience studies and historical analysis – the so-called historical turn of the new film history. There is solace in eschewing methods that treat films as Rorschach tests and burrowing instead into archived documents and production histories, frame-counting, formalist analysis and collecting audience memories.[47] Or stepping back and viewing interpretation within the larger frame of reception studies, which suspends choosing among possible interpretations in order to explain the event of the film's interpretation among various 'reading formations', as Barbara Klinger calls them, and evaluating the competing investments in making sense of the film among constituencies such as fans, critics and also academics, whose very identity, living and professional advancement depend on innovative re-interpretation and discursive reframing.[48]

The boundaries between amateur and professional criticism and scholarship are ever more lax and permeable. As Totaro says, 'In film criticism, thanks in large part to the growth of online film communities (blogs, critical websites, file sharing networks, etc.) the gap between scholarly and non-scholarly film writing has narrowed.'[49] The point isn't that film interpretation is inherently conspiratorial, though it sometimes is, but that there is a fascinating overlap between academic interpretation and conspiratorial thinking as the interpretative strategy of the losing side, eager to discover reasons why the world doesn't turn out how they'd like.[50]

Playtime

Personally, I haven't vacated the playhouses of interpretation or film theory if they happen to suit my purpose (though right now I doubt I'll ever make much sense or use of Deleuze).[51] I'm not *that* nihilistic. I think of film interpretation as a curious mixture of professional obligation, a genre with flexible rules, and a private activity driven by fascination that strays casually in and out of communally accepted rules and boundaries, insofar as they exist.[52] Like Francine Fishpaw (Divine), in *Polyester* (1981), warily dipping into an issue of *Cahiers du Cinéma*, I'm sceptical but open to persuasion that interpretation is more than a game. Pace Shambu, I don't see why it shouldn't be a self-sustaining puzzle-solving Rubik's cube-like exercise using whatever talents and resources you have to hand. There isn't *that* much at stake. Why shouldn't an apolitical hermetic activity have its own justifications and rewards? Does such 'immersive criticism' make it a waste of time?

> It's a level of engagement that moves in two directions simultaneously:
> It bores deeper into the text (because the movie needs to be watched dozens
> of times, detached from the literal narrative) and catapults far outside
> of the celluloid itself (because the Immersion Critic has tapped into the
> private, interior world of the director's consciousness, at least in theory).
> It's like a conspiracy theory, except it isn't remotely harmful – it's simply
> a new way to make a complex film more important, highly secretive, and
> uncomfortably human.[53]

Instead, while admitting that film interpretation may indeed be a repetitive and sometimes crackpot waste of time, I'd like to put a positive spin on the activity by seeing it, reparatively, from a cultist point of view.

If society, including work, is seen as repressive and engaging us in continuous self-monitoring to become better consumers and obedient producers, cultism has a number of transgressive elements, which work both as a parody of consumerism (all that re-purchasing of DVDs in new editions and shelling out for memorabilia) and also precisely in terms of *waste*. In part this is because cult films themselves are often waste products – the detritus of culture, such as exploitation and trash films, to which the cultist pays exaggerated attention and lovingly elevates in defiance of perceived cultural value. Cult viewing of trash films involves a decision not to watch the 'good' films or the latest films or the most socially progressive films in favour of recycling old films and technologies and fetishizing the obsolete and transgressive. But cult film watching itself can also be seen as wasting time. This gives us an initial way of thinking of cult as a guide to life, or at any rate a guide to *using up* one's life. The time-wasting of cult, its frenzied idleness in binge-watching, watching films in surreal ways, over-interpreting them and spending hours exchanging ideas online, involves a 'deep' uselessness that is an affront to consumerism, which has its own tiresome ideas about how to colonize leisure, and to the time management schedules of work. At a time when, as Jonathan Crary argues, our days are being colonized 24/7 by work and consumption, time-wasting and reverie become a form of resistance through private projects of hedonistic aimlessness, much like the psychogeographical drifting of the Situationists.[54]

> One of the forms of disempowerment within 24/7 environments is the incapacitation of daydream or any mode of absent-minded introspection that would otherwise occur in intervals of slow or vacant time. ... There is a profound incompatibility of anything resembling reverie with the priorities of efficiency, functionality, and speed.[55]

Along with the Dionysian experience of the 'orgy', cultism stands for a refusal of productive uses of time, or as Mathijs and Sexton put it, 'The aspect of wasted time reflects on the unwillingness of cultism to slot itself into a conduct of time as prescribed by society.'[56] The importance of *play* is crucial here. Play becomes an escape from boredom as well as an attempt at mastery and projection of the self, and one of the many ludic tactics of overconsumption and overproduction is cult film interpretation.[57] This breaks not only from socially sanctioned regimes of film-viewing and reception but also from the progressive demand, implicit in academic interpretation, for viewing to a higher purpose, whether that means policing films for signs of political deviation or exposing their complicity in relations of power.[58] This is useful only because it is, like any aesthetic experience, gloriously *useless*, a testing of boundaries, an energetic display of cultural capital, and a finessing of one's sensibility and aesthetic resources:

> A cult-film experience relies on a drive, a search with a strong sense of involvement, without real aim, for some pure insight into a profound form of truth. ... The cult film experience is thus 'wasteful': a collective sentiment of shared emotions in the absence of purpose.[59]

Interpretation, to give it a cultist spin, is a self-reflexive aesthetic exercise, a way of understanding the world by exploring the texts that articulate our relationships to life. We can blur the annoying distinctions between meaning and use, conspiracy and rational interpretation, academic responsibility and amateurism, and settle on the emotional usefulness of what Jason Mittell calls 'forensic fandom'.[60] This is one way I'd think of cult interpretation, at its most extravagant in *Room 237*: a focused kind of time-wasting – or 'time out' – that through over-interpretation and perhaps over-sharing online reconfigures the film in order to suit your desires. Such interpretation is, in Smith's phrase, 'imaginatively accommodating' and a royal road to the hedonic bliss.

For myself, as an example of this, there is one possible entry-point into the Kubrick universe that I have been grappling with, though I probably shouldn't – the films of Peter Hyams, who, with one of those curious coincidences that paranoids delight in, directed not only *Capricorn One* but also *2010* (1984), the sequel to *2001*. I started, after a few drinks, to wonder if there was more to this, and have since spent many happy aimless leisurely hours working away at this maddening conundrum when I should have been doing something more profitable and accountable. Immersively I've watched those two incriminating films as well as Hyams's *The Relic* (1996) and *The Sound of Thunder* (2005), and 'uncovered' their connections to Kubrick. I haven't got to the point, and probably never will, of doing the right academic thing and writing it up fully – or turning it into a blog post or online video. The emotional satisfactions so far have nevertheless been immense, as has the bathetic and rather Pooterish sense of aesthetic and professional revolt. As I make notes, the ghostly possibility of other, considerably more sophisticated readings is ever present, overlooking my trivial piecemeal efforts – Jungian ones, Žižekian ones, Marxist ones, postcolonial ones (*The Relic* is perfect for those) – but I haven't delved into them yet. Like Bartleby, I prefer not to. Anyway, when it comes to such theories, you don't have to believe them. You can just use them as entertaining fictions that enable shapely reconfigurations of the film that connect it to the personal obsessions or political beliefs to which the film, ultimately, will be forced to yield – even if you end up, like Jack Torrance in *The Shining*, typing out meaningless nonsense and wasting my time and yours.

Chapter 4

Cult Adaptations

Adaptation can be a shock, a betrayal, a resurrection, commercial cash in, homage, act of loving remembrance or even a deadly curse. The cult French novelist Boris Vian actually died watching the film adaptation of his *I Spit on Your Graves*.

This chapter is about adapting cult novels and how their cult qualities, as it were, might be transferred to film. We often speak of adapting the 'spirit' of a book rather than attempting absolute fidelity to it, but how could the evanescent quality of 'cultness', donated, like 'classic', to the afterlife to the novel, ever be ported over safely to a movie? Adapting a cult book, whose cult incorporates a sense of its accessibility only to an exclusive readership of the elect, is arguably perilous. Adaptation may be seen by fans not as a welcome canonization or legitimization of the book, but as a threat insofar as it commercializes the book's unique pleasures. Adapting a cult text may therefore require delicate handling – or it might not matter at all if the fans or cultists can be safely ignored in the interests of expanding the potential audience.

That cult films are sometimes the product of adaptation is not surprising given that adaptation is the rule in cinema rather than the exception. Most films are adaptations of one sort or another and most filmmakers, even the most auteurists like Hitchcock, Ford and Visconti were essentially adapters, initially from screenplays of course, but also from commercially viable pre-existing properties. *Casablanca* was based on an unproduced play, *Everyone Comes to Rick's* by Murray Burnett and Joan Allison; *Rocky Horror* on a stage musical. *Blade Runner*, *Picnic at Hanging Rock* (1975), *The Warriors*, *Fight Club*, *The Searchers* (1956), *It's a Wonderful Life*, *A Boy and His Dog* (1975), *A Clockwork Orange* and *Get Carter* – all were derived from novels or short stories, and some such as *The Terminator* and *Hardware* (1990) from sources not revealed in their credits. Although *Blade Runner*, for example, was based on a novel, *Do Androids Dream of Electric Sheep?*, by a bona fide cult writer, Philip K. Dick, few of these sources were themselves cult or indeed especially well known in their own medium. They were certainly not adapted 'as' cult films, which given that cult invariably means box-office failure or at best succès d'estime would be a perverse ambition indeed.

That said, it is striking how many cult films are *not* adaptations of the straightforward, licensed kind. Casting an eye over the canonical midnight movies of the 1970s, I am struck by how few had a single originating source to which the film was expressly tied: *Harold and Maude* (though based on a student film), *El topo*, *Night of the Living Dead*, *Eraserhead*, *Pink Flamingos*, *The Harder They Come*, *Reefer Madness*, *The Texas Chain Saw Massacre*. None of these are adaptations. The reasons are multiple. Some were horror and exploitation films, which tend not to be inspired by the literary (studio films like *Rosemary's Baby*, *The Exorcist* and *The Sentinel* (1977), on the other hand, were). Others were idiosyncratic independent or underground films, removed from the mainstream commercial convention of buying a usable property and refitting it for film. Although I wouldn't go so far as to hazard that cult films are *less* likely to be adaptations of novels than most movies, there is some logic to that broad assumption. Cult films whose sources are also cult are certainly unusual, such as *A Clockwork Orange, The Princess Bride, Fight Club* and *Trainspotting*, though that doesn't imply that the cultists of the book and the film, which may come years later, are necessarily the same. There are only a handful of canonical cult films based on classic novels (Peary lists one, Wyler's *Wuthering Heights* (1939)) and those that are, such as *The Holy Mountain* (based in part on René Daumal's *Mount Analogue*) and *Apocalypse Now* (1979), radically swerve from the source in pursuit of other intertextual aims; the cult of *Apocalypse Now* certainly incorporates knowledge of *Heart of Darkness*, but it depends more on the film's deranged production history, quotable lines and confusing philosophical import. With Altman's brisk revision of Chandler's *The Long Goodbye*, the auteurist takeover of the source contributed to the film's cult appeal to cineastes, while annoying unhip Chandler aficionados with its quirky and subversive updating. The same is true of *Starship Troopers*, which Verhoeven appropriated from Heinlein fans and turned to his own wickedly satirical ends. *Bad* adaptations, on the other hand, are more likely to have cultness forced upon them because of their camp inadequacy to their source (*Mommie Dearest, Catwoman, Battlefield Earth, Mortdecai* (2015)).

When films are based on a cult novel, the relationship may be irrelevant to selling the film and its reception context. The sadomasochistic *Gor* novels, for example, have a truly subterranean cult. Written since the 1960s by the academic John Norman, these began as relatively conventional sword and sorcery novels with an emphasis on male domination, much in the style of Edgar R. Burroughs and the frankly erotic fantasies of pulp fiction. As the series went on Norman focused more on the domination, exploring this also with philosophical manifestos that extrapolated from the novels' depiction of an alternative social system of slavery, in which women held positions either as free women or as slaves. The novels' escapism was founded in the author's Nietzschean world view, which legitimated the frequent recourse to speeches and dialogue promulgating it in the later novels. The *Gor* books became controversial and were often banned, but maintained their readership sufficiently to extend the series to over twenty extremely long instalments and to spawn a minor cult lifestyle based on the novels' BDSM framework, which really did take the books as a 'guide to life'. The lifestyle can itself be seen as an adaptation, the playing out of the philosophy of the novels and its libertarianism in the real world. It is difficult to know how many Goreans there are but they are pretty active on the internet. The books formalized imitable shared rules of behaviour and the characters which speak to those in the Gorean lifestyle, for whom the books are a utopian distillation of their preferred erotic identities, which it should be emphasized are consensual and based on 24/7 total power-exchange. I am not sure exactly when the Gorean lifestyle got under way; certainly by the time Norman restarted the novel sequence in the 1990s, the Gorean lifestyle had emerged as a distinctive lifestyle. However, *Gor* (1988) and *Outlaw of Gor* (1989), the two films based on the Gor novels during the fantasy boom of 1980s, were adaptations of the novels rather than responses to the lifestyle 'fandom' of the Goreans. They drew on such elements of the novels as aligned them with sword and sorcery and not the BDSM or the philosophy behind it. The sexism in the films was, as it were, more generic. Online discussions of the lifestyle, so far as I can tell, make no reference to the films. While the sales and notoriety of the novels made them candidates for adaptation for the same reason as most adaptations – in other words, that they were a pre-sold commercial proposition at a moment when the sword and sorcery genre on film momentarily sprang into life – this involved negating the philosophical elements because the films had to reach out to a larger audience. The cult readership was, in commercial terms, perfectly ignorable because adapting the elements that interested core readers would marginalize the films. Moreover, the way in which the books' philosophy was communicated was in the most unhelpful non-cinematic style – mostly monologues, glossing the elaborate world of the novels and its gradations of slaves and other classes. The cult elements were, in short, detachable from the genre elements, and while the films have cult potential as 'badfilms' their cult, such as it is, is unrelated to that of the books. There, in short, can be a tension between directing an adaptation towards a readership cult and making it work for a mainstream audience.

The Warriors, Walter Hill's film, was based on a 1960s novel by Sol Yurick, which so far as I did *not* have a measurable cult reputation though its content (youth gangs) know it ripe for cult appropriation. Though the subject matter was pulp, the treatment was literary and referential: it reads like a cross between *A Clockwork Orange* and the novels of Hubert Selby, Jr. *The Warriors* was based loosely on the Anabasis of Xenophon, flagged up in a quotation in the front of the book, and was therefore in a sense an adaptation itself, in that awareness of this distant source enriches understanding of the novel's purpose: the story of the Anabasis, the march of 10,000 warriors to the safety of the Black Sea, is sketched out in the book and when they reach the ocean, they cry 'The Ocean, The Ocean' as the warriors in the Anabasis cry, 'The Sea, The Sea!'[1] Hill's film is free to change the novel in ways unrestricted by audience expectations. Although the classical source is not acknowledged explicitly, Hill includes another reference to it, changing the name of the gang leader to Cyrus (to whom he is compared in the novel) and giving the gang members heroic names such as Ajax (one of them in the book is called Hector), so that the film is double-coded as an adaptation of the Anabasis as much as of the novel. In particular, the film is transformed into a heightened comic book version of the novel, inspired perhaps by the fact that in the novel one character reads a comic book version of the Anabasis, and is set in a dystopian future New York. As Peary remarks, the novel is very different – the Dominators, the gang in the book, are losers rather than heroes, and there is a good deal of sociological comment.[2] The film, however, restricts its social commentary to a few brief scenes and moments – the meeting with affluent kids on the subway, for example, and the final comment that they ran all night to get back to *this* (Coney Island). The key change that is made is reorganizing the plot around fight scenes and adding an antagonist. In the novel Ismael (the Cyrus character) is killed by an unnamed someone in the crowd, but in the film it is made a specific person, whom The Warriors confront at the end. The cult of the film, as is generally the case, was inspired by extratextual factors unrelated to the book, notably the association of the film with riots and violence during screenings that led it to being pulled from cinemas. What seems to make the film persist as cult therefore is not its relation to the novel, but its fights, stylization, borderline trash artiness, the use of rock music as commentary, its comic book existentialism (very much in keeping with Hill's *The Driver* (1978) and later *Streets of Fire*) and of course its inflammatory reputation. Reference back to the novel, while instructive (as would, incidentally, be comparison with screenplay drafts and access to fly-on-the-wall discussions among the creative team), wouldn't give you much sense of the contingencies that turned the film into a cult; moreover, it wouldn't necessarily set terms for understanding the film – its use of music, genre, Hill's authorship, and its relationship to other contexts (urban hell films set in New York, gang films like *The Wanderers* (1979)) would do that equally effectively. As a rule, what makes a film cult is not elements taken from the source, but rather pleasures that are cinephile and distinctly *non*-literary. On the other hand, cult films are far from stand-alone texts but they 'adapt' by being exceptionally intertextual in so far as they play with or bolt together references to multiple sources (genres, for example). *Taxi Driver* is crammed with references to Godard, Bresson and *The Searchers*, while cultists have their work cut out catching the allusions and homages in a film like *The Big Lebowski*. A clearer sense of how *The Warriors*' cult elements could be mobilized would be apparent if there was a remake, in which case the original's status as a cult film rather than its source novel would present severe problems to negotiate. As it is, the film was 'adapted' further in a Director's Version, which added comic book elements which Hill said he didn't have time to do in the original because of a rush to get it into the cinema before *The Wanderers*, a similar (and now cult) film based on a novel by Richard Price. The lack of any baggage for the film, the novel being virtually unknown, freed the director into appropriating the novel for his own purposes.

These two somewhat random examples show the issues involved. Adapting cult novels may require adapting what made the novels cult; but it may not. A cult film may be based on a novel but its cult may have little to do with the novel's content or reputation. Drawing on cult material may marginally enhance a film's commercial and critical chances, but it may also imperil them. As Simone Murray says of all literary adaptations:

> The sector of the film industry focussed on literary adaptations constantly walks this fine line between cultivating the prestigious associations of critically celebrated and often prize-winning properties, while simultaneously ensuring their screen adaptation secures vastly more in box office returns and subsequent media sell-throughs than even a bestselling book was likely to have achieved.[3]

But before we ask how the books are adapted and the key problems involved, which can only really be addressed on a film by film basis, we have to wrestle with defining what a cult novel is in the first place.

Cult Novels

It is difficult to establish a canon of cult books. Cult film has at least the period of midnight movies to offset the inevitable circularity of defining the category. Any list of cult novels is likely to seem partial and random, Eurocentric (though there are manga and Murakami) and probably stuck in the 1950s and 1960s. A cult novel is, you might haplessly admit, whatever gets described as a cult novel; it is another discursive category defined by repeated use rather than by any definable textual quality. If we look at the few books that do categorize novels as cult, they generally list novels and authors from the late twentieth century and mostly, as you'd expect given their readership, from Anglophone countries or novels known in translation. Calcutt and Shephard, for example, define the cult novel essentially as outsider fiction with a bohemian, Left Bank sensibility: 'literature from the margins and extremes'.[4] Their authors are 'those who seem to have lived as saints, seers or pioneers of consciousness at its extremes'.[5] Clive Bloom meanwhile opts simply to define it in terms of pulp.[6] One can track a novel's entry into the cult pantheon much as one would a film's – by attending to its sales (slow but sure) and influence over time, to references to it in other books and in popular culture, to the appearance of societies and clubs devoted to the author, and to how the book gets repackaged and sold, much as one would its elevation into that similar category, classic (or modern classic). But each novel, like each cult film, has its own cult trajectory according to how it is recontextualized by new possibilities of subcultural relevance (feminist classic, drug classic, queer text and so on), and by its being taken up by various readerships after its publication. Cult novels may hang together but ultimately the reasons for the cult need to be explained text by text.

As a discursive category the cult novel – to restrict it to just that and avoid outliers like the Book of Mormon, the Koran and the foundational texts of Scientology like *Dianetics* – can be traced back historically to Goethe's *The Sorrows of Young Werther*, which is frequently cited as the first.[7] It inspired suicides after the fashion of its hero, and, as Whissen says in *Classic Cult Fiction*, it is the proto-novel of later cult novels' trademark theme of male existential ennui and anguish, as well as the cults of Romantic outsiders like Byron, Baudelaire and Rimbaud.[8] *Young Werther* can 'serve as a mirror in which the alienated see themselves reflected – and rejoice.'[9] But as a model for cult as a distinctive recherché taste, influential but seemingly marginal, Huysmans's *Against Nature*, linking Pater, Wilde, Mallarmé, aestheticism, and Houellebecq (whose *Submission* is a homage to Huysmans), is the definitive example. Whissen includes 'behavior modification' as one of his criteria for cult books, and while *Against Nature* has yet to be adapted, its central conceit of a young man's alienation and outsider lifestyle runs through so many films, it might as well have been. Huysmans's book furnishes not only transgressive ideas but also material for imitation in one's own life, as we'll see in Chapter 9, and offers a powerful aesthetic model for living aslant to the indignities of modern vulgarity and endeavouring to blur art and life. The transition to modernism saw a number of key minor writers whose works, like Huysmans, encouraged cult attention and have moved from outside the literary mainstream to acceptance within it, like Ronald Firbank, Arthur Machen and H. P. Lovecraft. But it is not just minor writers. Some modernist novels seem hardly readable at all without the close and sustained attention of cult commitment, notably Proust and Joyce. *Finnegans Wake* is an exemplary cult novel from that perspective as well as a modern classic.

However, this is rapidly descending into mere labelling, without the comparative rigour of a canon or a consistent timeframe to guide me. A definition of a cult novel or writer that embraces, say, Jane Austen, Proust, Rimbaud, Angela Carter, Richard Allen and Bret Easton Ellis is next to useless. A more sensible way of tracking what is meant by cult is to align the novels with readerships starting in the 1950s and 1960s, where the books were both inspiration and documentation of what might be called existential mythification, at the heart of which was fantasy and science fiction and dreams of exotic escape, both inward and outward. Whissen writes that the rise of cult novels was 'clearly located in the United States where, in the first few decades following World War II, the growing number of books that became underground or campus favorites turned the phenomenon of the cult book into a discernible movement.'[10] They include surprise bestsellers, beyond the control of author or publisher, such as *The Lord of the Rings, Stranger in a Strange Land*

and *Dune*, and transgressive Beat and genre writers such as Burroughs, Ballard, Selby, Vonnegut and Jim Carroll. These authors have a family resemblance in their depiction of transgression, underground lifestyles and their focus on male spiritual journeys and autobiographies. They are sacred texts that take time to read and be absorbed in, are sometimes difficult or esoteric, are complexly coded (for example, in terms of sexuality), and interest in them spills over into the author, the milieu (alternative lifestyles, drug culture, imaginary worlds), the locations of the novels, and the philosophical significance.[11] Cult novels describe existential situations or spiritual journeys away from social and ethical norms. Think (another list) of *Steppenwolf*, *The Outsider*, *Atomised*, *Siddhartha*, *Zen and the Art of Motorcycle Maintenance*, *The Dice Man* and *American Psycho*. These student favourites invent large philosophically charged worlds that enable one to lose oneself in allegorical pursuit of the largest significance. Think too of *The 120 Days of Sodom*, *The Lord of the Rings*, *The Magus*, *Moby-Dick*, *Gravity's Rainbow*, *Infinite Jest*. They are cult, sometimes, in their sheer length and the devotion required to finish them, but also in the fascination of their authors' lives. For a cult author, minimal productivity helps (Salinger, Ralph Ellison, Harper Lee, John Kennedy Toole), but so does maximal novel writing – Proust, Powell, Melville, Pynchon, David Foster Wallace, especially when accompanied by a sufficient authorial myth (such as Pynchon's anonymity). Indeed it might be more accurate to describe these as cult authors rather than producers of cult novels, which are as often as not one-offs, the rest of the author's works being relatively unknown. More to the point is the cult around genre authors who by reason of their outsider status, extremism, uncertain literary status and perceived difference from the mainstream of genre, have been detached from their genre or pulp origins and inserted into the literary canon – Dick, Jim Thompson, Robert Anton Wilson, Burroughs, Ballard, Vian, Bukowski, Alan Moore, Poppy Z. Brite – where genre is turned against itself into something more avant-garde and liminal. Such cult authors inhabit the zone between the literary and genre, between literary and autobiography or confession, between the novel and the anti-novel. Sarah Martín Alegre further distinguishes between the two kinds of cult novels, writers' and readers':

> Readers' cult novels [like Frank Herbert's *Dune*] depend essentially on the reader's identification with a strong individual character of mythical dimensions, whereas writers' cult novels [like *Naked Lunch*] are enjoyed because the author is admired by aspiring or established authors due to his or her condition as a highly original (Romantic) artist. This explains, in addition, why cult books are found at either side of the canonical divide and why they cannot simply be identified with pulp or popular fiction.[12]

As we'll see, their adaptation on screen, while often prompted by their cult at a moment when their reputation is secure, is nevertheless uneven and difficult. These films suffer from the obvious disadvantage of adaptations of cult books.

Cult implies a small, dedicated readership that is caught up in the novel's world, its ideas and perhaps the myth of the author, but the appeal of the novel, which is its spinning out of a coherent world view, is also likely to alienate wider readerships by its idiosyncrasy, claustrophobia, excess of detail and marginality.

Spoilers

Here I want to say more about adaptation generally, as it'll also be the topic of the new four chapters.

What I mean by 'adaptation' is not just novel to film, though that is the chief definition of it. Adaptation, to take a wider view, involves more than such direct remediation across media in the age of franchises and media spin-offs and embraces the recycling of textual material in such diverse forms as sequels and remakes. The key is the foregrounding of a film's derivation from a pre-existing text. It is this which frames the film as an adaptation, and presents it as a secondary text. Adaptation studies, a field of scholarly activity that has revived over the last twenty years, used to focus on the translation of books, especially 'classic' and literary novels, into films and TV series. Recent scholarship works with a much broader definition of adaptation, no longer taken to mean simply novel-into-film (with the assumption being that 'the novel is better') but also films derived from such non-literary sources as comics, trading cards and theme park rides. Emphasizing intertextuality over fidelity, the best work in the field locates adaptation within a range of long-established industry practices that spin out and recycle narratives in the form of remakes, sequels, hyphenates, novelizations, videogames, DVD extras and 'world-building' franchises as well as straightforward 'films of the book'. Adaptation, from this point of view, is a rational commercial strategy for commodifying textual material by disseminating it across numerous media. In fact, it is extremely difficult to find any film that is not involved in a relation of adaptation or indeed multiple, overlapping kinds of adaptation and textual extension. Linda Hutcheon asks, 'What is *not* an adaptation?' one might equally ask, 'What is *only* an adaptation?'[13]

Analysing adaptation as an industrial process therefore involves more than directly comparing books with films, using fidelity as the key yardstick. Adaptation, much like genre, is a method of standardizing production and repackaging the familiar within an economy of sameness and difference. There is a danger here of expanding the definition of adaptation so loosely that it loses specificity. As a rule, not all films are 'marked' as adaptations. Some films are inevitably so in their publicity and other ancillary materials, so that audiences are primed to view it intertextually. It is hard to see how a new version of *Pride and Prejudice* or *War and Peace* or an adaptation of a bestseller like *Gone Girl* or *The Girl on the Train* could be delivered to the world without trailing expectations and some promise of fidelity, even to audiences who have not read the book, or who remember nothing about it, but for whom the film is a legitimized encounter with the text or a substitute for reading it. But other films, either because they are not shadowed by their source's literary merit or because no one especially cares if they are adaptations, do not tout their derivative status. I doubt many people judged *Die Hard* (1988) according to whether it lived up to Roderick Thorp's novel, *Nothing Lasts Forever*; and the scathing reviews for *Mortdecai* rarely touched on its basis in the sublime cult novels of Kyril Bonfiglioli.

The problem with discussing adaptations is deciding why one should bother in the first place, given the ubiquity of adaptation as an industry practice. It is true that researching sources and seeing how they are transformed is instructive, whether that is how Shakespeare revised *King Leir* to produce his versions of *King Lear* or how new variations of that material (*Ran* (1985)) subsequently rework it in the development of what Sarah Cardwell calls a 'meta-text'.[14] In researching adaptation, is one tracking down 'sources' and 'influences' in a somewhat old-fashioned scholarly manner, as one might with Coleridge's borrowings for 'Kubla Khan'? Or is one gauging technical prowess, admiring the skill with which elements of the original have been put to use and transferred to the new medium (which could equally apply to putting the screenplay on screen), on the assumption that making one thing somehow resemble another is itself an achievement? This is to see adaptation, like translation or producing a digested version of a text, as a technical issue. How, one may ask, is a problem solved, such as communicating a tone or voice (as in *A Clockwork Orange*), a narrative crux, the look of a character, or meeting (or elegantly thwarting) audience expectations – whether it is ensuring the 'Bondness' of the latest Bond film or ensuring that the expected elements of a Marvel comic turn up in the film that is, for certain audiences – a pleasurable re-encounter with cherished material or worlds? This issue of teachable craft, especially at the level of screenplay, is, however, also about negotiating the particular context of adaptation, and that can only be understood in relation to the determinants of the production circumstances (the need to placate authors, for example, like E. L. James who oversaw the adaptation of *Fifty Shades of Grey*), the expectations of various audiences, and above all commercial imperatives. The approach taken to adaptation in reviews is essentially judgemental, offering a platform for reviewers to display their knowledge of the original novel and explain, as often as not, why a film version doesn't live up to its source. With classic adaptations, there is an undertone of disappointment in the film medium itself, which, however apt to replicate the plot points of thrillers, is held incapable of doing what serious novels achieve terms of depicting interior states and intellectual content. The relationship between novel and film is, as George Bluestone said, 'overtly compatible, secretly hostile'.[15]

To figure out how any particular adaptation works must involve not a point by point comparison with the original but a sense of the reasons, contexts and objectives of the adaptation. These are guessed more easily from ancillary materials, advertising and the reception context (chat about the film) than from the text itself. One needs to see how films are framed, or not framed, as kinds of adaptations by the discourses around them. It is true that adaptation studies has often been plagued by its piecemeal approach, dealing with adaptations within discrete case studies rather than offering theories of adaptation. This can be tiresome. But, as a rule, understanding adaptation is best approached on a case by case basis, for the reason an adaptation turned out as it did tends to be due to very local circumstances, a vector of forces that has little to do with a single-minded intention to make a faithful copy of a book. The novel, above all, is a resource rather than a template for imitation. While it is interesting to see how one differs from the other, it is hardly decisive: 'Every adaptation is an authored, conscious response to or interpretation of a source text, one that may or may not be concerned with "fidelity", but is necessarily concerned with the creation of an independent film or television text.'[16]

What links cult and adaptation for our purposes and makes them a semi-useful pairing is emotional investment. In other words, by bringing audiences and reception into the picture, we can focus on *caring* not only by distraught authors at what adaptations have done to their novels, but by readers of cult novels, whose relationship with an adaptation might be conceived as an emotional arc – from anxiety to relief or disappointment depending on the perceived success of the adaptation. Recent work on adaptation melds perfectly with cult in its emphases on intertextuality and emotional investment, and it also allows us to reinvigorate the idea, ritually overturned by adaptation scholars, of 'fidelity'. While fidelity has little analytical use, it is nevertheless still important not only to reviewers anxious to share their view of what *Pride and Prejudice* or *The Great Gatsby* are *really* about, but also to audiences who've already cast and screened novels in their minds' eye and may be disturbed by film's lack of faithfulness. Specific audiences, such as those for cult novels, may see adaptations differently from those without specialized knowledge, and it may be crucial in the promotion of films to engage directly with those audiences in careful ways. Again, understanding this may involve analysing not the film itself but the mediating discourses that present it to audiences. At the same time, one must be aware of competing and contradictory cults in relation to adaptations – the Dick cultist may disapprove of *Blade Runner*'s lack of fidelity; the Verhoeven enthusiast or Schwarzenegger fan may not care less that *Total Recall* isn't a slavish homage to the original Dick short story. Most audiences of course may not care at all.

This was brought home to me when researching Peter Jackson's adaptation of a cult novel, *The Lord of the Rings*, when it was clear that, though the film had to work for mainstream blockbuster audiences who would not necessarily care about the film's fidelity to Tolkien, the novel's cult readership had to be kept on board by presenting the film as a loving rendition by suitably devoted fans.[17] Jackson and his co-authors went to great pains to double code the trilogy with allusions, acknowledgements and moments of fidelity that fans demanded.

Fan audiences can be a pain in the neck, given the requirement to 'get things right'. This is more the case with novels with mass fandoms, such as *The Lord of the Rings*, *Twilight* and comic book adaptations, especially these days when a film's production and release are pored over and critiqued by fans online. But outlier audiences like fans are also a resource for contemporary filmmakers as Simone Murray comments, referring here to readers of literary novels, 'loyal readers of an acclaimed novel are important chiefly as opinion-setting early-adopters'.[18] Getting the fans of *Twilight* involved, keeping them sweet, has paid tremendous dividends in spinning out the franchise; equally making *Star Wars: The Force Awakens* essentially a rejigged *Star Wars* brought back on board many alienated by the prequels' attempt to be experimentally different from the original trilogy. Cult and fan audiences, in other words, are both a potential hindrance to adaptations, because they might loudly reject the film, but they are also lucrative small cohorts worth reaching out to.

It would, however, be perverse to expect any special relation of fidelity between a cult novel and a cult film, or indeed between any novel and what emerges as a cult film. Cult films, as we've noted, tend towards bricolage – a process that can 'wrench representations from their naturalised and centralised positions' so that 'any sense of a legitimacy or true place for the original representations becomes exactly what is under attack'.[19] If cult films are destabilizing and self-referential, this more so than with most adaptations works against fidelity. The source text is likely to be just one reference point in the intertextual whirl.

Incidentally, if you take an even wider view and consider adaptations of cult *films*, both informal and official, then adaptation and cult have a closer relationship. Some cult films have had their universes expanded. *Blade Runner* begat sequel novels, and a sequel film is in the offing too; *Rocky Horror* was followed by a film sequel *Shock Treatment* (1981), which owed little to *Rocky Horror* beyond music and attitude. *Quadrophenia* was adapted from the Who's album and then novelized, the novel incorporating the Who's lyrics. Many cult films have supplementary texts, such as novelizations (including such unlikely candidates as *Performance*, *Deep Throat*, *The Devil in Miss Jones* and *Taxi Driver*), annotated screenplays (*El topo*), audience participation guides (*Rocky Horror*) and numerous 'making ofs', while the films themselves have been re-produced in limited edition box sets, which finesse the films' cult credentials in the market place. These supernumerary texts, not to mention the mash-ups, fan homages, slash fiction and so on that the films inspire, and of course the generally ill-fated remakes of cult films, further cultify the material and monetize fandom.[20] We'll consider this again when we look at '*Jaws*ploitation' films.

Cult and the Unfilmable

Coterie enthusiasm for the difficult and transgressive, as a kind of elite sensibility not above slumming but intent on overturning literary taste, has some parallels with cult in film. There is an obvious rapprochement with underground and midnight movie tastes. In the light of this, you might have thought that, given their similarity to midnight movies, cult novels would transfer easily to film. It is striking, however, what cult novels have *not* been filmed and those which, once filmed, have acquired the status of 'failed adaptation'. Many cult novels tend to inhabit the category of the 'unfilmable novel', which is reflected in the negative reception of the novels that did make it to the screen. In theory being unfilmable applies to all books and their mediation; plots can be carried over, their cardinal points, as McFarlane calls them, safely reconfigured, but their style and spirit remain elusive.[21] This seems especially to apply to cult books, which expressly defy the cinematic by their inwardness, density of information, spiritual or religious overtones, sheer size and by their idiosyncratic style and structure. This is true not only when they are on boundary of the trashy and avant-garde but when they are genre novels or middlebrow texts insecurely related to the canon, such as the complex worlds of *The Lord of the Rings*, *The Magus* and *Atlas Shrugged*. The unfilmability of a novel can become part of its aura. The list of cult novels that have not been filmed is very long. Some, such as *The Catcher in the Rye*, have escaped because the writer didn't want them to be filmed. Others had long unsuccessful gestations, such as John Kennedy Toole's *Confederacy of Dunces* and D. M. Thomas's *The White Hotel*, 'the very definition of the unfilmable book', which at one point was to be made by David Lynch from a script by Dennis Potter.[22] Jodorowsky was going to make *Dune*, in which emotional investment in the text and a desire to match it with an equally grand authorial vision helped bring the project to nothing; it would have starred Salvador Dali and run at fourteen hours.[23] *Naked Lunch* was to have been made in the 1970s by Burroughs's friend, Antony Balch. *The Dice Man*, according to Calcutt and Shephard, has been nearly filmed several times since 1971, with a screenplay by Rhinehart. Donna Tartt's *The Secret History*, as yet unadapted, has an active fandom online which suggests possible ways to film it.

An unfilmable novel that did make it to screen is Hermann Hesse's *Steppenwolf*. First published in 1927, it was firmly canonical but, like Hesse's *Siddhartha*, gathered its cult audience in the 1960s as a counterculture favourite. Hesse became a cult figure – the fourth wave of enthusiasm for him, according to his biographer – with the publication of *Siddhartha* in paperback in 1957, after encouragement by Henry Miller.[24] *Steppenwolf* featured as a key novel in Colin Wilson's *The Outsider* and was lauded as a psychedelic classic by Timothy Leary, creating for the counterculture what Freedman calls 'an almost entirely different Herman Hesse', a 'new ahistorical Hesse' far removed from how he was understood in Germany. Hesse became a sage for young people inspired by the mystic East and the possibilities of spiritual resistance. The 1974 film wrenched the novel away from the author and its original context and offered it within this new cult framework, as a kind of hippie head film. Both it and 1973's *Siddhartha* aimed at the counterculture audience that Hollywood, in the wake of *Easy Rider*, signally failed to reach out to with films like *Zabriskie*

Figure 10 Psychedelic revelations in *Steppenwolf.*

Point and *The Strawberry Statement* (1970). Both Hesse adaptations were commercial flops:

> For as texts of instruction and edification, they were not suitable for visual representation. The figures that enacted the various changes of the hero's psyche were so clearly dreamlike and allegorical that the partially realistic setting contradicted the anticipated dreams.[25]

This underlines a few key points: first, that such an adaptation adapts not the novel itself but its public reputation; second, that a cult audience is not only unlikely to be large enough to make the film a hit but its rejection of the film can hurt it; and finally, that without intersecting with other cults, the film is likely to fail. Audiences in search of spiritual cinema would look to films like *El topo* instead, which were the thing itself and not *aides memoires* to reading experiences. By the time the film of *Steppenwolf* was released, it was already out of date.

In regard to contemporary adaptations of cult novels, one noticeable factor is that adaptation, when it does happen, often occurs years after publication, so that adaptation is an act awkwardly combining homage and mainstreaming. The books may have literary prestige but the film does not necessarily come hotfoot after its commercial success. *Naked Lunch, Crash* (1996), *Atlas Shrugged* (2011), *The Killer Inside Me* (2010), *The Lord of the Rings, Fear and Loathing in Las Vegas* (1998), *Where the Wild Things Are* (2009) – all these came years after the period not only of the book's publication but of the institution of its cult, at the point where the book was passing into classic status. This may be to cash in on the cult appeal of an old book taken up by a new audience (like the adaptations of *Steppenwolf* and *Siddhartha* in the 1970s, and Ralph Bakshi's psychedelic cartoon version of *The Lord of the Rings* (1978)), but it may also be cult adaptation as vanity project – it happens when the director, say, or star is old and established enough to get his or her favourite book or author on screen. The adaptation is likely to work most plausibly within the independent or art film category, perhaps filmed by a cult director, and will tend to imitate the recognizable but commercially double-edged style of a cult film. With such delayed adaptations, readers have to be especially cultivated. As Murray says, 'A film is "made" in terms of its popular perception as much by its marketing campaign and distribution pattern as it is by the images and sounds recorded upon its negative.'[26]

Without offering a taxonomy and bearing in mind the elusiveness of the cult novel, the following strategies seem plausible in adapting them so as to keep their cultness intact and commercially useful: (1) emphasizing the fact of adaptation, as that it may in certain instances be a selling point for small-scale films anxious to situate themselves culturally; (2) positioning the film as homage and even as partial version (as in Proust adaptations like *Time Regained* (1999) and *Swann in Love* (1984)) or flagging up its unfilmability (*A Cock and Bull Story* (2006)); (3) focusing on the figure of the author (*Barfly* (1987), which is as much about the cult of Bukowski as about his novel) or integrating the author into the text, for example, by conscripting the author to give approval to the adaptation (Tom Robbins doing the voiceover for *Even Cowgirls Get the Blues* (1994), which established the film's authenticity but did not prevent it being a critical disaster); (4) adapting according to the context within which the novel became cult, its underground status, for example; and (5) adaptation by a cult director or with a cult star (*Fear and Loathing in Las Vegas*, which is directed by Terry Gilliam and stars Johnny Depp, both cult figures though rarely to their commercial advantage). In these circumstances adapting a cult novel generally involves either adopting the stylistic traits of a cult film or emphasizing the independent cult status of the adaptors.

Bret Easton Ellis's 1991 *American Psycho,* for example, was also in the unfilmable category for its extreme violence and sex, though also its ambiguity, not least the suggestion that the entire novel is a fantasy in its protagonist's crazed mind. The book's refusal of generic norms as well as its visceral quality made it a problem for adaptation, given that what made it cult also made it resistant to being turned into the most commercial format for the material, the serial killer movie, which achieved peak popularity in the early 1990s with *The Silence of the Lambs* (1991). While the novel was about a serial killer, and highly referential to films such as *Body Double* and *The Texas Chain Saw Massacre*, its methods were very different from police procedurals. It consists of a long numbing monologue by the central character, Patrick Bateman, which veers indifferently from surface descriptions of fashion labels, to mini-essays on banal pop culture, to excruciating flat descriptions of murders. Sadean in its emphasis on the algorithmic abstraction of language, which distances it from the concrete factuality of film, the novel seems deliberately unfilmable, as if unfilmability were a mark of its literary status. The book was therefore a problem, though the unfilmabilty of the novel would also be a selling point. As with Kubrick's *Lolita*

(1962), audiences familiar with the novel's reputation might be drawn to find out how the problem was solved. After numerous misfires, with directors from Paul Schrader and Oliver Stone to David Cronenberg attached to it, *American Psycho* was finally put on screen in 2000 by Mary Harron, with a script by Guinevere Turner. Being made by women was presented as both legitimizing the misogynistic material (adaptation as correction, as it were) and enabling its recasting as unambiguous black comedy and satire. The long descriptive passages were relegated to voiceover, and the serial killer film was turned into an art-house film. The result became, insofar as these things can be judged, a cult film itself, partly because of the novel, partly because of the cult persona of Christian Bale, who played Bateman, and partly because it worked within the tropes of the kind of smart, blackly comic independent film that appealed to young audiences. In short, it was a programmatic cult adaptation.

David Cronenberg's *Naked Lunch* might, however, be seen as the optimum cult adaptation, as the final result could *only* be a cult film, yoked to its source and destined to be judged alongside it. As with *Crash*, the film seems as much about the unfilmable status of the book and the myth of the author, proffering the usual biographical explanation of creativity as a sort of madness. The extratextual insistence on Cronenberg's respect for and fidelity to the material and the appeal to film cultists whose taste would overlap with the counterculture vibe of the book ensured a 'fit'.[27] Most important was the fact that Cronenberg himself was a cult director, and the film was not so much a vanity project but an expression of a shared world view – the fit between Burroughs and Cronenberg was such that they achieved, as often remarked, fusion. As Ernest Mathijs remarks, even before *Naked Lunch* Burroughs had been isolated as a key influence on Cronenberg, who was being propelled into auteur status and away from the horror film: 'Burroughs' novel combined high critical esteem with an enduring cult reputation that resonated well in literary circles that crossed over with art-house audiences.'[28] As Mathijs also notes, *Naked Lunch* was one of several films in the early 1990s that adapted cult – or 'cool' – texts about writers, such as *Henry & June* (1990) and *The Sheltering Sky* (1990), which resituated them as historical films. It is a process of adaptation close to what Dudley Andrew called 'intersecting':

> Here the uniqueness of the original text is preserved to such an extent that it is intentionally left unassimilated in adaptation. The cinema, as a separate mechanism, records its confrontation with an ultimately intransigent text ... in this instance we are presented not with an adaptation so much as a refraction of the original.[29]

But, crucially, *Naked Lunch* was a relative commercial failure – an ongoing theme of cult adaptations:

> The way it settled Cronenberg's name with a core audience that *Variety* described as 'buffs' and 'highbrow audiences in general' and the manner

Figure 11 Visualizing the unfilmable in *Naked Lunch*.

in which it found a hardcore cult of 'cool literature' and chic post-horror in Europe added more depth and substance – more flesh – to Cronenberg's reputation as a respected cultural force.[30]

As with *A Clockwork Orange*, where a novel with subcultural cachet was adapted by a cult auteur, the cults reinforced themselves, but in this case the cult material restricted the film's commercial chances while elevating Cronenberg from horror director to auteur of adaptation (turning to literary adaptation is often a way in which genre directors establish more 'serious' credentials).[31]

What *Naked Lunch* does show, however, is that there is a certain kind of filmmaking available for adaptations of cult novels – essentially independent art-house films by cult directors whose films are aimed at what passes for a cult audience nowadays. One can, tentatively, make a similar case with Paul Anderson's 2015 film of Thomas Pynchon's *Inherent Vice*, which, for Pynchon, is relatively adaptable (though there is, apparently, a short film version of *Gravity's Rainbow*). I'm on stickier ground here, because although the novel is only cult in the sense that all Pynchon is cult, the film hasn't yet fully set out on its lonely trek towards cult status on the grounds it was a commercial failure but moderate critical success. The film was praised for adhering respectfully to the Pynchonesque, but this was partly because it also cleaved to a recognizable kind of cult film, itself Pynchonesque – critics referred repeatedly to *The Long Goodbye* and *The Big Lebowski* as its closest cinematic relatives as a 'stoner comedy'. It also depended on the pre-existing cult status of Anderson, a critical darling even though many of his films, like *The Master* (2012), were significant flops. *Inherent Vice*'s ambling plot line, noirish incomprehensibility which required multiple viewing, homage to critically lauded periods of film, and the cultural capital accruing to its status as a Pynchon adaptation underwritten by a credible auteur (one, moreover, who was taught by Pynchon's 'heir', David Foster Wallace), makes it *feel* like a cult film, as well as a party to which most viewers had not been invited. As with *Naked Lunch* the fit of material and author enabled it to work critically as a success while not making an impact on the public.[32] Intriguingly this suggests a new definition of cult, which, rather than focusing on active audiences, might focus on *critical* love for films that the mass public don't like (critics taking over from cultists as arbiters of taste, you might say) and is *condemned* to be nothing else than cult. In that sense, 'cultishness' – an appeal to a limited pool of cineastes, critics and art-house audiences – works in the film's favour, as a generic kind of niche adaptation. Here 'cult adaptation' works as a genre, reflecting the degree to which independent films style themselves as cultish films for self-selecting audiences.

With most cult films, their status as an adaptation is, as with most adaptations, only as interesting as one cares to make it. Most people haven't read the original if there is one, though it may become for cultists of the film another extratextual source of fascination (as David Pinner's novel *Ritual*, allegedly a source for *The Wicker Man*, has become for that film's cultists). With cult novels, however, there are distinct difficulties deriving from their characteristic unfilmability, one reason for their cult status in the first place, and those films regarded as succeeding as adaptations often do so by reproducing the given textual characteristics of cult films (that is, by and large, independent auteurist art movies), at the expense of box-office success. Cult is a treacherous category for adaptation, a marketable category certainly, but paradoxical insofar as there is slippage between cult as applied to a novel, which resists adaptation because it is authentically itself, and a film. Success in attracting a mass audience with fan-favourites, such as young adult novels, is one thing; success in making commercially viable a film based on a novel whose appeal is not its genre but its modality as a cult text is altogether more unlikely. Their chances at the box office, unlike adaptations of books with a considerable and more easily cultivated fandom, are predictably slim.

Chapter 5

Exploitation as Adaptation

It is better to fail in originality than to succeed in imitation.

Herman Melville, *Moby-Dick*

This shark, swallow you whole.

Quint (Robert Shaw) in *Jaws*

One frequently overlooked mode of cult remaking is the exploitation film. This chapter argues, first, that exploitation remakes can be usefully thought of as a branch of adaptation; and, second, that this throws light on '*Jaws*ploitation' films – the franchised sequels, unlicensed rip-offs and other imitations that followed the unprecedented success of *Jaws* in 1975. These exploitation versions – recently dubbed 'mockbusters' or 'knockbusters' – from *Grizzly*, *Tentacles*, *Tintorera* (1977) and *Piranha* right up to *Deep Blue Sea* (1999), *Lake Placid* (1999), *Open Water* (2004), *Adrift* (2006), *Rogue* (2008), *Shark in Venice* (2008), *Piranha 3D* and *3DD*, *Sharktopus* (2010), *Shark Night 3D* (2011), *Bait 3D* (2012) and *Sharktopus vs. Whalewolf* (2015) attest to *Jaws*'s memetic vitality and continuing cultural impact. My intention is to pursue '*Jaws*ness' across numerous adaptations from copying and plagiarism to parody, homage and glancing allusion. *Jaws* lends itself to this kind of cinephiliac intertextual *dérive* more readily than pretty much any other film, except perhaps *King Kong*.[1] Certainly, few movies have given rise to such an extravagant surfeit of imitations, so much so that the '*Jaws* rip-off' film is virtually a horror subgenre in its own right.

Adaptation as Exploitation

Roughly speaking, an exploitation movie is a low-budget feature film which caters to a specific demographic, often to the pointed exclusion of other audiences, and which advertises material unavailable in mainstream cinema. The 'classical' exploitation film emerged in the United States in the 1930s with independently made films dealing with topics prohibited by the Production Code.

Films like *Maniac* (1934) and *Reefer Madness* offered simultaneously prurient and self-righteous *exposés* of taboo subject matter, which, in order to appease censors and legitimate the public's curiosity, adopted a moralistic and educational manner. With the waning of classical exploitation in the 1950s, 'exploitation film' acquired a more wide-ranging and largely descriptive application. No longer referring to a discrete mode of film production, 'exploitation' became an all-purpose label for cheap sensational movies that were produced in cycles, intensively promoted and distributed to a sectionalized market.

Exploitation is an all-purpose and invariably pejorative label for cheap sensational movies distributed to a sectionalized market, nowadays mostly straight to DVD. What has usually been exploited since the period of 'classical exploitation' in the 1920s–1950s is a controversial topic like sex or drugs, presented in a luridly voyeuristic manner.[2] But exploitation films often explicitly imitate other movies, cannibalizing their titles, concepts and publicity gimmicks. Sometimes this gives rise to a tightly defined cycle of films inspired by a mainstream or exploitation success – a slew of blaxploitation films after *Sweet Sweetback's Baadasssss Song* (1971) or Hells Angels films after *The Wild Angels* (1966) – but it may involve aping, more or less faithfully, the most exploitable elements of a specific high-profile movie. Such exploitation versions – low-budget and invariably low-grade – piggyback on the hype accompanying a major release. Blaxploitation films (action films of the 1970s aimed at black audiences) ripped off mainstream successes – *Hit Man* (1972), for example, relocated *Get Carter* to the ghetto (though like the Stallone remake it credits Ted Lewis's novel as its source). This was Roger Corman's signature production method with *Bloody Mama* (1970) and *Boxcar Bertha* (1972) (cashing in on *Bonnie and Clyde* (1967)), *Death Race 2000* (1975) (*Rollerball* (1975)), and *Carnosaur* (1993) (*Jurassic Park*, which it pipped to the box office by three months).[3] Even though exploitation versions may borrow little more than a title, concept and poster design, that is more than enough to secure a potentially lucrative association with the original.

For example, the internet buzz around *Snakes on a Plane*, whose outlandish title earned it a cult following during production, inspired *Snakes on a Train* (2007), which was released to DVD three days before the cinema release of its big-budget rival. While *Snakes on a Train* pilfers *Plane's* title and basic premise, its supernatural back story, emphasis on body horror and curiously serious tone are sufficiently different to avoid a plagiarism suit. Some contemporary companies are wholly dedicated to pre-emptive straight-to-video imitations of blockbusters, notably the Asylum, which produced *Snakes on a Train*, *The Da Vinci Treasure* (2006), *Transmorphers* (2007), *AVH: Alien vs. Hunter* (2007) and *I am Ωmega* (2007), and Seduction Cinema, which specializes in such softcore versions as *The Lord of the G-Strings: The Femaleship of the Ring* and *SpiderBabe* (2003), *Kinky Kong* (2006), which seize on appetizing textual material and rework it in a lower – or since the originals are rarely art films, even lower – cultural register. Unlicensed adaptations often illuminate their originals by modifying and correcting their subtexts and implications. The possibility exists, though most parodies don't take advantage of it, that they 'might exercise their pedagogical vocation by revealing with clarity and irony the ideological significations embedded in the entertainment values of Hollywood high-tech spectacles'.[4] As we'll see in Chapter 7, even softcore and hardcore porn versions such as *The Lord of the G-Strings* and *A Clockwork Orgy* (1995) can been seen as potentially creative appropriations at the limits of copyright rather than simply as parodic rip-offs.[5]

Imitation is, of course, standard practice across all entertainment media. Hollywood minimizes risk by sticking closely to generic formulae and updating familiar properties in disguised versions. Thus, in ascending order of cynicism and postmodern homage, *Sleepless in Seattle* (1993) reworks *An Affair to Remember* (1957); *Barb Wire, Casablanca*; and *Disturbia* (2007), *Rear Window* (1954).[6] This might reasonably be described as exploitation, the economical reuse of pre-existing narrative resources (though unlike natural resources, stories proliferate rather than deplete with exploitation). Exploitation films, insofar as exploitation still remains a distinctive mode of production, are set apart chiefly by independent production, video or DVD distribution, vanishingly small budgets, an emphasis on nudity and violence, and often nowadays a self-consciously trashy air of camp parody.

On the one hand, exploitation is a minor, left-handed form of adaptation; on the other, it is adaptation's shadowy Other (as exploitation is also mainstream cinema's) – for *all* adaptation, by a certain way of thinking, is exploitation. Mainstream cinema adapts novels for the same reason exploitation films latch onto hit movies – it makes financial sense to capitalize on products pre-tested in the marketplace. Even with an eminently respectable heritage movie like *Pride and Prejudice* (2005), the purpose of adapting Austen's novel for the umpteenth time was to secure commercial advantage from its familiarity, Janeite fan base and literary reputation. Exploitation and adaptation differ insofar as adaptation typically implies an acknowledged and, if copyright is relevant, legitimately purchased relationship with a prior text usually in another medium. An exploitation film that copies another film, as a short cut to establishing a relationship with an audience, is constrained to play a different intertextual game from a conventional adaptation. While emphasizing marketable similarities to its unlicensed 'hypotext's' selling points, an exploitation film must nimbly evade the legal problems that would attend genuine fidelity; duplication must pass as generic similarity.[7] Crossing the line from exploitation to outright plagiarism (exploitation's own Other, one might say) can prove an expensive mistake, as in the case of *Queen Kong* (1976), whose release was blocked by the producers of the 1976 remake of *King Kong* because it violated their copyright on oversized lovelorn gorillas.[8]

If adaptation often invokes metaphors of adultery (a bad adaptation is guilty of infidelity), exploitation suggests other crimes – theft, con-artistry or rape. Even so, the most literary of literary adaptations shares with the most tawdry exploitation movie (and, one might add, with all remakes and sequels) this fundamental and troubling similarity – both are 'copies' typically regarded as inferior to their sources and even as *necessarily* inferior to them. This is no less true of Oscar-bait like *Atonement* (2007) than of trash like *Snakes on a Train*. Unnecessary supplements, both films exist in derogatory relationships of parasitism and anxious dependency on their pre-texts.

Jaws *and Intertextuality*

Jaws is based on the novel by Peter Benchley, a bestseller whose paperback rights were sold for half a million dollars and whose movie rights went before publication for $150,000.[9] The film's status as adaptation was emphasized in its publicity – which made sense since the book had become a publishing phenomenon.[10] The film acknowledges its source directly both in the text – Benchley has a cameo as a news reporter – and in its advertising, the poster design, for example, being carried over from Paul Bacon's artwork on the US hardback edition.

It is important to note, as I said in the last chapter, that not all adaptations make much of the fact. Adaptation is an optional frame of reference in the film's publicity as well as in the minds of audiences and critics. The frame's usefulness depends on whether the source's literary cachet or commercial success justifies discursively identifying the film as an adaptation in posters, trailers, press kit and other 'paratexts'. 'These secondary, ancillary and satellite texts', as Martin Barker argues, 'shape in advance the conditions under which interpretations are formed.'[11] 'Architextuality', Genette's term for how texts anticipate their reception by invoking other texts and contexts, prepares audiences to make sense of a film, manages their expectations of it, and retrospectively shapes their understanding of its meaning and significance.[12] In the case of *Atonement*, framing the film within a discourse of adaptation (indeed, one of authentic and faithful adaptation) was both unavoidable and commercially essential, given the high profile of the source novel and the advantages of aligning the film with the prestigious and lucrative 'genre' of literary adaptations.[13] Catherine Grant remarks, 'The most important act that films and their surrounding discourses need to perform in order to communicate unequivocally their status as adaptations is to [make viewers] *recall* the adapted work, or the cultural memory of it.'[14] The same is true of exploitation versions, whose ancillary materials discursively anchor them to their objects of imitation.

In fact, there are good reasons, even in the case of the most faithful literary adaptation, to argue against necessarily prioritizing the novel as the film's determining inter- or pre-text (strictly, if fidelity is an issue, a film should be judged by how far it realized the potential of its screenplay, which is the most immediate and authoritative pre-text).[15] As Sarah Cardwell notes, in any film adaptation 'a considerable proportion of the filmic text … is not explicable in terms of the source book.[16] This is certainly the case with *Jaws*, which, though obviously indebted to the novel for its characters, storyline and defining gimmick of the man-eating shark, is complexly related to numerous genres and texts ranging from canonical classics to camp trash.

Briefly and in no particular order of relevance, Benchley's novel shares discursive space (allusion, influence, similarity) in Spielberg's film with Melville's *Moby-Dick* (of which *Jaws*, as Susan Sontag remarked somewhere, is the fish fingers version); Hemingway's *The Old Man and the Sea* (1952); Spielberg's TV movie, *Duel* (1971), also about a relentless behemoth; 1950s monster movies such as *The Creature from the Black Lagoon* (1954) and *It Came from Beneath the Sea* (1955); Ibsen's *The Enemy of the People* (1882), also about a cover-up; the films of John Ford (the motif of the obsessive hunt echoes *The Searchers*; 'Shall we gather at the river?', which appears in several of Ford's movies, is whistled by two hapless amateurs shark-fishing with the Sunday roast) and Howard Hawks's (the theme of male camaraderie); and crucially Hitchcock's *Vertigo* (the track in and zoom out '*Vertigo*' shot when Brody sees the attack on the Kintner boy), *Psycho* (1960) (the first shark attack intricately re-imagines the shower scene), and *The Birds* (1962). An important precursor in raising public awareness of Great Whites was the documentary, *Blue Water White Death* (1971), in which Ron and Valerie Taylor, who later filmed the shark footage in *Jaws*, go in pursuit of the elusive beasts (the film also inspired *The Life Aquatic with Steve Zissou* (2004)). The thudding rhythms of John Williams's unforgettable score – only matched by *Psycho* as meme – draws on Stravinsky's 'The Rite of Spring', which filmgoers of Spielberg's generation might recognize as the soundtrack to the dinosaur sequence in *Fantasia* (1940) – an entirely appropriate reference point for *Jaws*' invocation of ancient primeval terror. (Some of the cues of *Creature of the Black Lagoon*'s composite score of original and reused music, for example at 21 and 24–5 minutes, are echoed in *Jaws*.) A more complex intertextual secret sharer is Disney's *20,000 Leagues under the Sea* (1954). Captain Nemo, who rams ships with his shark-like submarine, the Nautilus, is like Ahab, another prototype for Quint's obsession with nautical revenge. As well as Monstro the Whale in Disney's *Pinocchio* (1940), Spielberg's mechanical shark pays homage to *20,000 Leagues*'s giant squid, the most celebrated SFX sea beast before *Jaws*; both were designed by Robert A. Mattey. And both films allude to the horrors of the Bomb: the Nautilus is driven by atomic power, while Quint survived the sinking of the USS Indianapolis, which delivered the Hiroshima bomb to the island of Tinian in 1945. *Jaws* also belongs with two specific generic trends of the early 1970s – disaster movies such as *The Poseidon Adventure* and *Earthquake*, in which ordinary people confront natural catastrophes; and 'revenge of nature' horror films such as *Willard* (1971), *Frogs* (1972), *Ben* (1972) and *Phase IV* (1974). *Jaws*'s anthropophagous oral fixation aligns it too with the cannibalistic themes of *Night of the Living Dead* and *The Texas Chain Saw Massacre* and, on a Freudian level, with the porn film, *Deep Throat* (1972), which is name-checked when a fisherman remarks of the gaping maw of a strung-up tiger shark, 'It's got a deep throat, Frank.' An allusion to Watergate is perhaps also intended (Deep Throat being of course the cover name of *The Washington Post*'s high-placed informant), for there are other sly references to the scandal: the mayor is a ringer for Nixon and the medical officer for Kissinger.

One could try to pin down the different kinds of adaptation involved here, ranging from direct translation of the novel to the unsystematic allusions characteristic of New Hollywood's playful cinephilia (though Spielberg's key reference points are much the same as the other Movie Brats': *The Searchers*, Corman, Hawks, the American Hitchcock), allusions that, like wormholes, connect the film to very different intertextual worlds.[17] Adaptation studies is fixated on taxonomies minutely separating out and defining the different orders of adaptation and 'transtextuality' but it is difficult to do this here with any great accuracy (or enthusiasm).[18]

Take, for example, *Moby-Dick*, which *Jaws* in one way or another resembles, or is inspired by, or riffs on, or degradingly popularizes, or indeed exploits (though, according to John Baxter, Spielberg 'complained the book had a little *Peyton Place*, a little *Godfather*, a little *Enemy of the People* and plenty of *Moby-Dick*' and that he 'spent a lot of time taking out the similarities between … Melville and Benchley'.)[19] *Jaws* the film has obvious parallels to Melville's novel – the white shark recalls the whiteness of the whale; Quint's obsession mirrors Ahab's; it all culminates in a sea chase. In Benchley's novel the shark dies (or seems to die) spiralling downwards with Quint strapped to it as Ahab was to the whale, which being an archetype survives. Spielberg's ending, in which the shark is defeated, wrenches the material away from Melville and locates it firmly within the tradition of the horror film. But as Dean Crawford notes, it is the film that ironically is perhaps in the end more faithful to Melville:

> While both the movie and book versions of *Jaws* owe considerable debt to Melville, Spielberg's is greater since his shark is the more mysterious monster, a malevolent counterforce to our own species. Whereas in Benchley's *Jaws* nature strikes back unwittingly, Spielberg's shark, like Melville's white whale, appears to operate with a motive at least as methodical as Ahab's madness.[20]

There are other echoes of *Moby-Dick* in the film – the song 'Farewell and ado to you fair Spanish ladies' is in both but as it is a traditional sea shanty, this may really just be coincidence.[21] (It later crops up as a tantalizing echo in *Master and Commander: The Far Side of the World* (2003).) Allusions to the *novel* of *Moby-Dick* are in any case questionable, since they might equally well refer to John Huston's 1956 film version; which would be in keeping with Spielberg's method of displacing literary references by cinematic ones. Indeed an early draft screenplay showed Quint laughing at Huston's *Moby-Dick* in a cinema (the object of mirth is perhaps Gregory Peck: miscast by Huston, he would have made a pretty good Quint) – an adaptation of that scene turns up in Scorsese's *Cape Fear* (1991) (another Peck remake, to continue the game of movie connections). Although Quint is generally taken to be a parodic Ahab, his unusual name has resonances not only of Queequeg but we might also pick up – to *The Turn of the Screw* and Jack Clayton's adaptation, *The Innocents* (1961), in which Quint is a malevolent supernatural perversion of masculinity; and to *The Nightcomers* (1971), Michael Winner's exploitation prequel to *The Turn of the Screw*, in which Marlon Brando's Quint represents, like Shaw in *Jaws*, a style of working-class masculinity made obsolete in the New Hollywood by ordinary bourgeois guys like Scheider and Dreyfuss. Quint also carries faint echoes of Queeg, the mad captain played by Humphrey Bogart in *The Caine Mutiny* (1954), though Quint is the gamey consummation of every movie sea dog from Ahab to Captain Bligh. These allusions, if that is what they are, should not lead us to conclude that *Jaws* is not an adaptation of Benchley after all or that *Moby-Dick* is not worth comparative study.[22] They simply confirm that films have their own referential ecology and multiple lines of intertextual descent. Christine Geraghty puts this well: 'The complex textual referencing of many adaptations, their layering of genres, performances and settings, provides evidence for how they work as films, not as versions of another form nor as a whirl of references without their own shape.'[23] Indeed, the crucial intertextual relationship informing *Jaws* aesthetically is arguably Hitchcock, who is evoked through allusions, rather than *Moby-Dick*, which is the film's mythic prototype, or Benchley's novel, which supplied most of its cardinal functions.

Jaws*ploitation*

The success of *Jaws* led to (and pioneered the idea of) multiple sequels as well as prompting dozens of *Jaws*ploitation movies from as far afield as Italy, Brazil, Mexico and the Philippines. There were also numerous licensed spin-offs such as comic books, toys and board games – indeed *Jaws* is credited with inspiring the first, albeit unofficial, video game adaptation, *Shark JAWS* in 1975. A couple of hours with IMDb, Wikipedia and amazon.com's recommendations page throws up a frankly deranging series of 'movie connections' for *Jaws*, mostly linking it with the products of the US and Italian exploitation industries. I shall not attempt to list them all.

*Jaws*ploitation films essentially came in two waves. The first, on the heels of the film's release, was a model exploitation cycle capitalizing on *Jaws*-mania. These films, parasites borne along on the success of their host, reworked *Jaws*'s plot to showcase a variety of killer beasts – not only sharks (*Mako: Jaws of Death* (1976), *L'ultimo squalo* [*Great White/The Last Shark*](1981)) and shark-like monsters (*Up from the Depths* (1979)), but barracuda (*Barracuda* (1978)), grizzly bears (*Grizzly*, the top-grossing independent film in the United States in 1976; *Claws* (1977)), octopi (*Tentacoli* [*Tentacles*], memorable for its surreally heavyweight cast of Hollywood veterans (Henry Fonda, John Huston, Shelley Winters)), shark-octopus hybrids (*Shark: Rosso nell'oceano* [*Devil*

Fish/Devouring Waves] (1984)), piranhas (*Piranha, Killer Fish* (1979), *Piranha Part Two: The Spawning* (1981)), killer whales (*Orca* (1977, producer Dino De Laurentiis' follow-up to his remake of *King Kong*), crocodilia (*Alligator* (1980) and a belated Australian contribution, *Dark Age* (1987)), a beach (*Blood Beach* (1981): tag-line: 'Just when you thought it was safe to go back in the water, you can't get to it') and cod (*Bacalhau* (1975)).[24] There was very nearly, till funding was pulled, a British version of *Jaws* by the Manchester-based specialist in straight-to-video exploitation, Cliff Twemlow, starring Joan Collins and based on Twemlow's 1982 novel, *The Pike*, about a marauding fish in Lake Windermere.[25] Not all of these ripped off *Jaws* directly (*Killer Fish*, for instance, exploited *Piranha*'s box-office success), and not all were cheap drive in fodder (*Orca* was a major Hollywood release) but they certainly aimed to hook audiences with comparable pleasures. The Italian films, such as *Tentacles* were consistent with Italian *filone*'s usual short-term strategy of churning out imitations of currently popular genre hits:

> Italian film producers of popular cinema in the 1960s and 1970s were a fickle bunch tied to the vagaries of public taste and international trends (especially American cinema). As a funny expression of this, director Loris Cozzi once said that when you bring a script to a producer they don't ask, 'what is your film like', but 'what film is your film like?'[26]

Jaws was also doubtless the inspiration for the shark versus zombie wrestling match in Fulci's *Zombi 2* (1979), in which the shark for once comes off worse.

Jaws also led to celebrity status for sharks in general and two US TV cartoon parodies starring the fish were produced in 1976, *Misterjaw* and *Jabberjaw*. Allusions to *Jaws* flourished almost as soon as it was released and, as J. Hoberman remarks, 'There were few American fears that were not displaced onto the shark in parodies of *Jaws*'s poster'.[27] Few films remain so identifiable from the smallest visual or musical clue, whether it is a shot of a fin in *1941* (1979) and *Airplane II: The Sequel* (1982) or a brief 'dum *dum*' in *Never Say Never Again* (1983), or from Cameron Diaz as she drunkenly awaits a telling off in *In Her Shoes* (2005). In *Swingers* (1996) the theme plays as a girl advances ominously towards Vince

Figure 12 Bear versus helicopter at the climax of *Grizzly*.

Vaughn and again when Jon Favreau goes 'sharking' in a bar. A lengthy list could be compiled of such aural allusions, which, except when the two notes are farted as a joke in *9 ½ Weeks* (1986), invariably denotes approaching danger (an exhaustive list is available as '*Jaws* connections' on IMDb). In *Brenda Starr* (1989) a variation of the shark theme warns of a nearby crocodile. In *Caddyshack* (1980) the theme strikes up when a Babe Ruth bar mistaken for a turd causes panic in a swimming pool while in *Bloodbath at the House of Death* (1984), the source of the alternating bass notes turns out to be Kenny Everett playing a cello in the lavatory. In *Crush* (2001), cleverly acknowledging one of Williams' sources, a few bars of 'The Rite of Spring' is used instead.

Many other nature-running-amok thrillers of the period might be classed among *Jaws*ploitation films, such as *Squirm* (1976), *The Food of the Gods* (1976), *The Pack* (1977), *The Car* (1977), *The Swarm, Empire of the Ants* (1977), *Long Weekend* (1978) and *The Day of the Animals* (1977). They are certainly influenced by *Jaws*'s visual tropes (for example, the ants' tessellated point of view shots in *Empire of the Ants*). But it is likely that the success of *Jaws* simply perpetuated what Tarantino called the early 1970s' 'Mother Nature goes ape-shit kind of movie', and also encouraged that cycle's combination with the disaster film in, for example, *The Swarm* and to some extent the remake of *King Kong*.[28] More fundamentally *Jaws* also bore out the efficiency of what Noel Carroll called 'perhaps the most serviceable narrative armature in the horror film genre' – the 'Discovery Plot', with its four movements: 'onset' (the monster is revealed), 'discovery' (the monster is discovered by a person or a group, but its existence is not acknowledged by the authorities), 'confirmation' (the authorities are eventually convinced of the monster's threat), and 'confrontation' (the monster is met and usually killed).[29] It is hard to disentangle the influence of *Jaws*, in creature features from *Empire of the Ants* to *King Cobra* (1999) and *Crocodile* (2000), from adherence to general narrative conventions of the horror film that *Jaws* happened to reinvigorate and perfect.

This first cycle of *Jaws*ploitation continued till roughly 1987 and the release of *Jaws the Revenge*, which is memorable only for its star Michael Caine's remark that 'I have never seen the film, but by all accounts it was terrible. However, I have seen the house that it built and it is terrific.' Among the last in the cycle were Joe D'Amato's *Sangue negli abissi* (*Deep Blood*) (1989), and *Killer Crocodile* (1989), a remarkably close imitation, which was shot back-to-back with its sequel, *Killer Crocodile 2* (1990). A second, continuing wave of *Jaws*ploitation films followed Spielberg's *Jurassic Park*, itself a reinvention of *Jaws*, which reinvigorated the creature feature with the twin novelties of computer generated special effects and the theme of genetic manipulation. Most of these were TV and straight-to-video movies (the TV remake of *Piranha* (1996); *Alligator II: The Mutation* (1999); *Croc* (2007); *Lake Placid 2* (2007); *Primeval* (2007), and *Shark Swarm* (2008) in the Sci-Fi Channel's Maneater series), but they included some mid-budget thrillers, such as *Anaconda* (1997), *The Relic* (1997), *Lake Placid, Eight Legged Freaks* (2002), *Gwoemul* [*The Host*]

(2006), and the wave's most self-aware and influential evocation of *Jaws*, *Deep Blue Sea*, which ushered in a new wave of mostly self-parodying cable films. The latest burst of sharksploitation consists mostly of deliberately bad camp films such as *Mega Piranha*, *Mega Shark versus Giant Octopus* (2009), *Sand Sharks* (2011), *Shark Avalanche* (2013), and many others, often produced for SyFy, of which the most noteworthy is *Sharknado* if only because of its brief cult status when its premiere on 12 July 2013 inspired up to 5,000 tweets a minute. The 3D remake of *Piranha* in 2010 inspired a number of 3D shark films, such *Shark Night 3D* and *Bait*, set bizarrely in a shark-infested flooded supermarket.

Roughly we can divide the *Jaws*ploitation movies of both waves into two categories: creature features and sharksploitation films.

Creature features play a kind of commutation game, substituting for sharks some other malevolent rogue species alluded to in the film's title. Their plots had similar cardinal functions to *Jaws*, with the same kind of events taking place in much the same order. This was not especially taxing to contrive since *Jaws*'s 'Discovery Plot' is so stripped to the bone (beast attacks people, people kill beast) that, like *The Most Dangerous Game* (1932), its barest essentials could be lifted without risk of plagiarism. Of the films in the first cycle, before *Jaws* was established as a pop culture myth, three are especially interesting in their different modes of adaptive exploitation, namely imitation, revision and parody.

Grizzly (*Claws*, as reviewers tended to rename it; a documentary extra on the DVD is 'Jaws with Claws') recapitulates *Jaws* in some detail – oversized bear, represented by point-of-view shots and accompanied by percussive chords, attacks attractive young women, man kills bear, blowing it up with a rocket launcher. There is even a recap of Quint's Indianapolis speech, when one character gives a hushed campfire rendition of a story about 'a whole herd of man-eating grizzlies ... tearing up Indians'. *Orca*, more ambitiously, develops and inverts *Jaws*'s theme of personal revenge in its tall tale of a killer whale pursuing the shark hunter who harpooned its pregnant mate. The film is an eco-friendly reshuffling of *Moby-Dick* in that a whale pursues Ahab, a woman loses a leg, and the whale wins. *Orca* (the name of Quint's boat) came up against a limitation of the *Jaws* formula. It is certainly true that *Jaws* grants the shark a degree of motive and intelligence ('Smart fish,' Quint remarks wonderingly when the shark goes under the boat). But unlike King Kong, the shark – or its equivalent in the exploitation versions – needs to be mythically charged but essentially characterless, more a symbol, narrative function or malevolent agent of external evil (as in *Piranha*) than a thing capable of anthropomorphism and sympathetic humanlike emotion.

The standout film of the first *Jaws* cycle is *Piranha* (1978), produced by Roger Corman and directed by Joe Dante. Intended to cash in on the production of *Jaws 2* it is a droll prefabricated cult movie, which introduced an anti-establishment agenda typical of Corman – the military bred, titular, super-aggressive 'mutant cannibal piranhas' for use in the Mekong Delta during the Vietnam War: 'radiation, selective breeding; they called it Operation

Razorfish'.[30] As in *Grizzly*, in which one female victim is killed while topless under a waterfall, *Piranha* adds nudity to *Jaws*'s 'PG'-rated mix. The plot follows *Jaws* quite closely (the story goes that Universal wanted to sue New World for plagiarism but dropped the suit after Spielberg approved of the film), but also introduces numerous allusions to other films (*Citizen Kane* (1941), *Invasion of the Body Snatchers* (1956)) in what would become the signature manner of exploitation auteurs like John Carpenter and Corman alumni such as Dante (*The Howling* (1981)), and John Landis (*Into the Night* (1985)).[31] *Piranha* is wittily knowing about both itself – a shot near the start of the *Shark JAWS* arcade game situates the film among the numerous unofficial *Jaws* spin-offs – and *Jaws*'s intertextual debts: a girl is seen reading *Moby-Dick* on the beach, while references to *Creature from the Black Lagoon* and a clip from *The Monster that Challenged the World* (1957) firmly reclaim *Jaws* for the tradition of 1950s SF. Indeed Jon Davison, one of *Piranha*'s producers, insisted that *Piranha* was targeting not *Jaws* but one of its key precursors:

> Everyone talks about what *Piranha* owes to Steve Spielberg and *Jaws*. What it really owes something to is Jack Arnold and *The Creature from the Black Lagoon*. *Jaws* was really nothing more than an expensive 50s monster-on-the-loose picture. So *Piranha* may be a rip-off of *Jaws*, but I prefer to think of it as a rip-off of *Black Lagoon*.[32]

The same line of parody was taken in *Alligator*, also written by John Sayles and packed with filmic in-jokes (as a rule the most effective approach for an exploitation version; as Dante said, 'A picture of this type made on this budget just couldn't play on a serious level').[33] Like *Piranha*, *Alligator* claims *Jaws* for 1950s science fiction and the association of monsters with mad science in such classics as *Them!* (1954) and *Gojira* [*Godzilla, King of the Monsters!*] (1954), to which *Jaws* paid subtle homage in Quint's Indianapolis speech, which implied the shark was metaphorically if not literally a product of the Bomb.

Figure 13 Paying homage: the *Shark JAWS* arcade game in *Piranha*.

It is worth briefly mentioning two erotic parodies. *Deep Jaws* (1976), a softcore sex film whose title ingeniously links *Jaws* with that other instantly proverbial film of the period, *Deep Throat*, is about a film studio that decides to make a sex film about mermaid fellatrices. *Gums* (1976), which I'll discuss further in Chapter 7's Appendix, replaces the shark with a mermaid who, with 'a different set of jaws', as *The Rocky Horror Picture Show* poster put it, gives blow jobs to unsuspecting swimmers. (An Australian shark called Gums, as my colleague Peter Wright reminds me, also featured in a British comic, *Monster Fun*, which was launched in 1975. Gums, whose strip debuted in issue 35 in February 1976, was so called because he was toothless and wore false teeth). Both films are tedious and daft but as so often with exploitation versions they draw attention to perverse subtexts repressed in the original. *Gums* neatly literalizes and defuses what Jane Caputi claims is *Jaws*'s violently sexual evocation of 'the castrating female, the terrible, murderous mother of patriarchal nightmare and myth'.[34]

Sharksploitation, the second category of *Jaws*ploitation films, initially either loosely remade *Jaws* (*L'ultimo squalo* remade it so closely that it was pulled from cinemas and has still not been officially released in the United States) or, ignoring the plot of *Jaws* entirely, was simply films with sharks in them. Given energetic advertising, this was sufficient to strike up a rewarding affiliation with *Jaws*. *Jaws*'s official sequels were especially inhibited from deviating too far from the template, which in any case allowed for little variation. *Jaws 2* (1978) was a teen slasher film; *Jaws 3-D* (1983), a technological upgrade with unconvincing 3D effects; and in *Jaws the Revenge*, the shark pursued a comically personal vendetta against Chief Brody's widow. *The Deep* (1977), interestingly, was also promoted as a sequel to *Jaws*.[35] A maritime yarn based on Benchley's follow-up novel, it is not a shark film at all and boasts few dangerous creatures except a moray eel. But its publicity material centred on its legitimate contiguity to the *Jaws* brand in that it shared the same writer and also starred Robert Shaw. As *The Deep*'s producer, Peter Gubar, remarked, 'Anyone who reads the book can see immediately that *The Deep* cannot even remotely be construed as a "sequel" to *Jaws* ... . The *Jaws* association, however, is a potent one in the film industry, and ... our only real ace in the hole'.[36] The poster graphically reinforced this relationship and instead of a shark depicts a young woman in snorkelling flippers struggling to the ocean surface. Exploitation versions, as one might expect, slavishly imitated Mick McGinty's iconic design for *Jaws*'s poster as being the most economical way of signalling a connection with its promise of titillating thrills. The posters for *Tintorera*, *Grizzly*, *Tentacles* and *Up from the Depths* feature their respective beasts menacing a single young woman, and even now the posters or DVD covers of second-wave films like *Deep Blue Sea*, *12 Days of Terror* (2004), *Spring Break Shark Attack* (2005), *Rogue* and *Shark in Venice* tend to show monsters in vertical ascent towards attractive starlets, as do *Mega Shark in Malibu* and *Piranha 3D*.

Of the first cycle of sharksploitation films, *Mako: Jaws of Death* is one of the most imaginative. Despite the title it is actually about a loner with a mystical connection with sharks who protects them from fisherman and other enemies. Although the title draws the film into *Jaws*'s orbit, it is much closer to *Willard* in its progressive depiction of sharks as victims of human predation, and thus anticipates *Deep Blue Sea; Sangue negli abissi*, in which an ancient Native American spirit takes the form of a killer shark; the anti-*Jaws* shark-ecology documentary, *Sharkwater* (2006); and Peter Benchley's later non-fiction books on shark conservation, which made amends for *Jaws*'s demonization of Great Whites.[37] *Mako* is a good example of exploitation securing its commercial viability by referencing another film in its title and publicity, and then through incompetence, negligence or creative necessity, doing something entirely different. This is perfectly in keeping with exploitation practice. Once the audience has been lured into buying a ticket or renting the DVD, a film has achieved its purpose and its actual content is irrelevant, but sometimes divertingly adrift from what is promised in the ancillary materials. The same is true of *Tintorera* (actually based on a novel), which is not the gore-fest depicted on its poster but a soapish drama about a couple of shark-hunting beach bums with barely a handful of scenes involving the promised tiger sharks. The film is not very good (though Wikipedia claims it has a cult reputation in Mexico), but often fascinating in its attempt to square picaresque romance with the demands of sharksploitation.

Aside from *Aatank* (1996), 'the Bollywood *Jaws*', most of the recent sharksploitation films are straight-to-video and TV movies, often filmed in South Africa and Bulgaria. The leading specialist is Nu Image, which produced the *Shark Attack* trilogy (1999–2002), *Hammerhead* and three films helmed by the Israeli director, Danny Lerner – *Shark Zone* (2003), *Raging Sharks* (2005) and *Shark in Venice*. This last, a sort of *Raiders of the Lost Shark*, is a deliriously trashy generic hybrid inspired by *National Treasure* (2004) and *The Da Vinci Code* (2006), in which the Mafia release sharks into the canals of Venice in order to protect Medici treasure. Among bigger-budget films *Deep Blue Sea* was probably the most significant and influential. A playful, postmodern splicing of *Jaws* and *Jurassic Park*, it acknowledges the impossibility of escaping *Jaws*'s gravitational pull by killing off its genetically engineered super-sharks in the manner and order of the ones in *Jaws* and the first two sequels (namely, gas explosion, electrocution and explosion). This theme of genetic mutation was subsequently taken up by *Shark Attack* (1999), *Shark Attack 2* (2001), *Blue Demon* (2004), *Hammerhead* (2005) and *Shark Swarm*, in which pollution causes Great Whites to swarm and kill for pleasure, but it was actually anticipated by Benchley's novel *White Shark* (1994) about a shark-human hybrid, which was filmed for TV in 1998 as *Peter Benchley's Creature*.[38] Jurassic sharks are another recent innovation, appearing in *Shark Hunter* (2001), *Shark Attack 3: Megalodon* (2002), as well as in the continuing parallel tradition of *Jaws*-inspired novels, such as Steve Alten's *Meg* (1997).[39] Other films, such as *12 Days of Terror*, about the New Jersey shark attacks of 1916 (mentioned in *Jaws*), filled in some of the back story of *Jaws* and the history that inspired it (*The Mission of the Shark: The Saga of the USS Indianapolis* (1991), a TV movie, had already dramatized the story made notorious by Quint's monologue). By now *Jaws* was a classic film rather than a hot property to exploit. Recent shark films do not attempt copies (with the odd exception like *Cruel Jaws*) but rather engage in citation and homage (*Shark Hunter*: 'We're going to need a bigger sub'), acknowledging *Jaws*'s determining association with sharks and its continuing supremacy as a model for thrillers about man versus nature. The same is true of the creature features. In *Anacondas: The Hunt for the Blood Orchid* (2004), for example, one character scares his companions in an Amazonian swamp by humming the *Jaws* theme moments before he is swallowed by a CGI snake. No longer a cycle of exploitation films cashing in on a blockbuster, these work variations on a horror subgenre, the creature feature, which preceded *Jaws* but is now wholly inextricable from it. For example, Barry Levinson's found footage movie, *The Bay* (2012), about an East Coast ecological disaster on the Fourth of July (a significant date in *Jaws*, of course) is littered with references to its defining predecessor, whose plot is melded with the body horror of *Shivers* (1975) and returned to its roots in 1970s eco-horror: a sequence of giant parasites attacking a young woman is indebted to the opening scene of *Jaws*, the parasites are initially thought to be sharks, and the mayor's name in the film, Stockman, is the same as that in *Enemy of the People*.

Open Water and *Adrift*, low-budget, independent and character-orientated rather than exploitation movies, are two of the best recent *Jaws*-related films. *Open Water* is a high-concept hyphenate, as the DVD box notes: *Blair Witch* meets *Jaws*, a formula successful enough to inspire two excellent Australian crocodile films, *Black Water* (2007) and *Rogue*. *Open Water* and *Adrift* are both small-scale dramas about people stranded in the ocean, in which *Jaws* is an intertextual resource rather than the target of imitation; the relation is one not of exploitation so much as of silent evocation.[40] *Open Water* does pay direct homage to *Jaws*, in that the main characters have the surnames Watkins and Kintner, the names of *Jaws*'s first two shark victims, but otherwise builds tension by subtly working against *Jaws*'s unrealistic representation of the 'rogue shark'. *Open Water*'s sharks, filmed for real on location, are smallish, hunt in groups, and bump victims before testing them out with a bite; in short, they behave like the sharks, presumably also Oceanic whitetips, which Quint describes in his Indianapolis speech. The intertextual relation with *Jaws* no longer needs to be stressed; it is simply and inevitably there and used to great advantage not only by inciting audience awareness of 'Jawsness' to produce suspense, but by 'correcting' the inaccuracies of the hypotext and negating audience expectations in a suspenseful and creative way.[41]

In *Adrift*, by contrast, there are no sharks at all, except ambiguously when one seems to nudge a character underwater. *Adrift* was opportunistically

Figure 14 Watkins and Kintner: *Jaws* references in *Open Water*.

advertised in the United States as *Open Water 2: Adrift*, though it was an unrelated production. (A classic exploitation strategy is to rename films and promote them as unofficial sequels – Bava's *Reazione a catena* (1971) became *The Last House on the Left, Part II* and, in Italy, *Zombi 2* purported to be a sequel to Romero's *Zombie: Dawn of the Dead* (1978).) *Adrift*, framed as a sequel to the 'shark movie' *Open Water*, rather than as a stand-alone film with a remarkably similar set-up, is a different and potentially frustrating experience. As one disgruntled poster to IMDb complained:

> Open Water 2 was so annoying that I found myself rooting for gigantic man-eating sharks to devour this pack of treading water whiners. And guess what? No sharks!!! Why bother doing a sequel to Open Water if your going to forget the most terrifying aspect, the eaten alive by sharks in the ocean part. That's like Snakes On A Plane Part 2 forgetting the snakes.[42]

The absence of sharks is dramatically a strength, for it enables the film to swerve away from the obvious narrative development (and from *Open Water*, which it is otherwise in danger of plagiarizing) in favour of a story about friendship, materialism and female strength. *Jaws* is so powerful a precursor text that the threat of sharks in the ocean could be taken for granted. But for audiences misled by *Adrift*'s discursive framing as a sequel to a shark movie, the absent sharks implied only that the budget couldn't stretch to filming them.

Fin *de siècle*

So why was *Jaws* so especially, perhaps even uniquely, resonant and imitable? There are two reasons, quite apart from its greatness as a work of film art. First, its narrative structure is of surpassing elegance and simplicity. The shark is little more than a lethal narrative device, albeit one with disturbing sexual overtones. This crucially influenced the slasher film and its offspring – *Halloween* (1978), *Alien* (1979), *Murder by Decree* (1979) (Jack the Ripper's murders are portrayed in point of view shots to the accompaniment of percussive music), *The Terminator* (1984), even the henchman, Jaws, in *The Spy Who Loved Me* (1977) – in which imperturbable killing machines arguably embodied both anti-feminist backlash and the affectless malevolence of capitalism; in fact, the slasher film is itself a cycle of *Jaws*ploitation in its obsession with point of view shots and eroticized serial violence, which *Jaws* adapted from Hitchcock.[43] *Jaws* also had an air of myth or urban legends (carried over into the slasher film too), so that *Jaws*ploitation films play like variations on archetypal fears rather than rip-offs of just one movie.

The second reason why *Jaws* was so easily made over as exploitation is that it was of course essentially an exploitation film, albeit one blessed with a large budget and stunning craftsmanship. This was not unnoticed on its initial release – '*Jaws* and *Bug* – The Only Difference is the Hype', as Stephen Farber put it in the headline of his *New York Times* review, alluding to exploitation producer's William Castle's 1975 film.[44] *Jaws*'s graphic qualities, its poster with the implied sexual threat to a nude female swimmer, and its debt to 1950s B-movies all underscored that like many other films of the 'Hollywood Renaissance' it was upscale exploitation fare, though more tailored for a family audience than the novel, with its gratuitous sex scenes between Hooper and Ellen Brody. By the 1970s exploitation cinema in the United States was threatened on two opposing fronts. On the one hand, the New Hollywood encroached on its territory with an unprecedented wave of violent and sexually explicit films; while, on the other, the legalization of hardcore made available the kind of pornography for which sexploitation had always been a poor substitute. Exploitation filmmakers had to find innovative ways to distinguish their films from both the Hollywood of *The Exorcist* and the hardcore chic of *Deep Throat*. New subgenres sprang up establishing fresh directions for exploitation, such as the slasher film (*Halloween*), the ultra-gore movie (*Maniac* (1980)), and the self-abasing, intentionally bad trash film, contemporary versions of which include the output of Lloyd Kaufman's Troma Films, such as *The Toxic Avenger* and *Class of Nuke 'Em High* series. A number of New Hollywood directors were alumni of Roger Corman's production outfits and their films expensively revisited what had once been strictly bargain basement genres. As Corman complained:

> The major challenge has been finding new markets and recouping costs while the majors have dominated the exploitation genres with budgets ten times higher than ours … . It was Vincent Canby of *The New York Times* who once wrote, 'What is *Jaws* but a big-budget Roger Corman movie?' But when Spielberg and the Lucases make technically exquisite genre films, they cut deeply into the box-office appeal of our kind of picture.[45]

Carol Clover dubbed this process 'trickle up', reversing the usual relation of exploitation to its source:

> When I see an Oscar-winning film like *The Accused* or the artful *Alien* ...
> I can't help thinking of all the low-budget, often harsh and awkward but sometimes deeply energetic films that preceded them by a decade or more – films that said it all, and in flatter terms, and on a shoestring.[46]

The difference between mainstream and exploitation was increasingly the budget rather than the topic, level of gore and nudity, or distribution or promotional techniques. *Jaws*, for example, had a summer opening, TV ads and saturation bookings, all promotion strategies pioneered by exploitation that soon became standard throughout Hollywood. At the same time *Jaws*, like its shark 'a perfect engine' (as numberless critics have remarked), became the template for the new Hollywood blockbuster, so that in a sense all subsequent films were adaptations of its successful formula and the big-budget B-movie became the staple of mainstream production. The film's most famous, improvised line, 'You're going to need a bigger boat', was a warning to Hollywood that it would need to upscale to face the future.

Jaws was also a gift to exploitation filmmakers because, unlike *King Kong* and *Jurassic Park*, which self-reflexively celebrated the display of special effects, the shark was defined by *not being seen*, except briefly, till it belly-flops onto the *Orca* at the end of the film and is revealed as a rubbery disappointment. This suspenseful technique of withholding a clear view of the shark, initially enforced by the mechanical sharks' failure to work, legitimized the representation of monsters by shoestring methods such as point of view shots, metonymic close-ups of paws and claws, and scrappy bits of stock footage. Until the digital innovations of *Deep Blue Sea*, the sharks in sharksploitation films are surprisingly absent as coherently presented creatures. As in *Jaws* they tend to be a digest of poorly matched documentary footage, model work and briskly edited close-ups. A postmodern extreme of bricolage is achieved by *Cruel Jaws* (1995), in which the shark is represented *entirely* by footage lifted from *L'ultimo squalo, Deep Blood* and the first three *Jaws* films.

In spite of its basic simplicity, *Jaws* was wildly overdetermined by metaphorical and symbolic contexts, cannily solicited in the film. Watergate, paranoia, styles of masculinity, the myth of the hunter, allegories of class, misogyny, guilt over Hiroshima and Vietnam – all these interpretative possibilities were highlighted by contemporary reviews and have been elaborated on by academic critics ever since.[47] The film proved an irresistible combination of high-concept premise and 'metaphorical polymorphousness'.[48] As soon as the film was released critics swiftly set upon it with their diagnostic tools: 'The shark reflects a disguised hatred of women and the preoccupation of our society with sadistic sexuality, a view of business as predatory and irresponsible in human terms, and a fear of retribution for the atomic bombing of Hiroshima.'[49] Walter

Metz, more recently, combines these in reading *Jaws* as a Cold War updating of *Moby-Dick*, not only a backlash film against the Women's Liberation Movement but also as a Vietnam War film:

> When Chief Brody stuffs an oxygen tank down the shark's throat and uses his rifle to blow him up, *Jaws* is producing a multifaceted image. After Brodie [*sic*] blows up the shark, it sinks to the bottom of the ocean, looking distinctly like a sinking submarine. Thus, Brodie [*sic*] is able to avenge the shark's murder of his friend [*sic*] Quint, which is polysemically also revenge against the Japanese who traumatised him via his experience on the USS Indianapolis.[50]

Metz then goes on to argue that Brody killing the shark with the cylinder 'has frightening allegorical consequences on the 1975 context of *Jaws*':

> For if the use of the nuclear bomb at Hiroshima is celebrated by Quint … then the film's positioning of Brodie's [*sic*] lesson as doing the same to the shark means allegorically that the way to win Vietnam would be the re-use of similar atomic weaponry. Throughout the film, the shark is positioned as a Vietcong-like entity: skulking round an underwater jungle, unseen, ready to spring out at any unexpected moment. And after all, the beach is the safest place for Americans, both in Vietnam and in *Jaws*.[51]

My point (pace what I said in Chapter 3) is not to deride such interpretations, fanciful as they might seem, but to highlight the ease and seeming naturalness of the film's wide-ranging allegorical applicability.[52] If for Metz the shark is a vengeful phallus, the Vietcong, an offspring of the white whale and a Second World War–Japanese submarine, other critics maintain with equal plausibility that it is a vagina dentata, enraged nature, a rapist, Gloria Steinem, a Jungian archetype, the Bomb and Watergate and that its explosive death is Hiroshima, an orgasm and a symbolic castration.[53] I could go on. But, as Antonia Quirke suggests, 'The biggest blessing fate bestowed on Spielberg in the 1970s was an indifference to politics. *Jaws*, like *Duel*, is an intriguing allegory precisely because the young nerd had no agenda.'[54] The kind of strategic ambiguity engineered in *Jaws* is now central to Hollywood storytelling. With reviews and cult readings instantly available on the internet, it makes sense to cram films with competing possible interpretations that maximize the films' appeal and readability to multiple audiences. It was *Jaws*, the shark that swallowed the *Zeitgeist*, which more than any other film habituated audiences and critics to reading popular movies in extravagantly allegorical terms.

One final way, briefly, of thinking about *Jaws* is as a meme, Richard Dawkins's term for a proliferating unit of culture, which he introduced in *The Selfish Gene* (1976).[55] As Linda Hutcheon puts it, 'Memes are not high-fidelity replicators: they change with time, for meme transmission is subject to constant mutation. Stories too propagate themselves when they catch on: adaptations – as both repetition and variation – are their form of replication.'[56] Memetics – the science (or pseudo-science) of memes – is a controversial field and the meme is probably a useful metaphor rather than a truly scientific concept.[57] What does the *Jaws* meme consist of? A couple of notes ('dum *dum*'), a shot of a fin, a point of view shot (as already mentioned, *not* seeing the monster is a defining mark of *Jaws*ness), or some combination of all three? It is perhaps more accurate – but wholly unscientific – to say that the *Jaws* meme is just this: *shark*. The film has so thoroughly colonized the very idea of 'shark' that any representation of one, from Discovery Channel documentaries (*Air Jaws* (2001), about aerial attacks by South African Great Whites) to press reports of shark sightings and attacks, to novels like James Delingpole's *Fin*, about a man terrified of being eaten by a shark, Steven Hall's *The Raw Shark Texts*, with its 'conceptual shark' and Will Self's *Shark*, inspired by the Indianapolis speech, must silently acknowledge the film's lurking precedence, its authoritative discursive prefiguring of 'shark'.[58] *Jaws* has so recalibrated the cultural meaning of shark that it is now *the* determining intertextual reference point even when no specific allusion is intended. All films with sharks, all cultural representations of sharks, are *Jaws*ploitation now.

If that is so, the most complete adaptation of *Jaws*, and the perfect *exploitation* of its meme, is Damien Hirst's visual one-liner, *The Physical Impossibility of Death in the Mind of Someone Living* (1992) – the tiger shark in a tank – which combines the minimum of transformed content with the maximum of implication. Instantly memorable, it is a precise memetic summary of *Jaws*'s massive semiotic presence. Hirst's shark is essentially a 3D still capable, on the one hand, of an exceptionally high degree of accuracy in replication and transmission (as when Hirst repeated the gesture with *The Kingdom* (2008), another production line pickled fish) but, on the other, sufficiently high-concept to be copyrighted. As high art Hirst's shark seems an unlikely addition to the roll call of *Jaws*ploitation – and admittedly I've simplified vastly what happens when exploitation goes so upmarket – yet its impact is wholly parasitic on *Jaws*'s supremacy as the apex predator meme in the domain of representing sharks. Hirst's art uses, in a more elevated register, much the same appropriative recycling procedures as video mashups like *Must Love Jaws* (2006) and slash fiction.[59] Indeed when Hirst came to release a children's *ABC* illustrating each letter with a detail of his work, his shark stood not for 'S' but for 'J': Jaws.[60]

We have drifted a long way from discussing either trashy exploitation films or theories and methods of adaptation. But I hope I have demonstrated that exploitation and adaptation are not opposite means of deriving one text from another. As so often in adaptation studies, this is an apparent binary – like 'original' and 'copy', 'faithful' and 'unfaithful', 'parasite' and 'host' – in need of summary deconstruction. The perceived differences between exploitation and adaptation are the product of, first, the cultural politics of legitimacy and, second, the vicissitudes of copyright legislation. I find it more useful to redescribe exploitation as unlicensed adaptation and adaptation as licensed plagiarism, questioning the distinction between exploitation and more 'respectable' modes of intertextuality in order to emphasize crucial similarities of commercial motive and aesthetic technique.

John Ellis remarked that 'adaptation into another medium becomes a means of prolonging the pleasure of the original presentation, and repeating the production of a memory'.[61] The same is true of exploitation versions, which mutate their sources to ensure their usefulness and viability in the textual environment of low-budget cinema. As with all modes of adaptation, their purpose is not only to exploit, but also to salvage, resurrect and preserve.

Chapter 6

EROTIC INFERNO

Britain, it is fair to say, is not renowned for its contribution to erotic cinema. There are very few British films with the iconic status of France's *Emmanuelle* (1974), Italy's *Last Tango in Paris* (1972), or Sweden's *I am Curious (Yellow)* (1967), and, with the possible exception of the art film directors Nicolas Roeg, Ken Russell and Peter Greenaway (for *The Cook, the Thief, His Wife and Her Lover* (1989)), no British *auteurs* of erotic cinema to compare with masters of sexploitation like Jean Rollin, Jess Franco, Just Jaeckin, Radley Metzger and Tinto Brass. Eroticism is more usually associated with 'continental' art cinema, while British cinema, perhaps in tune with the nation's proverbial suspicion of unabashed sexual pleasure, is awash with repression, sniggering and embarrassment. There are a few outliers, such as Roeg's *Don't Look Now* (1973), with its sex scene, erroneously rumoured to be real, between Donald Sutherland and Julie Christie, but my guess is that the most famous British 'sex film' remains *Confessions of a Window Cleaner* (1974). Nevertheless in the 1970s the softcore sexploitation film was one of the few relatively flourishing areas of British cinema at a low-point in the industry's history, and some of these generally woeful efforts, such as the *Confessions* series, were unlikely commercial triumphs.[1]

The British sexploitation film began in the 1950s with A-rated nudist films, such as *Naked – As Nature Intended* (1961), X-rated dramas like *The Flesh is Weak* (1957), and 'mondo' compilations of sensational footage such as *London in the Raw* (1964) and *Primitive London* (1965). The first outright softcore films were Norman J. Warren's *Her Private Hell* (1967) and *Loving Feeling* (1968), which posed as moral tales about the dangers of the sex trade, and dour 'permissive dramas', such as *Groupie Girl* (1970) and *Permissive* (1970), which documented changing sexual mores in the style of the social problem film. Throughout the 1970s hardcore erotica was banned outright and sexually explicit cinema fell foul of the tough regime of censorship of what was then the British Board of Film Censors. Sexual material was more heavily cut in exploitation than in art films, even after the relaxation of censorship at the end of the 1960s when the age of admission to 'X'-rated films was changed from 16 to 18. (Indeed, the modest number of celebrated British sex scenes of the 1970s were in *auteur* films such as *Don't Look Now*, Roeg and Donald Cammell's *Performance* (1970), and Roeg's *The Man Who Fell to Earth* (1976).) The British sexploitation film was dominated by comedies, which added nudity to the strain of British bawdy epitomized by *Carry On* and adaptations of stage farces such as *No Sex Please, We're British* (1973) and *Not Now Darling* (1973). The other thriving subgenre was the sex documentary, typified by educational 'white-coaters' like *Love Variations* (1969), a guide to sexual positions, and semi-humorous reportage on the subcultures of permissiveness such as *Commuter Husbands* (1972), *Suburban Wives* (1971) and *On the Game* (1973).[2]

Less discussed are the handful of attempts in the 1970s to make 'serious' and occasionally seriously arousing exploitation films on erotic themes. This is admittedly a fine distinction but one worth making, if films about sex and celebrating sex are regarded, as they should be, as legitimate exercises in arousing the senses, exploiting curiosity and exciting the imagination. Hence this chapter's title, which highlights the idea of *sexy* films designed to engage audiences erotically and showcase sexual liberation. Ranging from literary adaptations (*Mistress Pamela* (1974), *The Bawdy Adventures of Tom Jones* (1976), *Cruel Passion* (1977)) to outright softcore erotica (*Emily* (1976), *Erotic Inferno* (1975)), these films attempted to develop a distinctive market for British sex films despite stringent censorship and competition from American and mainland European product. They are engaged in the modes of exploitation we discussed in the last chapter in relation to *Jaws* – especially imitation and adaptation, and compromise.

Emily

The most influential and internationally successful softcore film of the 1970s was Just Jaeckin's softcore *Emmanuelle*, a hit in Britain where it was sold to a putative 'couples' audience. Although *Emmanuelle* prompted the *Carry On* team to spice up their final film, *Carry On Emmannuelle* (1978) (the aberrant spelling was to evade copyright), there were few British attempts to imitate its ambitious combination of literary pretension, pornography and art-house chic. In fact, there were precisely two such efforts in the 1970s: *Emily* and *Cruel Passion*, which shared a kitsch style of soft-focused artiness with Euro-softcore about pubescent girls such as *Bilitis* (1977) and *Néa* [*A Young Emmanuelle*] (1976). Like *Emmanuelle*, these were female-centred narratives of erotic self-discovery and identity formation, which, though owing little to feminism, at least emphasized female desire and the pleasures of sexual independence.

Emily, directed by Hugh Herbert (the Earl of Pembroke), emphatically recalls *Emmanuelle* from its title onwards. Set in 1928 (the date of *Lady Chatterley*'s first publication) and mounted like a period adaptation, it is actually an original story, lent a certain glossy charm by location shooting and a chirpy Rod McKuen soundtrack whose lyrics underline the film's voyeuristic fascination with Emily's 'awakening' and transition to 'womanhood' – 'Give her some room, She's blossoming soon, Sweet Emily.' (The film's alternative title was *The Awakening of Emily*, also used as the tag line on the British quad poster.)

Emily Foster (Koo Stark), who was born in New York and moved to London aged eight, arrives as a seventeen-year-old virgin at her mother's, Margaret Foster (Sarah Brackett), country house. Margaret, a prostitute of some sort, pays for the upkeep of the house with her immoral earnings. Richard Walker (Victor Spinetti) plays an equivalent role to Mario (Alain Cuny) in *Emmanuelle*, an older libertine and 'experienced observer' eager to teach the ingénue the ways of the adult world. From masturbation to lesbianism (in a shower; as usual in porn, lesbianism is merely a transitional recreation), Emily embarks on a series of incrementally more 'serious' sexual adventures that end with her 'deflowering', to use an appropriately vintage term. In another nod to *Emmanuelle*, her first sexual encounter is with Augustine Wain (Ina Skriver), who, like Bee (Marika Green) in *Emmanuelle*, is an older married woman. Being not only a bohemian painter but Swedish, and therefore an excessively overdetermined embodiment of sexual licence, Augustine inducts Emily into adult pleasures, which quickly also include cocktails and cigarettes ('Mrs Pankhurst would have been all for it,' Richard remarks of her smoking). Emily's awakening has a consciously Freudian underpinning and even hints at incestuous desires. Her father died when she was a baby and she seems in search of a father figure ('I'd like a father,' she says). She spins a tale to James West (Richard Oldfield), a young man with whom she enjoys some exploratory fumbles, about having sex at fifteen with an 'uncle' – 'I was curious, you see. It was in Brighton' – and finally consummates her paternal fixation by seducing Augustine's middle-aged husband, Rupert (Constantine Gregory). Such upper middle class and bohemian insouciance towards sex is contrasted with working-class respectability in a parallel plot of Raquel (Jane Hayden), a servant girl, and her soldier lover, Billy (David Auker), who are engaged but try to put off sex till marriage.

Emily's awakening is linked, oddly enough, to modes of vintage transport, the film's key on-screen signifier of its period setting and comparatively lavish production values, as well as an obvious symbol of male power and sexual energy. She arrives by steam train; meets Augustine out horse-riding; Richard fondles her in a horse-and-trap; she nearly has sex with James after a car ride; and it is while Rupert is driving her home that she strips and invites him to make love to her because 'I can't face my mother till I am a woman'. Most memorably, she almost causes James's bi-plane to crash because she is aroused by the vibrations of the joystick between her legs, prompting James to a scolding double entendre: 'The joystick is a very delicate piece of equipment. It has to be handled delicately.' The film ends with a freeze-frame of Emily, transferred safely from Rupert's car to James's, happily smiling as she goes to confront her mother, whom she caught engaged in group sex. It is left open whether she will marry James or, like her mother, embark on a career of numerous lovers. This is essentially a patriarchal narrative, and Emily remains a passenger rather than steering her own journey to sexual fulfilment, but it at least sets out the possibilities open to her, from marriage, adultery and promiscuity to bohemianism, lesbianism and prostitution.

The Bawdy Adventures of British Literary Adaptation

One way of looking at the British sex film of the period was that it eroticized familiar British genres such as comedy, social realism, horror and literary adaptation. The adaptations were loosely based on notorious classic historical novels and generally emphasized the frissons of sex across class boundaries and presented the past as an erotic playground, at any rate for men. In the 1960s the key erotic publications were themselves historical, from John Cleland's *Memoirs of a Woman of Pleasure* [*Fanny Hill*] (1748) to D. H. Lawrence's *Lady Chatterley's Lover*, while the republication of Victorian pornography such as *The Pearl* (1879–80) and *My Secret Life* (1888) helped to redefine the Victorians as hypocrites with a rich erotic subculture.

The key influence on sex films was Tony Richardson's *Tom Jones* (1963), in which the eighteenth century was depicted as a period of gleeful pre-Victorian licence, and the 1960s touted as a revival of the repressed energies of an older bawdy England. The subsequent handful of historically set erotic films – 'heritage sex' films if you will – were comedies in this tradition – *Carry on Henry* (1974); *Lock Up Your Daughters* (1969), set in the Restoration; *The Best House in London* (1969), about a Victorian brothel; *Joseph Andrews* (1977), Tony Richardson's follow-up to *Tom Jones* and another Fielding adaptation; and *Keep It Up Downstairs* (1976), which detailed the servicing of the gentry by their servants. *The Bawdy Adventures of Tom Jones*, adapting a stage musical, amounted to an 'exploitation version' of *Tom Jones*, and featured, like *Joseph Andrews*, that key figure in sex comedy, the picaresque working-class male hero. Tom Jones's unabashed sexual enthusiasm continued with Robin Askwith's Timmy Lea character in the *Confessions* films.

Mistress Pamela, produced, written and directed by Jim O'Connolly, is a cheap, talky and flatly filmed riff on Samuel Richardson's 1740 novel. The film, nominally a comedy, is remarkably short of sexual content (there are merely a couple of brief topless scenes), and though the BBFC seems not to have interfered with it, the action is nevertheless obscured during two mild sex scenes by blue shapes and on-screen messages that read: 'Pray be patient. We are being censored' and 'Later that same night. The censor struck again.' The most is made of the novel's prurient structure, with its repeated assaults on its heroine's virtue, which Fielding parodied in *Shamela* (1741) and *Joseph Andrews*. Nineteen-year-old Pamela (Ann Michelle) is pursued by Lord Devenish (Julian Barnes), who is raised from mere 'Mr. B' in the novel to the aristocracy to emphasize the class divide. Unable to believe that his feelings for Pamela might be love, Devenish concludes in bewilderment that they must simply be lust, since 'one does not respect a serving wench'. Devenish resorts (as in the novel) to keeping Pamela prisoner in his house in Lincolnshire, but she locks herself in her room and only relents when he promises to marry her in what transpires to be a fake ceremony. She escapes to a farm but he arrives on horseback to carry her off, whereupon she rather improbably forgives him.

The American one-sheet features Devenish spanking Pamela, a scene not in the film, with the tag-line: 'Once upon a time there was a male chauvinist pig ... and then he met Pamela.' Though hardly feminist, the film is in fact relentlessly focused on class and gender, emphasizing the limited ability of poor women to control ownership of their sexuality. It is especially sharp about the dangers of losing virginity, a woman's only bargaining chip in a male-dominated world, in which her 'virtue', wholly identified with virginity, is the chief mark of her independence. 'If a girl loses her virtue, she loses everything,' Pamela's father, a ditch-digger, declares. The rights of ownership of the higher class are brutally obvious. Devenish is bewildered that he can't simply own Pamela as he does everything else, and twice in monologues to the audience wishes he were 'queer' rather than put up with her intransigence. 'What's next,' he cries, 'armed insurrection?' The politics are underlined by Mrs Jelks (Anna Quayle), an older woman in service to Devenish and also in love with Pamela, who is threatened with imprisonment for knocking him out with a vase when he first assails Pamela's virtue. Believing that 'men are wicked, evil, all of them', Mrs Jelks declares that 'rich men make the law. Poor people like us go to prison.' Sexual possibilities for poor women are reduced to either virginity, marriage or becoming a whore. 'I will be no man's whore,' Pamela tells Devenish, but even so he pays her off to forget his assault on her, and she agrees to sleep with him to release Mrs Jelks from prison. Devenish's rakish friend, Percy (Derek Fowlds), in the most interesting scene in the film, sums up the prejudices of his class when he suggests that Devenish should 'think of women as sluts', 'strumpets all of them', and states that in 'hunting women' 'there are no rules'.

Percy draws the line at rape – it is no longer the done thing, he says, as it was for their grandfathers – but this is not the case in *Cruel Passion*, directed by Chris Boger, and starring *Emily*'s Koo Stark. This is a historically set adaptation, relocated to England, of the second version of de Sade's *Justine* (1791) and, according to the credits, 'other writings of the Marquis de Sade' (a version of *Justine* was finally published in Britain in the 1960s). The film's sadistic elements were doubtless intended to appeal to the abiding British liking for 'fladge'.[3] *Cruel Passion* was one of a number of de Sade adaptations of the period, mostly sexploitation or hardcore, such as Jess Franco's *Marquis de Sade: Justine* (1969) and Pasolini's *Salò, or the One Hundred Days of Sodom*.[4] De Sade's novel was to some extent a parody of Richardson's moral view of virtue rewarded. To what Tanya Krzywinska calls the 'the soft-core sexual initiation and self-discovery narrative formula', *Cruel Passion* adds romance elements in the gothic melodrama mode of Gainsborough's bodice-ripper *The Wicked Lady* (1945), but softcore tropes are combined also with those of the horror film.[5] The film is Sadean rather than a direct adaptation – 'arthouse meets grindhouse' as Sheridan put it – and focuses on repression, patriarchal violence and the exploitation of female sexuality.[6]

Cruel Passion starts as a rare British 'nunsploitation' film (the only other ones are Ken Russell's *The Devils* (1971) and Nigel Wingrove's *Sacred Flesh* (2000)). It certainly seems influenced by Russell, not least in the use of classical music (the overture from Wagner's *Tannhäuser* (1845) plays anachronistically over the opening titles) and in a lurid dream sequence in which Justine writhes surrealistically on a burning cross. Justine (Stark), who is sixteen, and her seventeen-year-old sister Juliette (Lydia Lisle) are orphans in a convent, which, as usual in nunsploitation, is a place of institutional hypocrisy and repression. Thrown out of the convent the sisters go to a Mayfair brothel to meet Juliette's friend, Pauline (Ann Michelle, from *Mistress Pamela*). The brothel scenes – overseen by Madame Lorande (Katherine Kath), who says 'A man is the only currency that a sensible girl needs' – seem more influenced by *Fanny Hill* than de Sade. There Juliette undergoes the 'education' plot, taking control of her sexuality in male fashion ('If I could be a man for just a day!') and devoting herself to wickedness, though this is defined as promiscuity rather than outright cosmic evil, as in de Sade: 'It is a simple rule of nature that the wicked will flourish and the good must founder. All I have learnt from the holy sisters is how to frig myself.' Justine keeps her virtue but Juliette accepts the 'first law of nature', as Pastor John (Louis Ife) who tries to rape Justine puts it, which 'is to survive', and 'seeks instruction' as a whore to 'embrace depravity' because it is one of the few ways to enjoy sex and attain some independence in a patriarchal world. The only alternative is to be a married 'drudge'. Even so, Juliette falls in love with Lord Carlisle (Martin Potter), a libertine and atheist ('religion is an illness to be cured'). The characters are tormented by the repression of their natural urges. A very modern, indeed post-Freudian, cynicism is expressed through one-liners inspired by de Sade: 'Modesty is a device employed by women to provoke,' the pastor cries, adding, 'We would often be ashamed of our kind actions if the world could see the motives behind them.'

Unlike the feistier Pamela, Justine holds on to her virginity through fear of Hell rather than a sense of virtuous self-preservation. Krzywinska argues that the film downplays Sade's point that 'Justine's adherence to piety is a form of arrogance and self-proving, a kind of self-serving pleasure, proving a parallel with the libertine'.[7] Stark's Justine, she argues, 'never solicits our interest in the use of virtuousness as a form of will to power'.[8] But Justine is, as the Mother Superior says, 'devout almost to the point of pride', and finds that her virtue is an incitement to assault rather than a last defence: 'In order to preserve that which she [Juliette] gives so free I should be led to so much suffering.' After escaping from the brothel and from the pastor, who falls from his death in pursuit of her, Justin falls in with some grave-robbers and highwaymen, led by a woman, Mrs Bonney (Hope Jackman). With a genuinely Sadean irony Justine stumbles into crime to survive and out of fear of hanging. Mrs Bonney puts a radical spin on the necessity of crime, echoing Mrs Jewks in *Mistress Pamela*:

Figure 15 A Ken Russell-ish composition in *Cruel Passion*, the first film shot by the great cinematographer Roger Deakins.

'The poor are always guilty. If the rich would open their purses and show us a bit of humanity, then we might show them a bit of virtue.'

Krzywinska reasonably calls the film 'a vaselined-focus lavish costume drama', which 'seems rather coy and seeks through various elisions to make de Sade's fiction more palatable for a mainstream audience'.[9] Indeed, though sadism is mentioned once in the film, it is when Carlisle calls Lord Claverton a sadistic swine for whipping Juliette. Sadism is a weakness and perversion rather than the philosophy of libertinage; George (Barry McGinn), for example, the simpleton Lord used to instruct Juliette, is into whipping. The film necessarily avoids Sade's more extreme scenarios, and has only recently been passed uncut in Britain, on DVD, having been cut by 2.46 on its original release and by 18 seconds on video in the 1990s. Cuts were to sexual detail and dialogue. In just Reel 3 – instructions to:

> Remove Madam's dialogue 'Hold it now, the master, see how it grows' and subsequent dialogue 'May place his organ between these mounds'.
> Remove sight of George making love to Pauline from behind as she kneels on the bed.
> Remove scene where Juliette performs fellatio on George as the two women hold his arms.

The rape at the end: 'Reel 6 – Reduce to establishing shot only, Carlisle raping Justine from the rear, removing vicious thrusting'. All shots of sadomasochism were removed:

> Reel 3 – Remove all sight of George whipping woman tied down on a bed.
> Reel 4 – Remove the scene in a room in a brothel where a naked woman is made to crawl and growl like a dog.
> Remove all sight of Claverton whipping Juliette as she lies tied on the bed.

Even so, despite the extensive cuts, *Cruel Passion* emerges as a very downbeat film. What begins as saucy satire in the convent and comic bawdy in the brothel scenes turns in its last twenty minutes, once Juliette drops out of the story, into a period rural horror film like *Witchfinder General* or *Blood on Satan's Claw* (1971). There is a brutal highway robbery involving a rape and the stabbing of a young boy to death; Carlisle, the supposed romantic hero, rapes Justine, is attacked by Dobermans and stabbed to death; and Justine is thrown into a lake and left for dead (a shot reminiscent of *Last House on the Left* (1972)). Outright rape is ruled out in the comic world of *Mistress Pamela*, but *Cruel Passion* ends more like Samuel Richardson's *Clarissa* (1748), in which the rake, Lovelace, eventually rapes the heroine out of frustration. Libertinism, for which we might read modern permissiveness at a time of waning social controls, seems only to release the natural violence of male sexuality. This echoes such British horror films of period as *Killer's Moon* (1978), about escaped lunatics attacking a bevy of schoolgirls in the Lake District, which, even as it cynically exploits schoolgirl fetishism, channels disquiet at the new sexual freedoms and their incitement to regarding all women as fair game.[10] Rape is the inevitable endpoint of permissiveness. Insofar as *Cruel Passion* draws parallels between eighteenth-century England and the 1970s, it emphasizes not only that Justine's virtue is outdated, superstitious and ineffective, but that choices for women under patriarchal permissiveness tend towards either becoming enthusiastic whores, exploiting their sexuality to control the unleashed demands of men or setting themselves up as victims of rape.

Erotic Inferno

Emily and *Cruel Passion* stood out because they imitated the gloss of *Emmanuelle* and the more respectable and aspirational end of the softcore market, such as magazines like *Mayfair* and *Club International*, which traded in discourses of liberation and naturalness and presented sex as one of the benefits to men of affluent consumerism. The one sex film that was neither glossy nor a comedy was *Erotic Inferno*, directed by Trevor Wrenn.[11] It was in fact a melodrama, in which the plot is driven by remarkably frequent softcore sex scenes of grunting and writhing bodies. It is only exceptional in that, as Simon Sheridan has rightly said, it is 'a bit of a British sex film rarity' and 'genuinely full of shagging'.[12] Unlike in most softcore rather than extended self-contained sex scenes, the film consists of more or less continuous parallel scenes intercut with one another. Consequently, in the uncut version later released on video, *Erotic Inferno* is probably the most explicit British film of the period. Unsurprisingly the BBFC insisted on numerous censorship cuts ranging from minor trims to detail and close-ups – 'Reel 1 – Remove the between-the-legs shot under titles', 'Reel 4 – In the sequence in which Martin makes love to Nicolle under the bed cover, remove shot of him opening her legs to perform cunnilingus' – to more significant edits – 'Reel 3 – Reduce "back-scuttling" sequence to remove implication of buggery'. The film was a hit and ran in Soho for nearly four years.[13]

The plot, which is set over three days, is about the sons of a wealthy industrialist, Barnard (Anthony Kenyon), who seems to have disappeared from his yacht, waiting for the reading of their father's will and manoeuvring to become his heir. Paul (Karl Lanchbury) and the boorish and dissolute Martin (Chris Chittell) are the legitimate heirs, while Adam (Michael Watkins), Barnard's butler and sometime pimp, is his embittered bastard son. Barnard's country house is locked up by Barnard's solicitor, Eric Gold (Michael Sheard), till after the will is read and the action takes place in the adjoining lodge, where the sons, Brenda (Jeannie Collings), Martin's fiancée, and Nicole (Jenny Westbrook), the housekeeper, work their way through numerous sexual permutations. Nicole, a 'nymphomaniac', is a perfect construction of permissive fantasy (Brenda: 'Is Nicole always this friendly?' Adam: 'Take no notice. She can't help it.'). Paul and Martin try to get the key of the house off Nicole, who wears it on a chain around her waist, so that they can dispose of any evidence that Adam is the rightful heir. This includes a farcical scene in which Paul tries to get the key while under a bed in which Martin and Nicole are having sex.

There is no propulsive narrative structure as such, and certainly no female-centred education plot. This is emphatically the world of porn, with its assumption of continual male priapism and female availability and submissiveness ('Oh you little hot sex kitten, this is what you want, isn't it, my little nympho', Martin says to Nicole as he playfully strangles her with his tie). The characters learn nothing through sex, which primarily an instrument of power and an expression of greed and, the film's key theme, rights of ownership. Adam and Martin fight over access to Nicole, who was also Barnard's lover, and the key to the house becomes a symbol of patriarchal control over both women and wealth (the two seemingly go together). The film's relentless cynicism is softened somewhat by Brenda and Paul – who has previously had sex with Nicole in the kitchen – falling in love (he chivalrously says he won't treat her 'like another screw') and Paul's subsequently losing interest in the inheritance. Lesbian sex scenes in a stable between Jane (Mary Millington) and Gayle (Heather Deeley) make up virtually all of *Erotic Inferno*'s genuinely caring and tender moments, a subversive touch for a film that 'often seems to get as carried away on male dominance kicks as its macho protagonists'.[14] Like *Straw Dogs*, this is a film about class and male rivalries played out in terms of the defence of property rights and the possession of women. When Mr Gold comes to read the will in the middle of the night, the father turns out to be still alive and enjoying himself with young women and champagne in the old house, having faked his death as a trap to see what his sons thought about him. Paul sticks with Brenda, but Martin, who shares his father's 'love and wine and lust for women', celebrates the old man's survival by partying with him and the girls in the old house. Adam is left alone, Nicole leaves him for Martin, and Paul and Brenda stay in bed rather than attend the opening of the will.

In *Erotic Inferno* there is none of the nostalgic yearning for innocence of *Emily*, the transgressive charge of defiling virtue of *Cruel Passion*, let alone the philosophical interest of *Emmanuelle* in sex as a method of testing boundaries and constructing a new erotic identity. Rather the film is an allegory of class struggle among men over the good life – in other words, women and money – in the 1970s, and the exclusion of working-class men from the promised spoils of permissive consumerism. As Nicole says, 'Money seems to have driven us all stark staring mad.' Paul and Martin, though hardly caricatures of the middle class or upper class, are described as public school educated and enjoy the usual trappings of the rich life (shooting, horses, housekeepers and stable girls). Adam's class rebellion is symbolized not only by his getting a shotgun and shooting at his brothers as they try to break into the old house, but by his attempt to possess all of the women on Barnard's estate, including Brenda – 'All you high class bitches are all the same' – whom he tries to drown in the bath, and Gayle – 'You're mine now, all mine' – who rejects him when he is too rough. Although Adam calls Barnard 'a dirty cheat', in the end, 'the old man is still king of the castle' and power stays firmly in the hands of rich patriarchal bastards.

The British sex film cycle collapsed at the start of the 1980s thanks to the end of the Eady Levy and the arrival of home video. Michael Winner's remake of *The Wicked Lady* (1983) was an explicit update of the Gainsborough melodrama, but the last genuinely sexy films to appear were belated adaptations of the key source texts of British erotica – Gerry O'Hara's *Fanny Hill* (1983) and Just Jaeckin's *Lady Chatterley's Lover* (1981), with *Emmanuelle's* Sylvia Kristel. The critical response to these, as to almost all the British sex films, echoed Kenneth Williams's appalled cry when Barbara Windsor's bikini top whacks him in the face in *Carry on Camping* (1969) – 'Matron, take them away!' Certainly, nothing in the 'lost continent' of British cinema is so despised and ridiculed as its forays into eroticism. Yet while we can dismiss all these films, from the unfunny sex comedies to the glossy imitations of *Emmanuelle*, as aesthetic failures, we obviously cannot be sure that they did not 'work' for many in the audience in the 1970s and, quite apart from speaking to novel anxieties about class and sexuality, engaged them with arousing scenarios and erotic 'punctums'. Perhaps, though, we should look elsewhere for the sexiest moments of British cinema of the 1970s. For none of these films may represent, at any rate to heterosexual male viewers of a certain age, the best remembered – indeed the most sublimely formative – erotic highlights of that far off era of the tantalizing 'X'-film. For those we might turn instead to memories of Britt Ekland in *The Wicker Man* and, above all, of Jenny Agutter from *Walkabout* (1971) to *An American Werewolf in London* (1981).[15]

Chapter 7

Tolkien Dirty

It is not at all clear that academics view porn in a way that is compatible with the way nonacademics watch porn.

Richard Burt[1]

One of the more unlikely spin-offs from Peter Jackson's film of *The Lord of the Rings: The Fellowship of the Ring* was a clutch of erotic spoofs and trash film parodies.[2] *Whore of the Rings* (2001), *Whore of the Rings II* (2003), and *Lord of the String* are hardcore pornographic movies; *Lord of the Cockrings* (2002) is a short underground film based on a stage-play; and *Quest for the Egg Salad: Fellowship of the Egg Salad* (2002) is a fan-accented gross-out comedy. The most engaging of these spoofs is *The Lord of the G-Strings: The Femaleship of the Ring*, a sexploitation film from Seduction Cinema, a New Jersey based outfit that specializes in erotic take-offs of mainstream films.

Seduction's distinctive brand of softcore straight-to-DVD parody has pumped new blood into the sexploitation market, and achieved a remarkable high profile with consistent package design, budget price point (in the UK, at any rate), and the promotion as cult figures of in-house starlets such as Misty Mundae, the pasty-faced, small-breasted lead in *Play-Mate of the Apes* (2002), *Roxanna* (2002) and *Lord of the G-Strings*. Seduction's highest profile films, such as *The Sexy Sixth Sense* (2001), *SpiderBabe* (2003) and *The Erotic Witch Project* (1999) rework their sources as ultra low-budget lesbian erotica, intended, like almost all lesbian-themed porn, for consumption by male audiences.

Softcore and Hardcore Versions

Sexploitation parodies are nothing new. Adult versions of fairy tales, classic literature and well-known films became popular in the 1970s – *Trader Hornee* (1970) sexed up *Trader Horn* (1931), while *The Opening of Misty Beethoven* (1976) transformed *My Fair Lady* (1964) into a classic of 'Golden Age' hardcore. Since the 1980s 'hardcore versions' of mainstream films have flourished on video, including such indicative titles as *A Midsummer Night's Cream*, *Harry*

Potter Made the Philosopher Moan, Lawrence of a Labia, The Ozporns, The Sperminator and *Yank My Doodle It's a Dandy*.[3]

These hardcore versions rarely go much further than punning on the titles and lifting the basic situations of the original films. The *Fast Times at Deep Crack High* series (2001, ongoing), for instance, alludes in its title to *Fast Times at Ridgemont High* (1982) merely to indicate that it is set around a school and features cheerleaders. Parody films, like most contemporary hardcore, largely jettison narrative in favour of uninterrupted 'gonzo' depictions of sex, and adhere tenaciously to what Linda Williams called hardcore's 'principle of maximum visibility'.[4] Some films do attempt a measure of fidelity to their sources, and shoehorn the obligatory bouts of sex into recognizable imitations of the originals' plots and themes. *A Clockwork Orgy*, for example, replicates not only the storyline of Kubrick's 1971 film but also its futuristic setting and hard-edged tone.[5] In general terms hardcore versions are raunchy reproaches to Hollywood's squeamishness about sex. As Constance Penley says,

> The knockoffs cannot be intended simply to ride the coattails of popular Hollywood films because most consumers know that the porn version seldom has much to do with the themes, characters and events found in the original film. What is more likely, as Cindy Patton says … is that they are meant as 'an erotic and humorous critique of the mass media's role in invoking but never delivering sex'.[6]

As a means of product differentiation in a notoriously repetitive genre and crowded market, the parody has become a key mode of contemporary professional hardcore on DVD, especially after the success of *Pirates* (2005), a glossy take on *The Pirates of the Caribbean: The Curse of the Black Pearl* (2003), which was touted as the most expensive porn film ever made.[7] Lynn Comella, reporting from the AVN Adult Entertainment Expo in Las Vegas, remarks:

> Jack Lawrence, who garnered a Best Actor nomination for his performance in *Reno 911: A XXX Parody* [2010], shared his thoughts about why porn parodies are doing so well: 'They are really the only things selling.' He theorized that because porn parodies are fun and playful, many men feel comfortable bringing them home to watch with their wives and girlfriends. Someone else offered a different perspective: people have a connection to the television shows and movies they grew up with. 'Who wouldn't want to have sex with Marcia Brady?,' one female performer remarked.[8]

The most high-profile recent parodies are the porn versions of superhero movies produced by Hustler and Vivid, for whom Axel Braun made *Avengers XXX: A Porn Parody* (2012) and *The Dark Knight XXX: A Porn Parody* (2012). Comparatively big-budget, these do attempt some measure of 'fidelity' to their originals and offer pleasures of recognition for fans, though plot development is usually brought to a screeching halt by the lengthy sex scenes.[9]

Although Seduction's erotic spoofs are softcore, they have a close affinity to hardcore versions. But whereas hardcore quickly abandons narrative for lengthy depictions of sex, softcore like *Lord of the G-Strings* pads out its length with story, dialogue and other erotically redundant business. An effort is made to reimagine *Fellowship of the Ring* rather than simply riff on its title. The plot centres on Dildo Saggins (Misty Mundae), a Throbbit of Diddle Earth, who goes on a quest with fellow Throbbits Spam (AJ Khan) and Horny (Darian Caine) to throw the legendary G-string, once worn by evil Horspank (Paige Richards), back into the Party-Pooper Volcano. Along the way they encounter Smirnof (Michael R. Thomas), a drunken parody of Gandalf the wizard; exiled Queen Araporn of Muffonia (Barbara Joyce); and a Gollum-like creature called Ballem. In pursuit are Sourass (John P. Fedele, in the Saruman role) and his Dork army. Since *Fellowship* is essentially a picaresque road movie, it yields easily to the requirements of pornographic narrative, which demands only that sexual encounters occur with the regularity of set-piece numbers in a musical.

Although its production values recall those of *The Blair Witch Project* (1999) – in other words, interminable footage of amateurs tramping through the woods – *Lord of the G-Strings* was actually something of a prestige project. Lavishly budgeted at $100,000, it was shot on 16mm film rather than Seduction's more usual videotape. Online reviews, taken aback by such unprecedented extravagance, generally rated the film Seduction's most successful to date; but were uncertain whether to judge it as a spoof with incidental sex scenes or as a porn film with occasional parodic flourishes.[10] The emphasis on parody and intertextual jokes is intended, perhaps, to extend the film's appeal beyond porn's core audience, and align it with one of the dominant modes of contemporary

Figure 16 Smirnof and various Throbbits in *The Lord of the G-Strings*.

Hollywood production – the compulsively referential comic parody (*Spaceballs* (1987), *Silence of the Hams* (1994), *Scary Movie* (2000)). Intertextual allusions in *Lord of the G-Strings*, however, tend to be scattershot and opportunistic, and it is difficult to attach any consistent satirical purpose to them (as, for example, when Smirnof, semi-quoting *American Pie* (1999), says, apropos nothing in particular, 'Once when I was at band camp I told this obnoxious little girl what she could do with her flute'). But it is worth noting that *Lord of the G-Strings*, in spite of its lowly position in the cultural hierarchy, is wholly representative of contemporary film practice in its reliance on pastiche, allusion and intertextuality.

Lord of the G-Strings is of interest, too, in representing a novel and distinctive mode of contemporary exploitation cinema, the trash film discussed in the previous chapter. Trash films, adopting the camp style pioneered by George Kuchar and John Waters (but not, in the main, their gay sensibility), revel in poor taste, gross-out content and reflexive pastiche of the clichés of low-budget filmmaking. The pleasure of watching them, as Carole Laseur remarks 'may well be precisely situated in the recognition of its satirical parody of a pompous high cultural (bourgeois) set of aesthetic proclamations'.[11] Their core constituency is young male connoisseurs of disreputable alternatives to the mainstream, the kind of films Jeffrey Sconce labelled 'paracinema'. Exploitation outfits that specialize in deliberate trash make a virtue of their films' sleaziness, gratuitous nudity and violence and contempt for politically correctness. By alienating the mass audience they enhance their appeal to trash aesthetes, self-selecting ironists who are proficient in cult appreciation. As Mark Jancovich has pointed out, a taste for paracinema is therefore curiously elitist in its preening, cliquey contempt for the mainstream and those who are satisfied by it; paracinema, he writes,

> is a species of bourgeois aesthetics not a challenge to it … . [It is] at least as concerned to assert its superiority over those whom it conceives of as the degraded victims of mainstream commercial culture as it is concerned to provide a challenge to the academy and the art cinema.[12]

Seduction's films fall squarely into this category of intentional commercial trash, setting them apart from both underground films and straightforward pornography. The calculated ineptitude of *Lord of the G-Strings* is designed to inveigle the viewer into mistaking what some might regard as incompetent rubbish for subversive self-reflexive fun. Trash films like this embrace their viewers as savvy and discriminating insiders, honoured participants in an exclusive postmodern cult. Seduction's brand of high camp trash is therefore an astute commercial solution to the dilemma of contemporary sexploitation. Recognizing the (paradoxical) mass cult appeal of trash films, Seduction offers DVDs like *Lord of the G-Strings* for sale as instant collectables rather than as anonymous soft porn – prefabricated cult movies for discerning aficionados of 'Alternative Cinema' (the revealing tie-in name of the company's website). To this end, and to position its films as *hommages* to the great tradition of exploitation cinema, the website advertises not only its own DVDs but vintage grindhouse fare. In short, Seduction peddles a curious kind of 'heritage cinema'; its films are paracinematic ready-mades, which mock the conventions of exploitation cinema even as they keep the ailing form alive.

'Description' and Masturbation

Craig Fischer has described how in porn films, and porn-inflected exploitation like Russ Meyer's *Beyond the Valley of the Dolls* (1970), narrative frequently collapses into what he calls 'description' – extended nude and sex scenes with no obvious purpose beyond the non-diegetic arousal of the audience.[13] These descriptive passages, which are generically essential to porn, are the kind of discursive but extraneous matter that classical Hollywood narrative omits in its pursuit of economical storytelling: 'The moments which define pornography as a genre are *descriptive* moments, independent of plot but concerned with rendering ... the properties of the human body, for voyeuristic purposes.'[14] Exploitation films generally fluctuate between storytelling and description, classical narrative and pornography. They may start out as narrative but 'the pre-eminence of sex and violence [in exploitation] breaks down narrative and replaces it with description of sexual acts'.[15]

This is certainly true of *Lord of the G-Strings*, which, hovering awkwardly between parody and porn, struggles to develop a coherent narrative while also serving up the necessary quota of descriptive moments of sex. The story is frequently held up by narratively redundant sex scenes, which get longer and more self-contained as the film goes on, and more severely disconnected from the on-screen diegesis. For example, immediately after the opening prologue, a longish sequence of Dildo masturbating brings the narrative to a grinding halt before it has even had a chance to get started. The result is very bad *classical* storytelling (because the scene is gratuitous vis-à-vis narrative development) but very good *porn description* (because Dildo gets nekkid, as Joe Bob Briggs would say, barely five minutes into the movie). The imperatives of narrative cinema, on the one hand, and porn's cinema of attractions, on the other, are in continuous warring opposition.

Subsequent sex scenes in *Lord of the G-Strings* progress from solo masturbation to one-on-one heterosexual fucking to a climactic lesbian orgy. None of the scenes moves the narrative along; mostly they are helicoptered in when a bit more sex is required and some are barely integrated into the plot at all. One lesbian scene, for example, takes place against a black background in isolation from storyline, diegesis and temporal location. The major sex scenes, incidentally, are spared the parodic handling of the dialogue sequences, which are steeped in camp irony, 'bad' style and the low culture equivalent of Brechtian alienation effects. The result is a weird inconsistency of tone: passages of comic narrative alternate mechanically with solemn bouts of sexual description, which seem designed – though it is hard to be sure – to enhance masturbation.

Pornography and Reflexivity

Lord of the G-String's ideology, insofar as it has one, is consistent with the libertinism of pornography. The Throbbits are 'trisexuals' – 'they'll try anything, the horny little bastards', according to Dildo – and Diddle Earth is a pornocopian land of single-minded sexual indulgence sans reference to marriage, monogamy or exclusive relationships (except for one poor soul jealous at being dropped by a Wood Dryad). Multiple partners and orgiastic promiscuity are taken for granted, and women are generally presented as strong and sexually active. (This modest feminism chimes with the latest wave of teen films, such as *American Pie*, which are more women-centred than predecessors like *Porky's* (1982) and *National Lampoon's Animal House* (1978) as well as more forthcoming about male inadequacy and sexual embarrassment.) Far removed from the moralism of classical exploitation, *Lord of the G-Strings* is evangelical about the virtues of masturbation, voyeurism, troilism, male defloration, lesbianism and lesbian sex.

Needless to say, the film's take on lesbianism owes little to the documented lifestyle of that social group, but rather corresponds to how lesbians *ought* to behave in the perfect porn universe. (Porn habitually presents women as its protagonists and narrators, a device intended to legitimate the male fantasies they are required to respond to and act out.) Pornography is an account of what men want sex to be like (in the case of lesbian sex, a sort of contact spectator sport with opportunities for audience participation). A chronicle of male yearning, porn registers disappointment in, rather than hatred of, the subtlety and difference of female sexuality, along with relief that women aren't actually so demanding in real life. The central fantasy of porn is that women are *up for it*; that, in defiance of their evolved sexual nature, they are no less indiscriminate and sexually driven as men.

Lord of the G-Strings is not only an exploitation film; it is also about how viewers ought to watch and respond to an exploitation film. First, in the accepted style of a postmodern trash film, it draws attention to its stupidity, gratuitousness and budgetary limitations. Second, and more interesting, it tries to second-guess and mirror back to the viewer his reactions to what he is seeing on screen – for example, in reflexive scenes of characters watching and commenting on the action as if anticipating the audience's response at home. This works both to naturalize the viewer's voyeurism (everyone in Diddle Earth does it, so why shouldn't you?) and also to indicate the kind of viewing situations most appropriate to consuming the film. The first lesbian scene, for example, is interrupted by male warriors led by General Uptight; the girls insist on carrying on making love but permit the men to watch. (One of the men is gay and agrees to watch only if he can imagine that one of the girls is a man). The resulting set-up, in which men ogle women who are performing sexually for them, is significant in two ways. First, it confirms that the sex scenes, even within the story, are public performances staged only in order to be observed and appreciated. Second, it constructs one preferred scenario for the viewing and correct appreciation of *Lord of the G-Strings* – as a sociable viewing activity with your mates, probably with a six-pack and a takeaway. Unlike hardcore porn, which smacks of furtive solitary entertainment, *Lord of the G-Strings* presents itself as ideal for collective laddish enjoyment. Its softcore naughtiness and referential humour identify it as titillating eye-candy for the guys rather than as straightforward pornography, a flat inducement to a lonesome wank (or, God forbid, circle jerk).

The implied audience for *Lord of the G-Strings* is therefore men young enough to get the references to contemporary cult and teen films. There are interesting moments, however, when the film's address to the audience switches and it seems to target women. For example, at one point the trio of female Throbbits ogle a sex session and the film adopts a nominally female point of view. Perhaps the film is suitable after all for viewing on a girls' night in. There is also a very peculiar moment during a dialogue scene when Sourass turns to the camera and says 'Hello girls', thus seeming directly to address women in the audience (or, possibly, since it is implied that he is gay, impertinently feminizing male viewers). He then becomes very self-conscious and, with one of his sidekicks, starts playing up to the camera. How do we read this? Camp improvization? Pretence that the film, against all generic logic, might count women among its viewers? Or simply a random moment of reflexivity, of a piece with the film's scrappily developed trash aesthetic? Reflexivity of this sort, acknowledging the viewer in order to unsettle his or her response to the film, is standard in parody films (*Airplane!*) and not unusual in pornography, which often draws the viewer's attention to its staged quality more powerfully to emphasize the reality of the sex. Richard Dyer has noted that gay porn lures the audience into the film by emphasizing its artificiality and hailing the viewer:

> Paradoxically there is a kind of realism in pornographic performance that declares its own performativity. What a porn film really is is a record of people actually having sex; it is only ever the narrative circumstances of porn, the apparent pretext for the sex, that is fictional.... . This realism in turn has the effect of validating the video and the genre to which it belongs. By stressing that what we are enjoying is not a fantasy, but porn, it validates porn itself.[16]

The reflexivity of *Lord of the G-Strings* can seem confusing if it's interrogated closely or taken too seriously. As I've suggested, the film's address to its audience as well as its generic self-definition are strategically inconsistent and opportunistic. This is partly because the film (like all exploitation films, perhaps) is interstitial between different kinds of low-budget movie – porn, trash film, sex comedy and so on – and their different but overlapping audiences. With its comic displays of tits-and-arse, *Lord of the G-Strings* is viable as a post-pub DVD for larky collective male viewing; or it might work as a couples' movie, a saucy bargain basement version of the mainstream parody film; it is also, primarily I'd argue, a trash film for the cult market and a must buy for paracinemaniacs. At the same time it is constructed in many scenes as straightforward pornography, whose extended sequences of sexual description invite the sticky-fingered attentions of masturbators.

In other words, it is hard to know exactly *how* the film is watched or indeed meant to be watched. The likeliest explanation is that Seduction is engaged in postmodern multiple coding. Just as every Hollywood film tries to reach out to multiple demographics, so too is *Lord of the G-Strings* making a play for the widest possible range of trash, erotic and parody movie fans.

Sexing up Tolkien

Finally we come to *Lord of the G-Strings*'s intertextual relationship with *The Fellowship of the Ring*, which I shall argue is not necessarily very important. It's certainly difficult to argue that there is a consistent purpose to its parody of Jackson's film, except insofar as it emphasizes that sex isn't prioritized in Middle Earth. Although *Lord of the G-Strings* is parasitic on *Fellowship of the Ring*, this is not the key determinant of its narrative structure, ideological content and address to the audience. Far more important, as I've suggested already, are the contexts of exploitation cinema, trash movies, pornography and mainstream parody films.

Nevertheless there are a few hints of subversive intent in *Lord of the G-Strings*. Although never cohering into a full-blown critique of *Lord of the Rings*, it does haphazardly unlock – or rather allow an enthusiastic critic to unlock – some of its repressions and erotic possibilities. The most outrageous aspect of *Lord of the G-Strings* is its overt sexualization of an imaginative world ostensibly purged of significant erotic reference. Indeed the sheer absence of sex in Tolkien's fantasy might be read by psychoanalytically-minded critics as a sign of massive repression and sublimation. Middle Earth cries out to be pornified, not in order to defile its innocence but rather to encourage a healthy return of the repressed. From this perspective, *Lord of the G-Strings* is neither lurid filth nor disfiguring graffiti, but a kind of wild overcorrection, substituting the single motivation of sex for Tolkien's complexly interwoven religious, philological and mythic concerns.

The Lord of the Rings (the novel) is arguably brimful with sexual tensions and aspects of inchoate erotic fantasy and repression. In particular, it is nervous about women (divided, in stereotypically Catholic style, into Madonnas (Galadriel) and whores (Shelob)) and deeply attracted to an exclusive and clubbishly homosocial world of men. It must be said that Peter Jackson, in all three films, is alert to the alleged misogyny and erotic subtexts of the novel, and to their relevance to its marginalization of romance, its vivid sexual symbolism and its bubbling currents of homoeroticism. (Given Jackson's background in trash exploitation, it is not surprising that he should relish lurid subtexts in respectable material; his *Meet the Feebles* (1989), a truly grotesque trash spoof of the Muppets, makes *Lord of the G-Strings* seem positively cherubic.) On the one hand, Jackson rescues the Aragorn–Arwen story from the Appendices of *The Return of the King*, which, along with boosting the role of Eowyn, enhances the role of women in the story; this acknowledges, too, that, post-*Titanic*, action films are well advised to build in plenty of love interest. On the other hand, Jackson points up the book's unconscious sexual imagery – the recurrence of swords as symbols of power and masculinity; the womb-like cosiness of hobbits' burrows; the terrifying anality of the One Ring; and the resemblance of Sauron's disembodied cat's eye to the vertical slit of a vagina. As Graham Fuller notes,

> This malicious gynecentrism, intended or not, is reiterated in the images of hapless males imperiling themselves by entering clefts, crevices, caves, and narrow doorways time and time again: the portals to Moria, the Paths of the Dead, Shelob's lair ... the scalding Cracks of Doom.[17]

Paradoxically, having intended to present *Lord of the G-Strings* as a parody of *The Fellowship of the Ring* and a sarky commentary on its sexual subtexts and repressions, I am forced to acknowledge that Jackson may well have got there first.

Lord of the G-Strings is, in fact, more usefully understood in cultural and generic terms as a trashy American retort to, on the one hand, the English prissiness of the original novel and, on the other, the middlebrow pretensions of the fantasy genre. Constance Penley and Laura Kipnis both describe porn as class antagonistic grossness and *Lord of the G-Strings* is indeed a low cultural fart in the general direction of (in no particular order) bourgeois propriety, sexual purity, good taste, bodily restraint and social hierarchy (though, admittedly, Gimli serves some of these functions in Jackson's films).[18] Given its multiracial casting, *Lord of the G-Strings* also vigorously rebuts Middle Earth's unrelieved whiteness, which is transferred wholesale into the film of *Fellowship of the Ring* with its persistent negative association of blackness with Orcs, Maori-ish Uruk-Hai and other subhumans from the East. In short, *Lord of the G-Strings* is, in very general terms, *Fellowship*'s generic Other – scatological, disrespectful, pervy, democratic (mostly) in its sexual tastes, racially relaxed, cheap, American, unpretentious and overrun with sexually confident female trailer trash.

Although widely read as an allegory of the Cold War, *The Lord of the Rings* can also be interpreted as a homoerotic sexual myth, which, in flight from female sexuality, constructs a fantasy world of sublimated homoerotic desire.

Consider, for example, Roger Kaufman's ingenious theory that Gollum is Frodo's homosexual other. Kaufman remarks that Tolkien 'created an incredibly rich and detailed fantasy world from which heterosexual romance is almost entirely absent, and none of the primary characters is married' and then offers a brisk reading of the novel from a revisionist Jungian perspective.[19] According to Kaufman, Sam is Frodo's 'Double' who accompanies Frodo on an archetypal 'hero's journey' of individuation towards his true actualized self. Because Sam is both Frodo's soul mate and erotically charged helper,

> the relationship between Frodo and Sam is not only an ode to same-sex love but also an archetypal dynamic within each gay man, where self-reflection may reveal the existence of an inner lover or a 'soul figure' and guide who loves us just as Sam loves Frodo, and who, like Sam, can spur us to reach our greatest potential.[20]

But to achieve individuation the hero, Frodo, must confront his 'shadow', the most shameful part of himself, represented here by Gollum, Frodo's dark, unconscious twin. Kaufman argues – oddly, in my view – that the films downplay the homoeroticism between Frodo and Sam in favour of an eroticized relationship between Frodo and Gollum (for example, when they struggle inside Mount Doom Gollum wraps himself around Frodo from behind as if endeavouring to bugger him). Gollum, Kaufman concludes, represents the gay man's feelings of inadequacy and inferiority, but he is also energetic and vital and 'in many ways the least repressed creature in Middle Earth'.[21] Frodo's growing empathy with Gollum (himself a divided creature) suggests how the shadow can be wrestled with, confronted and integrated into the self.

Jackson seems to acknowledge the homoerotic passion between Frodo and Sam. In *The Return of the King* (2003) Frodo comes across not only as gay (he exchanges lingering glances at Sam; nearly kisses him on the lips at the harbour; and goes off at the end with Gandalf, whose sexuality, inflected extratextually by Ian McKellen's, is fascinatingly indeterminate) but as a gay Christ, who says 'It is done' when the ring is destroyed and who must die to save the Shire ('it is saved, but not for me'). The crucial difference with *Lord of the G-Strings* is that, even if *Lord of the G-Strings* registered these layers of homoerotic implication, it could not deal with them, at least not openly. Although the film transforms the central characters from implicitly gay men into porn-lesbians, male homosexuality is strictly off limits as a sexual permutation. It is true – and a valuable inversion of Tolkien – that *Lord of the G-Strings* converts Middle Earth from a hierarchical, male-centred world into an erotic paradise. It is also true that, in turning the male characters into lesbians, the film asserts a sexual identity unthinkable in the original novel (and perhaps in the films, too) and cancels out its fear of women's sexuality. The price, however, is the elimination of male homoeroticism.

The preponderance of lesbian scenes in Seduction's films, as in porn generally, might be seen, in fact, as an attempt to neutralize the homoerotic aspect of viewing straight porn – that it involves men getting aroused by watching other men have sex. (Watching straight porn has unexpectedly queer possibilities. If men watch porn together, the event becomes discomfortingly homosocial; if one watches it alone and masturbates – well, masturbation is a species of homosexual act, in which a man has sex – incestuously? – with a man.) Since *Lord of the G-Strings* draws the line at male homosexuality (except as a joke), this unexpectedly renders it more homophobic than *The Lord of the Rings* films, if one is persuaded that they intentionally allude to homoerotic subtexts in the novel. For example, whereas the lesbians in *Lord of the G-Strings* are liberated, polymorphous and sympathetically portrayed, Sourass, the film's villain, seems to be a hostile depiction of gayness. Crabbily repressed and appalled by sex, he is a compilation of disgusted allusions to male homosexuality, which range from obscurely coded references to *The Wizard of Oz* (he calls the Dorks, 'my pretties', like the Wicked Witch of the West) to insistent anus and fart gags.

It is worth very briefly contrasting *Lord of the G-Strings* with 'slash fiction', which also appropriates *Lord of the Rings* for sexual fantasy.[22] Slash fiction is a genre of fan stories about homoerotic affairs between male characters in popular films and TV series, such as, classically, *Star Trek*. Slash writers are almost exclusively women, who, as Milly Chen remarks in a magazine piece on Sam/Frodo slash, find that slash 'lets them write about relationships without having to deal with traditional sexual power struggle' and 'take control of men's bodies for their own fun, just as men have been taking control of women's bodies for centuries'.[23] There is an extensive archive of *Lord of the Rings* slash at The Library of Moria (http://www.libraryofmoria.com), including stories like 'When the Wizard's Away ...' by 'Sam Littlefoot', which imagines Sam and Frodo making love under the friendly gaze of Aragorn:

> Sam stroked his fingers, in and out, touching Frodo deeply – massaging the opening to a body he knew almost as well as his own. Frodo's body arched with a cry as Sam touched that one special spot, the one that filled his lover with indescribable pleasure. Again and again he stroked the dark-haired Hobbit, watching him writhe each time the fingers found their mark.[24]

Not all slash is quite so 'NC-17' rated. In fact, according to Catherine Salmon and Donald Symons, who analyse slash from the perspective of evolutionary psychology, slash fiction seems to be as much about friendship and intimacy as sex; its core theme is 'building a romantic/sexual relationship on the solid foundation of an established relationship'.[25] Slash is a variation on the romance novel, whose goal is never sex for its own sake but rather the establishment (or in slash, the fulfilment) of a lasting pair bond: 'In mainstream romances love originates in sexual passion, whereas in slash it originates in friendship; slash protagonists were comrades long before the scales fell from their eyes and they realised the existence of mutual love.'[26]

Now, the comparison between *Lord of the G-Strings* and slash is not entirely apt; the former is a commercial film rather than a fan production, and therefore constrained by generic obligations that a slash writer may ignore. But the differences between the two – one essentially porn for men, the other fanfic by women – are nevertheless revealing. For, according to Salmon and Symons, porn and slash are wholly incompatible genres that reflect abiding differences between male and female psychologies and mating strategies. Whereas slash – as in the passage cited above – highlights emotional as well as physical intimacy, porn such as *The Lord of the G-Strings* is exclusively interested in maximizing opportunities for impersonal sexual encounters. Considered as porn, *Lord of the G-Strings*, for all its supposed 'lesbian' content, is a clear-cut product of the evolved characteristics of male psychology, and its vision of sex is anathema to the romantic, female world of slash. One interesting result is that slash, unlike straight porn and exploitation, can frankly cope with *Lord of the Rings*'s homoerotic subtexts (though lesbianism doesn't get a look-in); indeed it finds little else to write about.

In the end, one might conclude that porn versions cannot work as adaptations because the adaptation element is always displaced by the pornography. Whereas adaptation, parody and satire all require specificity of reference for their effect, porn usually tends towards the anonymous, conventionalized and ahistorical. Although *Lord of the G-Strings* starts off as a parody of *Fellowship of the Ring*, its sex scenes are interchangeable with the ritualized, nude caresses of countless other softcore movies. Richard Burt, discussing porn and trash versions of Shakespeare, argues that such versions do, in fact, add up to an ideological project: they 'rewrite Shakespeare so as to undo the romantic couple and the institution of marriage. They give reign to a sexual pornotopia, including gay and lesbian sex and even incest, rather than uphold heteronormative

Figure 17 Gollum given a porno makeover in *Whore of the Rings II*.

sexuality.'[27] But this is what happens when *any* text is reworked as porn and it tells us very little about the subtexts or repressed content of the original.

Burt also notes of Shakespearean porn that the porn elements cannot really function within the parodic frame. Since we do not know, for example, what 'Shakespearean sex' would be like, what we get instead is the standard repertoire of sexual acts. Similarly, with *Lord of the G-Strings*, there is nothing intrinsically 'Tolkien-esque' – if one can imagine such a thing – about the sex scenes. (*Whore of the Rings II*, by contrast, makes a couple of its sex scenes vaguely relevant to *The Two Towers* (2002); an Ent, for example, is fellated till it ejaculates out of a branch.) As soon as the sex scenes begin, the parody stops and all narrative coherence is lost.

Sex Work

In luridly re-imagining *The Lord of the Rings* as a sexual fantasy, one is struck by three thoughts: first, that it is quite easily done, if one is not too fastidious, and has a relatively dirty mind; second, that sexing up the classics has become an obligatory exercise given the post-Freudian belief that sex is the measure of all things, the *real* real signified; and, third, that *The Lord of the G-Strings* is, essentially, doing what is now standard practice among highbrow critics – recklessly queering the text and imposing its own grid of predictable obsessions. My conclusion is that a merely textual account of the movie, whether as exploitation or pornography or both, misses out what is crucial about it as a 'sex work', the BBFC's term for a film intended solely for erotic arousal.

It is perfectly reasonable to interpret *Lord of the G-Strings* in narrowly generic, ideological and historical terms, which is more or less what I've tried to do here. But pornography needs to be thought about in relation to its *use* and this is where my treatment of *Lord of the G-Strings* is seriously – if inevitably – flawed.[28] Although I've described the kind of audiences the film caters to – from trash film devotees to solitary masturbators – I have no idea how they actually use it in the sense of integrating it into their lives.[29]

This is an acute problem with erotic films because to understand the experience of watching them requires more than delicately unpicking their subtexts from a safe academic distance. As Jennifer Wicke remarks,

> It needs to be accepted that pornography is not 'just' consumed, but is used, worked on, elaborated, remembered, fantasised about by its subjects. To stop the analysis at the artefact, as virtually all the current books and articles do, imagining that the representation is the pornography in quite simple terms, is to truncate the consumption process radically, and thereby to leave unconsidered the human making involved in completing the act of pornographic consumption. Because of the overwhelming focus on the artefacts or representations of pornography, such 'making' has been

obscured in favour of simply asserting that these artefacts have a specific or even an indelible meaning, the one read off the representation by the critic. That act of interpretation is a far remove from what happens in pornographic consumption itself, where the premium is on incorporating or acquiring material for a range of phantasmic transformations. When the pornographic image or text is acquired, the work of pornographic consumption has just begun.[30]

So, for example, if an account of watching porn in a dedicated porn cinema assumed that viewers attended to the films no differently from in a multiplex, it would be leaving out everything that mattered about the weird, edgy and homoerotic world of the grindhouse – the comings and goings of the clientele, the shadowy assignations, the irrelevance of the film itself sometimes to the performances in the stalls. Similarly to make sense of domestically consumed porn and exploitation DVDs and videos, we need some sense of the context of their use and private significance – a phenomenology of wanking, if you like. We should consider the circumstances in which porn is enjoyed by viewers primarily engaged *not* in comprehending the narrative of a film but rather in the coordinated physical and cognitive task of *masturbating to it*.[31] As Laurence O'Toole remarks, 'It has never occurred to anyone to ask porn users what's going on. ... Folks think they already know all there is to know about porn users: they look at dirty images, they become aroused, they're sad.'[32] Crucial to understanding a film like *Lord of the G-Strings* are such quirky and impertinent questions as the following. Do people watch porn DVDs all the way through, or just in satisfying bursts? (One of the unusual characteristics of porn DVDs is that they are not necessarily intended to be watched all the way through in one sitting.) Do men always masturbate to porn, or are there more subtle, curious or sinister reasons to view it? Do men typically delay orgasm till the cum shot happens on screen? How often do men watch porn films communally? Do viewers *ever* interpret a porn film or care about its meaning?

Getting stuck into these questions is no less rewarding than textual analysis and theoretical speculation; it is just harder to do. I'd be fascinated to know how *Lord of the G-Strings* is actually viewed, consumed and used by people in the home, whether as amusing trash film, male bonding exercise, wannabe cult object or incitement to erotic play. My guess is that its parodic relation to *The Lord of the Rings* would quickly fall away as a topic of interest. More compelling by far would be an intimate exploration of its role in the life of an individual viewer, modelling one's approach, perhaps, on a closely focused study by Martin Barker of one fan's political engagement with *Judge Dredd*.[33] Admittedly, this sounds like a complete non-starter: it is hard to imagine *Lord of the G-Strings* securing in anybody's life – even in mine – a place of special cult affection or erotic significance. More valuable would be locating the film within the vast eroticized multiverse spun out from *The Lord of the Rings* in the form of fanfic, cos-play, slash fiction, film parodies and even cultist essays like this one; and discovering how all this creativity appropriates, sabotages, and, to borrow a phrase from the Surrealists, 'irrationally enlarges' Tolkien's world of fantasy.

Appendix

A couple of years after writing this chapter on *The Lord of the G-Strings* I leapt at the chance to watch not only *Gums*, which had finally broken surface on DVD, but also *This Ain't Jaws XXX*, which is a pornographic parody of my all-time favourite personal cult film. Unlike *Lord of the G-Strings*, *This Ain't Jaws* is not a playfully cultish sexploitation film but swims the warm waters of the sins of the flesh, as *Rocky Horror* put it, in the form of an industrial strength hardcore porn movie – in 3D. Produced by Adam & Eve productions and Hustler, presumably to cash in on the 2012 rerelease of *Jaws* to cinemas in a digital print, *This Ain't Jaws XXX* turned out to be woefully light on shark action but compensated by including explicit sex scenes conspicuously missing from the 'PG'-rated original. I thought it worth adding this short section to Chapter 7 in order, first, to expand discussion of the porn parody beyond sexploitation and into the more problematic realm of hardcore, and, second, to bring things full circle and up to date with *Jaws*ploitation.

*

On the face of it, *Jaws* seems an unlikely candidate for the porn treatment. Spielberg's film is entirely male-centred – so I guess a gay version with three-way romps on the *Orca* might make sense – but the characters' motivations have no obvious erotic component or indeed reference, aside from Quint calling out 'Stop playing with yourself, Hooper' to the lounging ichthyologist. Sex as a theme is not there to be exploited as with, say, *A Clockwork Orgy*, the porn version of *A Clockwork Orange*, which feeds off the obsession with sex, power and breasts that drives the narrative of the original. And the piscine motif of *Jaws* doesn't immediately suggest the erotic, unless one considers the 'eels for pleasure' section of the '*Animal Farm*' bestiality compilation video that did the rounds in Britain in the 1980s, or urban myths involving Led Zeppelin, a groupie and a shark. That said, it is doubtless true that any film can be 'pornified' insofar as narrative gaps in the original can be filled with sex scenes, and the characters' motivations refocused on seeking opportunities for them.

Jaws is not, however, *entirely* without legitimate sexual interpretation and erotic possibilities. The beach locations provide a valid excuse for *Jaws*ploitation films to dwell on the antics of bikinied and skinny-dipping beauties.[34] Recent *Jaws* films such as *Piranha 3D* and *Piranha 3DD* pick up on this sexploitation angle, with shots of attractive young women on Spring Break or, as in the most memorable scene in *Piranha 3D*, luxuriantly swimming nude underwater in homage to one of *Jaws*'s sources, *The Creature from the Black Lagoon*, in which the smitten creature swims under the gorgeous Julie Adams. Moreover, both *Jaws* and Peter Benchley's source novel, boast sexual subtexts worth spoofing by a canny satirist or pornographer (Spielberg initially misconstrued the title of the novel when he picked up the galley proofs: ' "What is this about?" he asked himself. "A porno dentist?" '[35]). The middle section of the novel, for example, is about an affair between the shark expert Matt Hooper and Ellen, Chief Brody's frustrated wife, ('There had not been much sex in the Brody household recently').[36] They share a brief unerotic sex scene, recalled by Ellen, in which Hooper's 'eyes seemed to bulge until, just before release, Ellen had feared they might actually pop out of their sockets.'[37] Spielberg, on astute aesthetic grounds, got rid of the affair to focus on the chase for shark and so eliminated the obvious resource for sexing the material up. The book is nevertheless haunted by sex, or more precisely rape. Hendricks, the deputy sheriff, reads a pulp novel, *Deadly, I'm Yours*, in which a girl is about to be raped by a motorcycle gang (15), and 'the summer before, a black gardener had raped seven rich white women, not one of whom would appear in court to testify against him' (16). In fact, the description of Hooper's 'obvious, violent climax' with Ellen and 'the ferocity and intensity of his assault' (161) not only suggests rape but aligns Hooper's angry primal appetites with those of the hyper-phallic shark.

The sexual overtones of *Jaws*, the film, dovetail with these allusions to rape and even expand on them with a sly Freudian emphasis. This was after all the period of *Deep Throat*, referenced (as I mentioned previously) when a fisherman remarks of a tiger shark strung up on the harbour, 'It's got a deep throat, Frank.' In the opening attack on the nude Chrissie, for instance, which is constructed as a symbolic rape in imitation of the shower scene in *Psycho*, Chrissie screams 'It hurts' as her would-be lover, sprawling drunk back on the beach, moans, 'I'm coming.' The shark is a phallic monster of the Id, whose power both mocks Brody's and Hooper's masculinity and complements and threatens Quint's. Some radical feminists, giving this a further psychoanalytic spin, read *Jaws* as a kind of backlash film, in which the shark evokes not a male fantasy of territorial control through rape. *Jaws*'s influence on the 'slasher' horror cycle re-emphasizes this. The slasher film, with its structure of set-piece murders of horny teenagers right after sex, does, in fact, offer one scenario for a porn film drawn from the template of *Jaws*. Horror films and especially slasher films lend themselves readily to porn parody, as with *The XXXorcist* (2006), *Porn of the Dead* (2006) and *Texas Vibrator Massacre* (2008).[38]

This Ain't Jaws XXX, made in 3D for 3D TVs, though a 2D version is also included in the DVD set, is essentially a series of sex scenes, moving tableaux uninterrupted by dialogue or motivated by anything beyond characters' unrelenting horniness. Though boldly touted as a parody on the DVD cover, the sex scenes are played more or less straight and any comedy is due to hammy performances and the 'badfilm' pleasures of poor CGI and irreverent dialogue references to the original *Jaws*. After a brief bit of the obligatory 'dum-dum' *Jaws* music to cue us in, *This Ain't Jaws XXX* begins with two young lovers, Cassie (Lily LaBeau) and Danny (Danny Wylde) having sex, only two and half minutes into the film, in a bamboo beach shack in studio. In the novel the equivalent characters, Tom and Chrissie, thrash 'with urgent ardour on the cold sand' on first page and the attack takes place while the man is asleep on the sand.[39] So this explicit expansion has at least an element of fidelity. The content and style of this sex scene typifies what follows – long takes (this one is twelve and a half minutes) documenting three or four discrete positions, with some cut-ins or camera pans to genital detail, and ending in a 'cumshot' or 'pop-shot'. After the sex and a cut to the ocean, the girl goes swimming, the shark closes in on her and she disappears, leaving only her necklace to be found (there is no gore in this retelling). In Mayor Vaughn's (Darcy Tyler) office, Vaughn and Chief Brody (Dale DaBone) engage in a mash-up of dialogue from the original before another sex scene in a tent between a teenager (Phoenix Marie) and a lifeguard (Rocco Reed), for which there is no equivalent in film or novel (narratively it replaces the Kintner boy's death). This is another uninterrupted sequence, twenty minutes long, consisting of just three positions and a climactic 'facial'. The staging of the sex scenes in a distinct pornosphere is emphasized by their being staged in obvious studio interiors, which could be re-cut into more or less any porn film whatsoever. Brody spots the shark feasting on another swimmer, and demands that that the beaches are closed. A shark expert is brought in (Alexis Ford, in the Hooper role – 'Sometimes the best man is a woman') and agrees to the beach closure, which prompts another twenty-minute sex scene, between her and the mayor. Evan Stone ('It's Quint—just Quint') offers to hunt the shark with Hooper. Meanwhile Brody goes off to have sex with his wife, Ellen (Darcy Tyler), another scene not in book or film but which undercuts the novel's subplot about the sheriff's sex-starved adulterous wife. Brody, Hooper and Quint go in pursuit of the shark, Quint threatening to hook it by dangling his 'big worm'. Hooper and Quint have sex after he seduces her with a Tijuana bible and some nautical jokes about his 'good sized tackle'. This sex scene, for once, is more obviously a 'Jawesome' performance, with Quint asking her to bite his penis like a shark. The shark, in a flurry of appalling CGI, then crashes the stern of the boat and eats Quint. This inspires Hooper to strip naked and dive in to try to kill the shark with a speargun, but she disappears and, as in *Jaws*, Brody feeds the shark an oxygen tank and explodes it, saying, 'Smile you son of a bitch.' The shark is killed and Hooper returns to the boat.

As this dreary summary suggests, *This Ain't Jaws XXX* 'parodies' *Jaws* by shoe-horning long stand-alone sex scenes into a rudimentary version of the film's structure while diligently salvaging some of its more quotable dialogue. Punning allusions to *Jaws* are indeed rife. 'Show me the way to go home,' communally sung on the *Orca*, becomes 'I wanna get blown', while Hooper mangles given Brody's classic improvised line, 'I think you're gonna need a bigger dick.' *This Ain't Jaws XXX* reverses how *Jaws* adapted its own source, which in classical Hollywood style meant trimming extraneous detail for the

Figure 18 The crew of the *Orca* in *This Ain't Jaws XXX*.

sake of plot momentum and character delineation. The structure of *This Ain't Jaws XXX* is indeed much like the slasher film, with sex scenes spacing out brief moments of shark attack.

Even so, I am frankly at a loss how the film evinces any '*Jawsness*' even at the level of parody. *This Ain't Jaws XXX* scarcely draws upon its source's sexual subtexts, though admittedly it is possible that off-screen in *Jaws*, Brody had hot sex with his wife, the mayor and Hooper made out in his office, and Quint seduced Hooper on the *Orca*. There are a few minor interesting alterations and emphases. Quint is here more obviously raucous working class, perhaps to align him with the conventional blue-collar *Hustler* reader. Changing the sex of Hooper underlines that this could have been a gay film (homosexuality is only allowed as lesbianism in commercial porn), and so mildly queers the text as well as drawing attention to the theme of feminized masculinity in the original. But otherwise – and it would be naive to expect anything else – *This Ain't Jaws XXX* eliminates all deviations from its sole purpose, which is not closely to imitate or subvert *Jaws* but to incite viewers to masturbate and, in intervening periods, to amuse themselves with echoes of a revered film otherwise sexually uninspiring except via strenuous symptomatic interpretation. The 'action' of the porn version degrades any sense of narrative progress. This is a film structured and paced for the stop-start rhythms of masturbation sessions. The story scenes, which bracket off the self-contained bouts of sex, are essentially padding, dead time (or down time, narrative refractory periods) that viewers are likely to fast-forward to reach the next usefully arousing sequence. In this it is unlike *Pirates*, which Hines argues does integrate the sex scenes within some vestige of narrative logic. Unusually for a hardcore version *Pirates* with its high production values manages 'to either imitate or adapt important elements of the mainstream original, including setting, special effects, story-line and character'.[40] *This Ain't Jaws XXX* just plonks them in the narrative rather than either replicate the pleasures of the original or attempt to parody and subvert them.

Comparing *Gums* with *This Ain't Jaws XXX* highlights differences between two versions of porn parody indicative of contrasting periods of porn production. *Gums*, which exists in two versions, a softcore print (66 minutes) and a hardcore one (79 minutes), belongs to the wave of porn parodies from porn's so-called 'Golden Age', when hardcore scenes were embedded in developed narratives. Unlike *This Ain't Jaws XXX*, *Gums* transforms the material. Goofy humour, songs and film references give it a tone similar to cult films of the period such as *Piranha* and, a more obvious comparison, *Flesh Gordon* (1974). In fact, it is rather like *Deep Throat* in being a counterculture relic, more like an underground film than a mainstream porn movie or a compilation of sex scenes. According to one of the stars, Jody Maxwell:

> It cost over a million dollars to make, and took over a month to film. The movie was made by Hollywood film makers who had NEVER made hardcore before, and were pretty clueless to some of what that takes ... . Yes, the movie was intentionally made hardcore from the very beginning, and was filmed accordingly. They also wanted to be campy, and satirize some hardcore practices. THEY thought it would be terribly funny to have a WHITE mayor and when I suck him to show him having a BLACK cock. It was totally deliberate!!!![41]

A sense of *Gums*, which looks nothing like a contemporary porn film, is given simply by a plot summary. When the penis of the latest victim washes up, Sheriff Rooster Coxswain (Paul Styles) closes down Great Head's beach, but the mayor, Ike White (Ian Morley), (who wears a grossly oversized necktie, white tails and a top hat) demands that he re-open it for tourist season. Coxswain calls on the help of Dr Sy Smegma (Richard Lair [Robert Kerman]), the world's leading fellatiologist, and Captain Carl Clitoris (Brother Theodore), the commander of the S. S. Cunnilingus. Clitoris, who could be a character out of Russ Meyer's *Up!* (1976), wears Nazi uniform, demands oil for his efforts, and has a pet buzzard that

Figure 19 Captain Clitoris (Brother Theodore) falls victim to the mermaid in *Gums*.

ejaculates copiously. The rogue mermaid (Terri Hall) subsequently fellates and kills the mayor, and the crew of the Cunnilingus set off in pursuit, luring her by throwing porn magazines overboard like chum. She kills everyone but is finally defeated by two pirate puppets that sport enormous erections and sing a lewd version of 'Mack the Knife' over the end credits.

Gums is designed for watching in a cinema pretty much as a cult film, with a transgressive and even generous enthusiasm about sex and a willingness to break the boundaries of porn in deference to humour and entertainment. There is a wholly unnecessary excess about its deviations, from the bizarre antics of Brother Theodore to the inclusion of gay characters and some extremely bois- terous and politically incorrect Jewish and racial comedy, as when 'black father' Tim (Marc Carvel) tells the sheriff, the mayor and local reporter Norm Gingold (Zack Norman) that his twin brother Kevin was sucked-off and killed while they were fishing in a rowboat, using fried chicken wrapped in tin foil as bait. The porn sequences are comparatively brief – the film 'works' equally well in the softcore version – and rather than grind through the usual acts, the posi- tions are orally fixated, as if US culture had, in the wake of *Deep Throat*, not yet got over the discovery of fellatio. As in *Deep Throat*, there is also a certain experimentalism of style. The sheriff's homosexual deputy Dick [Ras Kean] says, after finding and fondling the first dick that washes ashore, 'It looks like he's been sucked-off by a beaver!', prompting a cut to a stock shot of beavers in a river, which recalls the end of *Deep Throat* when Linda Lovelace's first orgasm is non-diegetically symbolized by footage of fireworks and a rocket launch. The film even pins down some references left unstated in *Jaws*, such as to Water- gate ('This will make Watergate look like a limp dick'), which shadowed *Jaws's* cover-up plot.

This Ain't Jaws XXX, on the other hand, is utterly mainstream by contempo- rary standards, with its identikit silicon-enhanced, tattooed, pierced and pubi- cally trimmed blondes. This is vanilla, hygienic and consensual stuff compared to the hard-edged porn online that caters to niche viewing. *Gums* seems glee- fully unrestrained by such standardization. While *This Ain't Jaws XXX* is less 'cinematic' than *Gums*, and far less amusing as a deconstruction of the sexual subtexts of *Jaws*, its 'failure' is, really, nothing of the sort. This is not so much an aesthetic disaster but a kind of finessing, adapting the material strictly to func- tion as masturbation material. Unlike *Gums*, *This Ain't Jaws XXX* is *all* porn, offering precisely and no more what the movie and its viewers need, which cer- tainly does not necessarily include winning reinterpretations of a 1970s action film. As Linda Williams says of *Pirates*, it is simply an 'imitation of an old- fashioned movie' that 'offers the sexual fantasy of spectacular male and female bodies in action'.[42]

This Ain't Jaws XXX suggests both the limits of the porn version and the limits of interpreting one in the manner of a 'regular' movie. Both it and *Gums* seem out of the mainstream: *Gums* because it is a parody from a time when porn could strive to be cult and *This Ain't Jaws XXX* because the experience of it is so different from watching a classical film or considerably less classy and plotless snippets of gonzo amateurism on the internet. *This Ain't Jaws XXX* exists in its own porn universe, in dialogue with the original, in that, it recycles quotations and memes, but its intention is not so much to adapt the original as to use it opportunistically as a framing and promotional device. Whether it 'works' depends on the individual viewer's active erotic response and tolerance for badly acted and eminently skippable filler. This is always an issue with porn versions, whether softcore or hardcore. Smith comments, of softcore versions, that 'the commercial tactic of imitative spoofing works in tension with the generic requirement for extended scenes of soft-core porn' – 'you need the spoofing to distinguish your pornography in the marketplace, but you find that, within the film itself, the spoofing actually gets in the way of the pornography'.[43] *Gums* solves the problem with Bahktinian comedy that opens up the original and revamps it for erotic comedy and droll ambiguously intentional commentary – the enforced blow jobs, for instance, can be read as shoring up *Jaws*'s oral fixation and making explicit its submerged rape imagery. *This Ain't Jaws XXX*, by contrast, all but eliminates the original in its necessitated focus on usable sex scenes. As its title insists, the film is *not Jaws* but something else, a self-contained, generically rigorous porn film that merely names the original rather than imitates, simulates or transforms the original.

This leaves us with a large question about how to make sense of pornography, at any rate in terms of the usual things we look for in movies, such as narrative, style and meaning.[44] *Gums* is, for all its amateurism and haplessness, a *movie* and no less comprehensible and interpretable than other proto-cult films for similar audiences such as *Pink Flamingos*. The same is true of sex films that break with pornography's 'aesthetic' of remorseless exposure and visibility and either align themselves with the art film, such as *9 Songs* (2004) and *Nymphomaniac Vols. I and II* (2013), or more conventionally adapt an erotic novel, as with *The Image* (1976).

This Ain't Jaws XXX seems, well, different. Is it a film at all, in the usual sense? Or is it simply a sexual aid? Reading pornography as a genre of cinema remains problematic for several overlapping and sometimes contradictory reasons. It is true that porn can be compared, tenuously, with the new 'cinema of attractions' of post-classical blockbusters – all that exciting and empty spectacle well in excess of narrative coherence. Equally sensible comparisons are with music or dance documentaries and sports footage, which seek to capture bodies in strenuous unmediated physical performance. The symptomatic interest of porn films may lie chiefly not in their aesthetic or expressive dimensions as much as in their inadvertent monitoring of haphazard generic and historical change; the digital sharpness of *This Ain't Jaws XXX* as well the actors' tattoos and shaved genitals announce that the film is a product of contemporary porn production, much as tight shorts and comedy perms date football footage to the 1970s. For example, how on earth does one judge *normatively* the erotic – and indeed other – qualities of a porn film? Judging a scene from *This Ain't Jaws XXX* by the standards of mainstream cinema – or indeed as an adaptation or parody of *Jaws* – arguably detracts from its pornographic aspects, which is to say its utility for arousal. *The Opening of Misty Beethoven*, often described as the 'best' porn film ever, is habitually praised for its characterization, camerawork, witty dialogue and parody of *My Fair Lady* – yet this somehow misses the straightforward erotic charge that pornography aims at – the raw depiction of sexual pleasure in fleshy desiring machines sufficiently enthralling to speak to and complement viewers' fantasies (*This Ain't Jaws XXX* certainly doesn't work for me on that level). As Clarissa Smith points out, in most discussions of porn, 'The possibility that the use of actual sexual interactions might signal an alternative logic of filmic production centred on the body is sidelined and questions of acting, performance and presentation of "real" sex are occluded.'[45] In other words, reading porn parodies as films, let alone as parasitic adaptations, is to miss the point comprehensively. Moreover, pornography can be removed from the sphere of film entirely. Anti-pornography activists think of it as having little to do with film and more to do with sex work and exploitation of the grossest and cruellest kind. It is an unfolding text that says nothing except reiterate porn's single ideological project; from this point of view, *This Ain't Jaws XXX* is just one more stylized performance of patriarchal oppression, CCTV from a crime scene, and reading it as an adaptation is an act of collusion rather than interpretation.

Pornography remains an outlier in the study of film and adaptation. While a film like *This Ain't Jaws XXX* is easy enough to describe, knowing how to interpret, analyse and judge it objectively remain curiously mysterious and even fraught. One is reminded just how different pornography really is from the methods, aims and effects of conventional cinema, even when it is 'adapted' from one of the most famous movies ever made.

Chapter 8

FROM ADAPTATION TO CINEPHILIA: AN INTERTEXTUAL ODYSSEY

2001: A Space Odyssey is one of the few Stanley Kubrick films that is *not* an adaptation. The end credits on screen simply read, 'Based on a screenplay by Stanley Kubrick and Arthur C. Clarke', and no other source text is mentioned. But *2001* is nevertheless shadowed, and its enigmas potentially explained by, other texts, towards which viewers are directed extratextually; texts which, as with any adaptation, precede the film, complement it and perhaps even complete it, and which may also frame and influence the film's reception, for example, by encouraging us to read it 'as' an adaptation. For viewers engaged in the longitudinal process of understanding *2001* or even, as cinephile cultists, acquiring an emotional investment in its production, meanings, authorship and 'secrets', these texts may become resources of additional knowledge and cultural capital that inform and modify their repeated encounters with the supreme masterpiece of SF cinema.

For example, 'everyone knows' that *2001*'s decisive, albeit unacknowledged, precursor was Clarke's 'The Sentinel' (1951) (originally published as 'The Sentinel of Eternity'), a short story about men discovering an alien object on the Moon and setting off a signalling device, which Clarke had offered to Kubrick in 1964 for adaptation.[1] Clarke's contract to work on *2001* included the sale of 'The Sentinel' and five other stories, with Clarke being paid specifically to write a treatment based on 'The Sentinel'.[2] This short story is reprinted as the film's source text in a number of satellite publications, such as Jerome Agel's *The Making of Kubrick's 2001* and Clarke's *The Lost Worlds of 2001* (and in Piers Bizony's later *2001: Filming the Future*, which refers to it as 'the starting point').[3] Although *2001* drew thematically on other Clarke stories such as his novel *Childhood's End* (1953), also about an alien master race overseeing human development, it is 'The Sentinel' that is now discursively fixed as the film's 'true' – if uncredited – origin. This might be seen as a case of 'unacknowledged adaptation', where only extratextual knowledge of a film's sources, generated by discourses around the film or intertextually signalled within it, primes audiences to approach it as an adaptation (or indeed remake or sequel or unauthorized version) – as with *Body Heat* (1981), for example, which riffs on *Double Indemnity* (1944) and James M. Cain's original novel without acknowledging either text in the credits or ancillary materials. *2001* is – depending on the terms you wish to use – a massive expansion of 'The Sentinel', which is folded into the film's narratives along with other intertextual resources, or a realization of what 'The Sentinel' only hinted at. But so slight is 'The Sentinel' that it is pointless to judge the film (and comparative judgement seems the default option for adaptation studies) by its closeness to or betrayal of it; and indeed I am not aware of any critical articles that do so. Clarke commented:

> I am continually annoyed by careless references to 'The Sentinel' as 'the story on which *2001* is based'; it bears about as much relation to the movie as an acorn to the resultant full-grown oak. Considerably less, in fact, because ideas from several other stories were also incorporated. Even the elements that Stanley Kubrick and I did actually use were considerably modified.[4]

Nevertheless, that *2001* stands in some relation to 'The Sentinel' is an established 'fact' about the film, even though the story is not flagged up as a source text on screen. This is a different relationship of precedence and adaptation from the cases of Kubrick's *A Clockwork Orange*, which he adapted quite closely from Anthony Burgess's 1962 novel, and *The Shining*, which Kubrick and Diane Johnson adapted from Stephen King's 1977 novel, improving it immeasurably, much to King's chagrin. *2001* cannot be expected to adhere to the 'spirit' of the short story and most audiences – certainly when the film was first released – would not frame it as a conventional adaptation. But even if 'The Sentinel' is not the true begetter of the film, or, at best, one staging post in the film's thematic development, its subsequent pre-eminence in accounts of the film's origins sends out the message that *Clarke* was the key source and the film a continuation of Clarkean as much as Kubrickean themes.

Yet if *2001* cannot be regarded as an adaptation of 'The Sentinel', it is nevertheless haunted, as bona fide adaptations are haunted, by another identically titled text in the marketplace. There exists what might be called a 'parallel adaptation' – or even competitor adaptation – of the material and screenplay. This is the novelization by Clarke (1968) which was published a few months after the film's release, and which is itself positioned (as novelizations usually are) as an adaptation on the same terms as the film – 'based on the screenplay by Arthur C. Clarke and Stanley Kubrick'.[5] Thomas Van Parys describes this as an example of 'simultaneous novelization':

> Not to be confused with novelisations (partially) credited to the director or screenwriter but really written by a hired author only, these are collaborative efforts in that film and novelisation have mutually influenced each other, and illustrate the kind of symbiosis that texts in different media may reach. They are also part of a larger group of novelisations that have been developed simultaneously with the film, which dismisses from the outset any clear hierarchy. Other examples of 'simultaneous' novelisations are Thea von Harbou's *Metropolis* (1926), Graham Greene's novella *The Third Man* (1950),

and Pier Paolo Pasolini's *Teorema* (1968). Often such novels enjoy the same respectability as the film; therefore it is telling that they are seldom considered novelisations, and sometimes even mistaken for adapted novels instead.[6]

In an unusual process of script development, Clarke and Kubrick produced, rather than a screenplay, a jointly written 'long, novelistic treatment', *Journey beyond the Stars*.[7] It was this extended screen treatment that was used to sell the project to MGM and became the basis for the screenplay.[8] Clarke reshaped *Journey beyond the Stars* as a novel by summer 1966 but it was subsequently revised with input from Kubrick and both novel and screenplay were revised jointly right up to production:[9]

> Toward the end, both novel and screenplay were being written simultaneously, with feedback in both directions. Some parts of the novel had their final revisions after we had seen the rushes based on the screenplay based on the earlier versions of the novel ... and so on.[10]

Kubrick finally allowed the novel to be published in July 1968.

Novelizations are paradoxical texts with a long history. Though they might seem to be, like adaptations conventionally, follow-up texts, they are usually written at the same time as the film is produced and are sometimes available before the film. Rather than transcripts of the visuals of the film, they are imagined from a draft of the screenplay, and frequently include scenes missing from the final cut. In the days before video and DVD, novelizations were a way to pre- or re-experience a film outside the cinema, 'in line with the double goal of the novelization throughout its history, namely as promotional material before the film release as well as a prolongation of the movie experience to capitalize on its potential success'.[11]

Unlike most novelizations, that of *2001* has considerable authority as an 'authentic' treatment of the story material. It is not a secondary text, a mere spin-off or piece of hackwork, but a novel developed by Clarke, in consultation with Kubrick, which offers an alternative version of the narrative and considerably clarifies various plot points and dilemmas of interpretation. Not merely a written-up version of the screenplay, it is, like the film, the end product of a long process of textual elaboration. As such, it challenges the film's realization (or adaptation) of the screen treatment and screenplay and its deviations from the film might be regarded as corrections, by an expert SF writer, of its generically wayward mysticism and ambiguity. For one thing, the novel brings the material into line with the conventions of the commercial hard SF novel, Clarke's realm of creative authority. As Carrol L. Fry notes, 'Clarke wrote the story in genre-correct fashion' so as to 'transform visual poetry into prose'.[12] Michel Chion remarks, perhaps overstating the case a little, that the novel 'rather cleverly adopts an opposite position to the film. Probably in order to avoid being merely a written paraphrase of the film, it describes and explains everything much more explicitly, leaving nothing to interpretation'.[13] The novelization is at once a stand-alone text within Clarke's oeuvre; a double adaptation (of the screen treatment/screenplay as well as the film, which it preceded rather than ekphrastically described); and, crucially, a handy primer and crib to a wholly unconventional film. Clarke said that the novel was 'an independent and self-contained work – even though it was created specifically for the movie'.[14] But one can imagine a viewer in 1968 who has read the book feeling not only better equipped to negotiate the eccentricities of the narrative but also in a superior position vis-à-vis interpretation of it, just as someone familiar with the source text of an adaptation may feel better prepared to 'get' the adapted film. Like a running commentary, the novel of *2001* clarifies textual cruxes in the movie and offers straightforward factual explanations of its mysteries. The film and book might even be seen as necessary guides to each other (which harks back to the role of novelization in the silent era, when novelization 'functioned as announcement, explanation and completion of the silent film'.)[15] Indeed, this was quickly recognized shortly after publication – 'Since the motion picture has its baffling moments, a perusal of the book will help, and, indeed, the motion picture helps elucidate the book'.[16]

There are numerous minor differences between novel and film – such as the astronauts' destination in the former being Saturn and not Jupiter (see Wikipedia for a comprehensive summary otiose here). Unlike the film, the novel provides detailed descriptions of prehistoric life, gives access to HAL's paranoid mind, and helpfully explains why Bowman ends up in a hotel room: 'So that was how this reception area had been prepared for him; his hosts had based their ideas of terrestrial living upon TV programmes. His feeling that he was inside a movie set was almost literally true'.[17] These 'facts' do not belong to the film itself but certainly offer a different route into its meanings for viewers who approach it with knowledge gleaned from the novel. For example, building on the revelation, inaccessible in the film, that the spaceship which the ape's bone cuts to is a nuclear weapon, the book ends with the Star Child exploding other such weapons orbiting the Earth: 'He put forth his will, and the circling megatons flowered in a silent detonation that brought a brief, false dawn to half the sleeping globe'.[18] As Krämer points out, this gives the novel an ambiguous ending, which could be read as the destruction of the earth. This was certainly not Kubrick's intention, though Clarke subsequently announced his ambivalence: 'Despite his original intention to offer an optimistic ending, Clarke later acknowledged the validity of a pessimistic ending as well, thus affirming the fundamental ambiguity of the ending'.[19]

At the same time the novelization is certainly misleading as to the 'feel' – the all-important *experience* – of the film and its depiction of the future. For some critics (especially those aligned with SF literature) the novel was essential to a complete experience of the film:

> Audiences were mostly baffled; the final moments, especially, are entirely unintelligible without Clarke's text. ... Only with its belated appearance ... was

the tension resolved between Kubrick's allusive visual suggestion and Clarke's open rationalism. This peculiar symbiosis of novel and film remains key to the appreciation of both as finished texts; it is doubtful whether either work would seem as impressive without the other.[20]

Yet the novel's reductive factuality reduces the polysemic openness the film strives for. Rather than explain the film, the novel explains it away. The novel is also thematically distinct from the film. For example, describing the trip to the space station, the book states, 'No matter how many times you left Earth, Dr Heywood Floyd told himself, the excitement never really palled.'[21] In the book this sequence begins on Earth, delivers a good deal of information about the population explosion, food shortages, belligerency between thirty-eight nuclear powers (41), and then gives details of take-off and the 'extraordinary euphoria' of the experience of space flight (44). This is certainly in the keeping with the film's rapt depiction of technological mastery and shares some of the same details – the stewardess's Velcro slippers, for example, and later, in the trip to the Moon, the zero gravity toilet (though that is not a moment of comedy, as in the film). There is also a sense of the extraordinary ease and normality of the journey: 'He had made, utterly without incident and in little more than one day, the incredible journey of which men had dreamed for two thousand years. After a normal, routine flight, he had landed on the Moon' (59). In the film Floyd spends the entire trip to the station asleep and the film goes out of its way to suggest the boredom of the journey and the dull inability of humans like him to feel a sense of wonder. Rather than Clarke's optimism, *2001* is a study of violence, boredom, failed communication and male inadequacy.

Even as the film dazzles viewers with special effects, with a droll interest in convincing small details, paying as much attention to the returning of a floating pen to Floyd's pocket as to the docking of ship and station, it lulls us with visual redundancy so that the sequence, with the music in ironic counterpoint, courts tedium and banality and mere description. Meanwhile we have time to note the visual rhymes between the rotating phallic spaceships and pen (this is a film of sly homoeroticism), and the sexual implications of the docking (especially

Figure 20 The banality of space travel in *2001: A Space Odyssey*.

if we remember the aerial intercourse between refuelling planes at the start of Kubrick's *Dr Strangelove or: How I Learned to Stop Worrying and Love the Bomb* (1964)). The slow pace enables us to look closely, drift intertextually, and ponder symbolism and other repetitions, or simply revel in the special effects as we adjust to the film's curiously long rhythms of visual description. The book fills in narrative gaps, but it describes a signifying universe absolutely different from the film. Kubrick hints at this:

> I think it gives you the opportunity of seeing two attempts in two different mediums, print and film, to express the same basic concept and story. ... I think that the divergencies between the two works are interesting. Actually, it was an unprecedented situation for someone to do an essentially original literary work based on glimpses and segments of a film he had not seen in its entirety.[22]

What are often held to be the surpassing advantages of the novel over film – interiority, access to consciousness, massive detail and the use of an authorial voice to communicate psychological complexity and ideas – seem, in the novelization, merely conventional and deadening, precisely what you would expect from a genre writer trying to communicate a 'sense of wonder' by means of the usual formulae and novelistic techniques. Although the involvement of Clarke on board aligns *2001* with the 'ideas-driven' extrapolations of literary SF, Kubrick's method of visualizing ideas is predicated on a refusal not only of standard tropes of the SF genre, but of the novel itself. Rather as certain novels are said to be 'unadaptable', so *2001* is designed to be an unadaptable film.

This difference between film and novelization was intentional. As Peter Krämer has argued, Kubrick in his pre-release edit of the film got rid of most of the explanatory material in order to heighten the film's purely experiential qualities, the theme of communication through images and its symbolism. While the film's grandeur and seriousness distance it from previous SF films, Kubrick also strove to distance the film comprehensively from both the novelization and written SF, and more fundamentally to distance cinema from print:

> The idea that the novel might be suitable for presenting explanations, while film would work better through a more open-ended narrative and ambiguous images, became ever more central for Kubrick's conception of the project. A kind of division of labour was slowly emerging whereby the film could afford to be mysterious because the novel would explain everything.[23]

Kubrick decided to drop the explanatory voiceovers a few weeks before release and put his faith in the power of the image.

Both film and novel are in a sense equally valid re-presentations of the material in the screenplay. Yet even if the novelization has its own integrity, it is the film that is generally seen as the superior if not necessarily the anterior text, neatly reversing the usual cultural assumption that novels are *a priori* superior to films. (There were some demurrals: Ray Bradbury said that Kubrick is 'a very bad writer who got in the way of Arthur C. Clarke, who is a wonderful writer'.[24]) With *2001* what the film 'means' is therefore more likely now to be approached by seeing it as a Kubrick film, interpreted according to the evolving themes of his subsequent work. Like many 'art films' *2001* 'foregrounds the *author* as a structure in the film's system. ... The author becomes a formal component, the overriding intelligence organizing the film for our comprehension.'[25] Audiences, baffled by its sudden temporal shifts, languid pace, narratives ellipses and redundancies and symbols, can assume that it all makes sense in the light of Kubrick's expressive intention. In 1968 the film more resembled the description of the monolith – its origin and purpose a total mystery (a comparison frequently made in the years since).

This is where the novelization came in. Looking beyond the film makes sense because *2001 requires* interpretation. It forces viewers to augment narrative comprehensive with symbolic unpacking. Even the most casual viewers, not just film critics or academics who are professionally obliged to hunt for meaning, must do *something* with the jump cut from bone weapon to orbiting spaceship, the significance of the monolith and the final image of the Star Child.

These might be crudely described as 'WTF' moments, puzzles that engage the audience in similar intellectual effort to the characters on screen – like dealing with images, pursuing clues, encountering symbols and undergoing existential transformations. Kubrick did this throughout his films, not so much to create a puzzle story or even as a mark of authorship but to confront viewers with images that undercut the story world, pose an insoluble enigma or offer a baffling (non-)explanation: the orgy fantasy at the end of *A Clockwork Orange*, the photograph of the New Year's party at the end of *The Shining*, much of the dream narrative of *Eyes Wide Shut*. The novel of *2001* offered an authoritative gloss to a film whose opacity more or less required recourse to explanatory texts. The film's difficulty catered to late 1960s audiences increasingly attuned to what would become cult film reading practices – cult being 'a meta-genre

Figure 21 WTF? The mysterious Star Child in *2001: A Space Odyssey*.

that caters to intense, interpretative audience practices'.[26] One of the key aspects of cult interpretation is watching and rewatching a film in order to unlock its mysteries, but with each re-viewing informed by extratextual information about the film – the sort of information that a skeleton key like 2001's novelization might provide. 2001 needs to be experienced (and mulled over) numerous times for its significance to emerge (this was also the case with Kubrick's Barry Lyndon (1975) and The Shining, which, as we saw in Chapter 3, met with lukewarm critical reaction before achieving their classic status). Indeed there were a number of 'recant notices' of 2001 in which, unusually, critics took a second look at the film and revised their earlier judgements (for example, the review in Variety, 15 May 1968). The ideal viewer of 2001 would watch and rewatch the film, literally revisit it in optimum Cinerama viewing conditions, having used the intervening periods following up intertextual clues and reading up on the 'hip cosmological discourse surrounding the film' – in other words, embarking on what we might now call a cult trajectory, a project of intertextual immersion that might last a lifetime.[27] The 'experience' of 2001 went beyond simply watching it, although that was unusually important: the film was a 'purely' cinematic experience, and was framed as such when posters for the 1969 rerelease, repositioning the film as a hippie cult item, declared it as 'the ultimate trip'.[28] You had to drop the film's acid in a cinema, not just read about it. For its 'young, quasi-"hippie" audience', as Variety put it, quoting a New York Times review, 'the film has broken loose from the novel and is exploring the possibilities of its own medium. "Space Odyssey" is poetry. It asks for groovin', not understanding' (Variety, 15 May 1968).

Each iteration of viewing would only be enhanced by preparatory extratextual exploration. Hence Clarke's advice: 'I always used to tell people, "Read the book, see the film and repeat the dose as often as necessary."'[29] But as well as reading the novel, interviews, sources such as 'The Sentinel', 'making of' books, Homer's Odyssey, Robert Ardrey (whose 'killer ape' theory influenced the 'Dawn of Man' sequence) and the Nietzsche of Thus Spake Zarathustra, viewers might be inspired to dig Ligeti, Khachaturian and the two Strausses. Like many of Kubrick's films, 2001 is a switchboard of cultural references, which reminds one of Clarke's description of the Star Gate: 'some kind of cosmic switching device ... a Grand Central Station of the Galaxy' – sending the viewer hurtling through not just time and space but also new worlds of intertextuality.[30] The ideal viewer, in other words, was (and remains) a cultist, who has a long-standing intellectual investment and emotional investment in the film, which would itself become an object of nostalgia and desire over a lifetime of educative re-viewings. One cultist, Robert Castle goes so far as to say that:

2001: A Space Odyssey (1968) has inhabited a large part of my life. ... How I have responded to the film reveals my growth as a thinker and critic, a growth I believe 2001 to be one of the causes. Not a dramatic growth that can be certified but one that effected an intellectual attention to the material/

subject on the movie screen. Accomplishing this growth, in a sense, never ceased. Seeing and interpreting the film over the last 30 years has become analogous to the very process of change and growth happening in *2001*.[31]

With *2001*, narrative comprehension ('Who or what is the baby?') has an unmistakeable edge of mysticism ('What does the baby *mean*?'), so that repeated viewings and 'deeper' interpretations are stages on a personal odyssey towards spiritual rebirth. Like other cult texts of the period, from *The Magus* to Carlos Castaneda, *El topo* and *The Lord of the Rings*, *2001* is an auratic text containing, within the structure of a Hero's Journey, a mythic, grandiose and endlessly interpretable lexicon of Jungian imagery, through which audiences can imagine they reconnect with collective unconscious experience. Encountering the film – which is to say, *re*-encountering it – can be life-changing and transfiguring if the viewer is able to submit, to think and *to care*.

As I said in Chapter 5, this notion of emotional investment in a film, obvious with cult films, emphasizes how much of our relationship with films is defined by what might be seen as intrinsic to adaptation – intertextual adventures across paratexts, pursuing allusions, comparisons, precursors, add-ons of all kinds. It is a relationship of *care* that takes place over *time*, from anticipation of the film to an embedded knowledge of it. Cultists care for texts in relationships of memory, nostalgia and anticipation; they have emotional investment in films, a sense even of ownership; they pursue the extratextual and seemingly irrelevant, specialize in breaking the boundaries of texts, and enthusiastically explore intertextual worlds, including texts that might further explicate bewildering films. This dynamic relationship between a film and accompanying texts is, of course, always present, but it is most obviously so among audiences of adaptations (some of whose audiences may care passionately about the success and fidelity of an adaptation, and read the film always in terms of the book) and among cultists, who invest massively in the films they love and the significance they can wring from them. With adaptations, audiences may be invited to anticipate, view, recall, review and discuss films in relation to the original novel. With cultism, audiences acquire and are offered extratextual information and supplementary texts to extend and deepen their appreciation of films. The novelization of *2001* and books such as Agel's *The Making of Kubrick's 2001* and Clarke's *The Lost Worlds of 2001* performed this role for early cultists of *2001*, at the very start of the cult phenomenon.[32] Nowadays, the delivery of gap-filling 'textual expanders' to exploit fans and encourage word of mouth is standard industry practice: 'In a universe of converging media, reception is now definitively affiliated with multiple platforms of access and the associative intertextualities they inspire.'[33] All interpretation of a film requires the film reader to work intertextually – aligning it with genre tropes, getting allusions.[34] Film-viewing is not just attention paid to a single text but, for certain audiences and most emphatically with cult audiences and those for adaptations, always about shuttling between film and novel, original and new version, to the point where the borders of the text are ambiguous. The texts that frame and reframe the film, which determine the audience's relationship to it and invite different kinds of relationships to it (that of a fan, for example), are strictly speaking outside the film, and therefore secondary to it, but they nevertheless determine how we make sense of the film. They are rather like what Derrida calls 'parergons', frames that while outside the text define the text, not outside or inside but rather indeterminate – in other words, supplements that might be essential to the text itself:

> A parergon comes against, beside, and in addition to the *ergon*, the work done [*fait*], the fact [*le fait*], the work, but it does not fall to one side, it touches and cooperates within the operation, from a certain outside. Neither outside nor simply inside … . It is first of all the on (the) bo(a)rd(er) [*Il est d'abord l'à-bord*].[35]

Obviously most of the time we do not especially relate to films in this way, although the marketing departments may wish we did; but cult films and their fans are an example of how this experience functions, and therefore illuminate how this works in relation to adaptation.

2001 is a marvellously bold and seemingly hermetic work of art and a work of precise cinematic machinery. But it is not a stand-alone object, or one whose meanings (thematic but also narrative) are to be discovered by textual explication of a single text. Rather than see the appearance of a film like *2001* as a simple textual event, one should regard it as the dominant text in a process of textual production that engages audiences – or, at any rate, audiences willing to be engaged – in an intertextual odyssey in search of the film's meaning – starting, perhaps, with the novelization. Yet *2001* is also, paradoxically, a film that seeks to escape its intertextual debts and connections. It is true that *2001* is an exceptionally intellectual film, which requires strenuous effort even to comprehend the narrative. Yet, inspired by the estranging formalism of art-house and underground cinema, it also aspires to the condition of 'pure cinema', communicating unparaphrasable visual and aural experiences as much as subtle and difficult meanings. The novelization, for neophyte cultists, offered some entry-level introduction to the 'world' of *2001* but necessarily falls short in making sense of its leisurely camerawork, enhanced sense of duration and rhythm and its immersion in abstractions beyond words. The film works on the emotions like music, even if it is the music of boredom and discomfort and incomprehension; and to that extent its meaning *is* the feeling the images and music evoke. *2001* is not least about the phenomenological experience of cinema itself, like a movie equivalent of a colour field painting.[36] *2001* is 'Kubrick's reaffirmation', as Fredric Jameson said, 'of the *flatness* of the visual screen':

> The visual features of *2001* were, on the one hand, the screen as a surface to be inscribed, and on the other, the window-cockpit traveling across

an expanse of landscapes. ... We are spectators seated comfortably in the speeding vehicle of a movie theatre soaring into infinity.[37]

In distancing the film from the novel, the visual from print, and celebrating the communicative power of the image in consort with music, Kubrick does more than claim the pre-eminence of the visual. He also offers, and thematically embeds in the experience of the film, the implication that cinema is an *evolution beyond* the novel, a uniquely, if ambivalently, powerful medium for triggering the unconsciousness, reproducing dream states and altering consciousness as well as subliminally manipulating the viewer (an idea explored further and more acerbically in *A Clockwork Orange*). The distance between the film and its novelization is key to this, because Kubrick is that paradox – an auteur of adaptation who in *2001*, as in *A Clockwork Orange*, *The Shining* and *Eyes Wide Shut*, foregrounds the written text only to swerve emphatically away from it. He adapts so as to *trump* the original rather than to pay homage to or to respect its inviolable spirit. As Thomas Leitch says, Kubrick 'earned his auteur status ... by taking on authors directly in open warfare'.[38] Because with *2001* there is no single originary text, the swerve away from the 'source', which is Kubrick's distinctive gesture of auteurist appropriation, is especially complex; numerous influences and anxieties must be confronted and overcome. In aiming to produce the consummate SF *film*, Kubrick must go beyond not only preceding SF cinema but also the literary SF tradition represented by Clarke and embodied in his novelization.

But if, for all Clarke's involvement, *2001* would ultimately be promoted and interpreted as a Kubrick film, it was the novelization that generated more direct textual offspring. Clarke went on to write three sequels without Kubrick's involvement (although Kubrick had shares in the property).[39] *2010: Odyssey Two* was adapted as a film, *2010*, by Peter Hyams. Clarke brought the novel of *2010* into conformity with the film of *2001* (for example, the destination planet is Jupiter, as in the film), but the film of *2010* nevertheless hinges on a reference to a key moment at the end of the novelization of *2001* that is

Figure 22 Communication through visuals and symbolism: the monolith in *2001: A Space Odyssey*.

not present in the film – Bowman crying, 'Oh my God – *it's full of stars!*'[40] Hyams's film is therefore a sequel to the *2001* novelization as much as either an adaptation of Clarke's *2010* novel or a sequel to Kubrick's film – 'something much more complex than a straightforward sequel to the earlier novel – or the movie'.[41] Although *2001* is invariably classed as a Kubrick film, his contribution to the *2001* 'universe' is dwarfed by Clarke's expansion (and ownership) of the material into a franchise over three decades. Even so, in returning the world of *2001* to that of literary SF, Clarke might be said to betray the spirit of Kubrick's extraordinary film as comprehensively as the generic ordinariness of Hyams's perfectly competent sequel/adaptation banalizes rather than enhances or retrospectively completes it.

Kubrick ensures that comparisons with such source or competitor texts demonstrate the inadequacy of words and the marvellous and troubling power of the visual, like music and often in combination with it, to possess, control, haunt, derange and unsettle. It was important to Kubrick that film should still be understood to be able to communicate ideas, and indeed a combination of intense visual experience and rigorous intellectual formalism is the most striking and characteristic quality of all his films. Kubrick said: 'Film operates on a level much closer to music and painting than to the printed word, and, of course, movies present an opportunity to convey complex concepts and abstractions without the traditional reliance on words.'[42] One of the clichés of opposing SF literature to SF cinema – usually as an indictment of SF cinema – is that the former is a medium of ideas while the latter 'expects much less intelligence in its audience' and 'with few exceptions, is no more sophisticated than was genre magazine SF in the 1930s'.[43] Kubrick was therefore engaged in a complex engagement with – and, crucially, disengagement from – a number of traditions and assumptions about SF, the relationship between SF film and SF genre writing, and the comparative abilities of cinema and literature, all of which determine his withdrawal of fidelity to the novelization. Simply put – the novelization of *2001* represents all that the film refuses and *transcends*. That is why Kubrick is so crucial to adaptation studies and its endless blasphemous refutations of the ineffable superiority of Word over Image. His films are *about* the evolution of image beyond word and of film beyond the novel. *2001* is a defining moment in, as well as a compelling allegory of, what Jameson calls the 'never-ending and unresolvable struggles for primacy between literature and cinema'.[44]

Chapter 9

Cult Film as a Guide to Life

Movies are about people who *do* things. The number one reason fantasy of the cinema is that we can do something – we are relatively impotent in our own lives so we go to movies to watch people who are in control of their lives.

Paul Schrader[1]

How the hell do I know why there were Nazis? I don't know how the can-opener works.

Hannah and Her Sisters (1986)

The most popular song at British funerals is apparently 'Always Look on the Bright Side of Life'. Cheerfully belted out by one of the crucified at the end of *Monty Python's Life of Brian*, this wonderful torch song both promulgates and ironizes keeping the British end up in the face of catastrophe. While ludicrous in its stiff upper lip parody of 'Whistle a Happy Tune' and 'Give a Little Whistle', Jewish foolish wisdom, and outdated middle-class British slang ('in the dumps', 'silly chumps', 'life seems jolly rotten'), the song is more subtle than it first appears (the line 'make you swear and curse' is rhymed with 'turn out for the best', while the better rhyme, 'for the worse', seems deliberately avoided; 'nothing will come from nothing' is a nod to that bleakest of masterpieces, *King Lear*). 'Life's a piece of shit' is scarcely a happy thought, and 'worse things happy at sea' merely a cliché, but the rest is in keeping with the Pythons' Buñuelian sense of the absurdity and meaningless of life and articulates a forthright atheism that would please the Richard Dawkins of *The God Delusion* – 'you come from nothing, you're going back to nothing. What have you lost? Nothing!'[2] It is taken further by 'The Galaxy Song' in the viciously anti-religious *Monty Python's The Meaning of Life* (1983), in which a pink-suited Eric Idle appears from a fridge and chirpily persuades Mrs Brown (Terry Jones) to donate her liver while still alive by serenading her with astronomical data about the vastness and indifference of the universe. His song similarly combines positive thinking – 'Remember when you're feeling very small and insecure, How amazingly unlikely is your birth' with forthright 'life is shit' bleakness – 'Pray that there's intelligent life somewhere up in space, Cos there's bugger all down here on Earth'. Like 'Always Look on the Bright Side of Life' it is a *reductio ad absurdum* of the daft consequences of worrying about the meaninglessness of life and the inescapability of death (think of young Alvy in *Annie Hall* (1977), depressed because the universe if not Brooklyn is expanding). Still, both are pretty good songs to listen to if you're in a dark place, and I can think of worse philosophies to live by.

Now, I wouldn't say that I learnt everything I know from cult films, but they certainly taught me life lessons; some, like Woody Allen's, because their philosophical insights are packaged in memorable one-liners and some, like the films of that other great Jewish New York intellectual, Stanley Kubrick, because they encourage thinking about large topics on an epic scale. Films become cult movies not just because they are quirky, funny or uncategorizable, but because they may offer clues on how to live and comport yourself public-wise, oh my brothers. On the one hand, they offer handy portable philosophies in the form of T-shirt quotations; on the other, watching them on repeat offers time and space for experiencing life meaningfully, precisely by following the way of the cultist.[3]

There is, as I've stressed throughout this book, more to watching and living with films than getting them right. This may certainly be crucial for fans and cultists – and an ethical imperative for academics – in relation to correct information about the films, but caring about cult films and making the best of them is equally important as seeing through them or applying the correct theoretical frameworks for ruining them altogether (which is what academics do, mostly). Laura Mulvey, in her classic piece, 'Visual Pleasure and Narrative Cinema' wrote that 'it is said that analysing pleasure, or beauty, destroys it. That is the intention of this article.'[4] This chapter intends to do the opposite. Focusing on the pleasures of cult (and their occasionally beauties) and the thrill of discovering, appropriating, revelling in and sharing films liberated from their original contexts, this final chapter takes a crack at showing how cult films might offer moments of spiritual and existential revelation and help steady the self during its emotional crises. (I won't pursue the alleged comparisons between cult or fandom and religion, though some of the therapeutic and philosophical aspects of cult viewing do overlap with religious belief.)[5]

The chapter goes on to think about trash horror films, which might seem as unlikely resources for self-invention or meaningful discourses about life.[6] Invoking the figure of the 'trash aesthete', who is a connoisseur of the low in preference to the 'ordinary', I'll discuss how he or she may find pleasure, solace and release from boredom in trash and thereby shore up his or her identity. I'll focus on the privatized aesthetic value of trash in opening imaginative and experiential possibilities of the sublime and Abject. I can hardly claim to be a representative trash aesthete, but drawing on my own, admittedly very specific and, as the jargon has it, intersectionally extremely privileged, tastes in a cinephile auto-ethnography is at least a starting point.[7] In all of this, as I freely admit, I am mostly guessing. If you want a pocket-sized primer to the big issues I recommend, with reservations, Terry Eagleton's *The Meaning of Life* and, with infinitely more reservations, Wayne Omura's existentially focused *Movies and the Meaning of Life: The Most Profound Films in Cinematic History*, or one of the many '*Philosophy and X*' books, which use films to explicate issues in ethics and ontology.[8] If there is a meaning of life out there, I haven't found it yet, and if I did find it, I probably wouldn't understand it anyway. Knowing my luck it is salted away in one of Gilles Deleuze and Felix Guattari's books.

Therapy and Self-help

Film has been used as therapy directed towards finding stories that inspire as well as distract and entertain. 'Reel therapy', a branch of self-help and psycho-therapy, enables troubled clients to find emotional connections and models of behaviour to empathize with or emulate whole films or instructive clips. More ambitious than the conventional understanding of films as mere escapism or ideology-machines, therapy latches on to them as philosophical resources that liberate you to talk about and overcome problems and thereby learn to see yourself and your lives differently. The films are invited to interpellate you, as it were, in valuable and functional ways.

Modelled on Karl Menninger's bibliotherapy which began to be used in counselling in the 1940s and 1950s, reel therapy has inspired a large literature and numerous links on the internet. Though it seems to have started in the 1980s, the movement swelled in the early 2000s, with numerous therapists and amateurs offering films as routes to self-discovery. Transactional analysis, such as that described by the improbably monickered therapist Fuat Ulus, is one of the main approaches.[9] Jungian perspectives are popular too in therapy, echoing the insistence in screenplay manuals that successful films, on the model of *Star Wars*, pursue a twelve-part Hero's Journey structure towards individuation and self-fulfilment; indeed contemporary fantasy films seem expressly designed to be therapeutic archetypal myths that work universally. In either case, there is an implication that popular films embody, and can instruct us in, the myths and values of our society, and that thoughtfully encountering films and chatting about them with others may integrate us more fully into the world (or, more appropriate to cultists, sharpen and justify their alienation from it).

In his 2008 book *Movie Therapy: How It Changes Lives*, Bernie Wooder, who advertises himself as Britain's first Movie Therapist, explains how films help patients engage with traumas by allowing them to externalize their responses.[10] Wooder's clients work through their personal narratives via films of all sorts and not just cult movies on the premise that 'moments from movies, issues contained within them or relationships between movie characters [help] to quickly identify the feelings, and later the reasons, for unconscious unhappiness'.[11] The case histories, which with one exception are those of women, are redemptive stories whose happy endings come with a breakthrough and self-realization. For example, one client showed a clip of Mrs Danvers from Hitchcock's *Rebecca* (1940) to her husband to indicate how she felt about his mother. Wooder does recount case histories incorporating cult films, such as *The Adventures of Priscilla, Queen of the Desert* (1994) (whose 'stunning cinematography stimulated [the client's] wish to drive across the country' (93)) and *Life of Brian* (which helped one woman 'recognise that we are all individuals and that being able to stand alone is not a sign of loneliness' (151)), as well as films with major fandoms, such as *Star Wars*, *The Sound of Music*, *Titanic* and *The Lord of the Rings* trilogy. As with the romantic comedies also used in his sessions, such as *Four Weddings and a Funeral* (1994) and *Bridget Jones's Diary* (2001), which a client valued for their depiction of 'the sharing of friendship' (214), the therapy is aligned with the purpose (ideological purpose, if you take the Mulveyan view) of the films – to cheer you up, rouse you emotionally and engage you in recognizing the heroic possibilities of ordinary lives. The role of films seems very like that of novels in reading groups, where the therapeutic aspect is unspoken but the novels are a means of exploring the world through conversations:

> For reading groups, the relationship between book and world is open; the book is expected to speak about the world, and the world (reading-group observation and experience) is brought to bear upon the book. The point is not to map book and life closely. ... but that the traffic should be two-way. Or rather three-way, to include the busy internal networks of the group itself.[12]

Film therapy does not necessarily involve cinephile responses to the films. Because a film may be chosen by the therapist rather than being a 'natural' personal favourite, responses to it are focused, pragmatic instances of what Jackie Stacey called 'cinematic identificatory practices'; fandom and any fantasy element of adoration or imitation of stars is much less important than plucking from the films hints for cure and self-recognition.[13] The film as conversation piece, transactional object and emotional anchor makes you, according to Wooder, 'feel better as a constant resource, until [you] naturally [integrate] the sense of wellbeing created in [you] by the film just by thinking about it rather than needing actually to see it' (214). This is rather like using films in a programme of mindfulness – the currently fashionable meditative practice closely related to Cognitive Behavioural Therapy in which one learns 'to pay attention, on purpose, in the present moment, without judgment, to things as they actually are' and attains heightened awareness of not only the moment but one's own routine cognitive processes.[14] The burden of the message tends to be, as Ferris Bueller says, 'Life moves pretty fast. If you don't stop and look around once in a while, you could miss it.' The films become not so much objects of fervid devotion as touchstones of cognitive and emotional utility with the power to release you from automatic negative thoughts and destructive behaviour patterns.[15] What matters is, on the one hand, just talking about the films and, on the other, scavenging ways of rebooting the self and communicating emotions, even if the films are accessible pop classics rather than, say, Andrei Tarkovsky's spiritual epics, of which he said, 'My purpose as far as possible is to make films that will help people to live, even if they sometimes cause unhappiness.'[16]

On a less scientific grounding, light-hearted self-help guides, such as *Advanced Cinematherapy*, offer checklists for women of films, chick flicks and beyond, on the intriguing grounds that 'women watch movies differently than guys do. For us, movies are more than just entertainment; they're self-medication that can help cure anything from an identity crisis to the codependent blues.'[17] *Cabaret* (1972), for instance, 'is a great movie to watch when you're on the brink of a personal world war.'[18] A chapter on 'understanding your man movies' includes a number of 'masculine' cult films such as *Taxi Driver* ('a classic example of the weird love affair that guys have with cinematic down-and-outers' (49)), *GoodFellas* ('a lot of men are really turned on the fantasy of becoming a sociopathic wiseguy' (59)), in which films are means to work out the mysteries of men through their off-putting tastes. Again, these are not fan responses as such, though the viewer may presumably resort to the film repeatedly and become a fan over time, but rather situational appropriations of the films to promote or complement a particular mood or to solve a particular problem (patriarchy, from the sound of it), which may include why men tend to like certain initially off-putting films, which, if you grasp their appeal, unlock secrets of gender difference. According to Deborah Yaffe, Jane Austen has been similarly incorporated into bibliotherapy to cope with borderline personality disorder and to understand autism, based, in the latter case, on comprehending signs of autism in the behaviour of characters such as the socially awkward Darcy.[19]

These kinds of personal reactions to films, some of them in specialized therapeutic contexts, might be seen as trivial uses of movies, much like bucket lists of films to see and places to go, but the banality is the point. If real viewers picked up on them – or the suggestions in *Time Out's 1000 Films to Change Your Life*– they would certainly be no less worthy of attention than cult or fan responses, though resulting in nothing much beyond better adjusted emotions and rewritten narratives of the self with pleasingly upbeat plot twists. 'Ordinary' uses of films are no less important than other models of engaged cult viewing and equally distant from notions of the passive viewer. To crib a line from the enigmatic cult road movie, *Two Lane Blacktop*, 'those satisfactions are permanent'. Such pragmatic dislocations of films from their 'real' meanings and history make them useful on one's personal trajectory towards self-realization or in framing a valuable conversation among people for a common purpose of self-reflection – as when Ulus recommends showing, to those 'that are not able to turn their words into the deeds', a scene from *The Good, the Bad and the Ugly* (1966) in which Tuco (Eli Wallach) shoots an over-talkative opponent before he can pull his trigger, declaring, 'When you shoot, shoot ... don't talk!' [20]

Earlier I cited Rorty's suggestion that in interpreting texts we should let go of trying to get the text right once and for all and 'just distinguish between uses by different people for different purposes'.[21] The therapeutic or self-medicating uses of film strike me as productive examples of how films can be put to work, as well as illustrating the casual uses of film as sources of meaning outside fandom, and the kind of role that films have in everyday life as objects of memory and discussion. As Annette Kuhn wrote about memories of cinema going in Britain in the 1930s:

> The formal attributes of memory texts ... often betray a collective imagination as well as embodying truths of a more personal salience. ... Thus memory texts may create, rework, repeat and recontextualise the stories people tell each other about the kind of lives they have led; and these memory-stories can assume a timeless, even a mythic quality which may be enhanced with each retelling.[22]

The obvious question is whether *cult* films, those films snatched from built-in obsolescence and made the subject of their own memory-stories, have any specific therapeutic functionality; are they especially potent resources for 'self-medication', which might explain their grip on fans' (or any viewers') imaginations and emotions? One reason for the imaginative traction of *some* cult films is that they represent, without any sense of documentary truth, a schematic and emotionally compelling world that enables both inward reflections on identity and, beyond that, suggests vivid and often troubling diagrams of how things are. Their role is not always to cheer you up, and one's pleasure in them may be compromised by their politics, offensive representations or other factors that make them painful viewing for you.[23] If you want a political spin on the idea, imagine cult films as optimizing an emotional and philosophical education that enables living productively within, or in spite of, consumer capitalism and fantasizing some momentary escape from it. You need to look at the 'world' of the films – the self-enclosed world, as Eco put it – and, in particular, the philosophical import of that world, and focus on how to act authentically and according to a code that will impose meaning on chaos and stake a personal claim in a limiting universe. Cult films home in on philosophical issues, mediating, to the possible discomfort of mainstream audiences, between the highbrow austerity of art movies and the immediate pleasures of genre films or even exploitation and pornography. What, asks *A Clockwork Orange*, is freedom? *Blade Runner* addresses what it is to be human, how far identity is fabricated from memories, and whether replicants, who burn so brightly in their short lives, might have an existential edge ('I've seen things you people wouldn't believe. Attack ships on fire off the shoulder of Orion. I watched C-beams glitter in the dark near the Tannhauser gate.') *Donnie Darko* is about time and reality. Others, such as *2001* and *El topo*, with their invitation to patient exegesis and lifelong commitment, are religiously charged explorations of nothing less than the meaning of life – they speak to a 'thirst for cosmic meaning', as Mathijs and Sexton put it.[24] *Dirty Dancing* and other rom-coms teach lessons about love, actually, and *Dirty Dancing*'s casual acceptance of abortion makes it, according to Hadley Freeman, an unheralded feminist classic.[25] *Life of Brian* puts religion in its place, while *The Big Lebowski* shows you how to convert reverie and laziness into an alternative lifestyle. So let's take a look at some high-profile cult films and consider what they might do for their viewers.

Some Films

The films of the midnight movie era, such as *Night of the Living Dead*, *El topo* and *Pink Flamingos*, were anti-establishment films whose emphasis on freedom, self-actualization and bleak prognosis of the chances of achieving them resonated with the desires of the counterculture. Those elements, especially the desire for self-actualization, continued in other later cult films, such as *The Rocky Horror Picture Show*, *Dirty Dancing* and *Showgirls*, whose protagonists achieve moments of freedom, however temporary.

Some cult films are outright feel-good movies in this mode and watching them can indeed improve your mood; sharing that pleasure ritually with others makes for a communal sense of belonging. That seasonal fixture in the United States, *It's a Wonderful Life*, which is not a joyful film for much of its length and especially in the noirish central section, ultimately affirms the value of community at its sentimental ending. The film's utopianism is hardly a feature only of cult films; arguably it is emotionally felt also in musicals, as Richard Dyer has claimed, and in the camaraderie of domestic screenings of films, such as *Mamma Mia! The Movie*, which encourage exchanging everyday life for boisterous silliness.[26] Repeated seasonal TV broadcasts of films such as *It's a Wonderful Life*, *Miracle on 34th Street* (1947) and, proverbially at Easter in Britain, *The Great Escape* (1964) have turned them into mass cult films, whose 'continued ritual television broadcasts', according to Ernest Mathijs, 'during a particular time of year construct a sense of tailored nostalgia, a nostalgia both predictable and manageable, yet still real in its emotional authenticity and physically present in its expressions'.[27] It may seem odd to class these scheduled re-encounters as cult since there is nothing particularly exclusive about them; perhaps it is more accurate to say that the ritual screenings allow you to be a cultist without even knowing it for a couple of hours (to become, gooba gobble, one of us, to quote *Freaks* (1932)) as you settle down to a recreation of national viewing before it was fragmented. Films like *It's a Wonderful Life* and *The Great Escape* have an emotional reach that is itself an artefact of nostalgia (utopia in a rear-view mirror), not least for the kind of old, unabashed and unironic films they don't make any more.

With *Harold and Maude* the spiritual resources to be tapped from its metaphors for coping with life are sufficiently explicit to have been formalized into a secular religion constructed of uplifting quotations of folksy philosophy. *Harold and Maude* was one of the archetypal midnight movies: 'When polling people as to their cult film list *Harold and Maude* was most frequently named first. If not, then the person would invariably chastise themselves upon realising they had forgotten it.'[28] It was written by Colin Higgins, initially from a UCLA student project, and directed by Hal Ashby, a hippyish New Hollywood director also responsible for *Shampoo* (1975), *Coming Home* (1978) and *Being There* (1979), films in which a constant theme is characters whose innocence and philosophy inspire others. After an initially poor reception (*Variety* said it had 'all the fun and gaiety of a burning orphanage'), *Harold and Maude* became a campus hit and played at one cinema in Minneapolis for three years; Ruth Gordon, its star, went to the thousandth screening. The film is a bad taste comedy, which reverses the counterculture's fetishism of youth by making an old woman, Maud (Gordon), an eighty-year-old concentration camp survivor, symbolize life and her depressive young lover, Harold (Bud Cort), the refusal of it. Its appeal to a countercultural youth audience during Vietnam is not hard to see. The film included attacks on military values, a message of freedom and anti-materialism, and showcased the life-affirming qualities of its eccentric characters. A term 'Maudism' has been coined to refer to Maud's positive philosophy. She is a remarkably good guide, too, and the film's cult is sustained, forty years after its release, by the therapeutic value of her wisdom, which encapsulates hippy optimism in the face of bleak reality without succumbing to the cynicism of other cult films of the midnight movie period:

> A lot of people enjoy being dead. But they're not dead really. They're just backing away from life. Reach out. Take a chance. Get hurt even. But play as well as you can. Go team go!! Give me an L. Give me an I. Give me a V. Give me an E!! L-I-V-E! LIVE ... Otherwise, you got nothing to talk about in the locker room.

Figure 23 Maude (Ruth Gordon) guides Harold (Bud Cort) through life in *Harold and Maude*.

To judge from moving testimonies online, *Harold and Maude* remains a go-to experience for self-therapy; not a cult experience as it was in the 1970s, in the sense that it requires a public gathering of emotionally attuned fans, but rather a discreet and privately significant communing which, as Wooder says, helps 'develop a place of self awareness from which we can witness our thoughts and feelings without being sucked in and contaminated by them'.[29]

Another abiding favourite for self-therapy, perched on top of IMDb's chart of the Top 250 Films, is *The Shawshank Redemption* (1994), which missed its audience at the cinema only to discover it on home video, where it was the top-renting title of the year before securing its audience in the United States by repeat screenings on TNT. A prison drama with overtones of fantasy and homoeroticism, *The Shawshank Redemption* is replete with religious symbolism, as Mark Kermode has argued, so that a scene in which the escapee, Andy Dufresne (Tim Robbins), drinks beer with other prisoners can be read as the Last Supper.[30] It also posits cinema itself as a mode of transcendence that can, Kermode says, 'transform the nature of one's surroundings, taking us out of the here and now and transporting us to the Elysian fields of the imagination, making us again free men'.[31] The hero not only sustains his sense of identity within a cruel regime but escapes at last through a tunnel of shit and is reborn into freedom, spreading his arms in an ecstatic cruciform welcoming of the world outside. Film is literally a sign of escape, given that Dufresne tunnels out behind a poster of Raquel Welch in *One Million Years B.C.* (1966) on his cell wall (though it is not explained how he pinned the poster back onto the wall once he is in the tunnel; the internet suggests some cunning solutions). The film's passionate fan base, which is cult in its intensity rather than deviant taste, seems to respond to the absolute literalism of the theme of escape into utopia, represented by the Mexican beach, Zihuatanejo, where Andy talks to Red (Morgan Freeman) about wanting to 'finish out my life, Red ... open a little hotel right on the beach ... buy some worthless old boat and fix it up like new ... take my guests out charter fishing'. Robbins comments:

> That no matter what your prison is – whether it's a job that you hate, a bad relationship that you're slogging through, whether your warden is a terrible boss or a wife or a husband – it holds out the possibility that there is freedom inside you. And that, at some point in life, there is a warm spot on a beach and that we can all get there. But sometimes it takes a while.[32]

This is Hollywood uplift taken to an unusually complete pitch of crowd-pleasing 'escapism'. So knowingly does it draw out the possibilities of the prison film as an inspiring metaphor of Stoicism, that one can imagine a Maudist religion based on it, the secular Passion of Andy transfiguring a male weepie into an emotionally satisfying working of profound unexpressed impulses to male companionship and leisured self-fulfilment. The religious impulse is converted into – or complemented by – quotable button slogans ('Get busy livin' or get busy dyin") and an instructional model of a life of forbearance and hope that, revisited and mulled over, contributes to the ongoing 'project of the self', as Abercrombie and Longhurst call it, in which creating a self-reflexive narrative for one's life from whatever significant materials are at hand is 'related to a modern quest for personal therapies of all sorts in which the security, maintenance and development of the self is seen as an all-important life aim'.[33] Like *Harold and Maude*, *Shawshank's* ultimately positive view of life amounts to an extractable philosophy of living in hope and acceptance.

Turning films into religions is associated with *Star Wars*, The Force and being a Jedi Knight, which an impressive number of alleged converts and definite jokers claimed for their faith in a recent British census: 390,000 in 2001 census, falling to 177,000 in 2011.[34] Also Zen-based, the most elaborate, albeit tongue-in-cheek, secular cult religion, however, was founded on *The Big Lebowski*. Like *The Shawshank Redemption*, this film acquired its considerable fan following not on first release but through 'replay culture': 'expanding outlets for reissues, convergence-inspired repurposing, the growth of the home market and its playback machines, and consumer activities responsive to this climate'.[35] Fans – predominantly white men, so far as I can tell – respond to the film's scatty humanism and the laid-back philosophy of the Dude (Jeff Bridges), which has been summarized and preached in several books as well by the Church of the Latter-Day Dude, whose certification of induction I downloaded from dudeism.com.[36] The film's encouragement to indulge in spiritually enhancing alcohol and drugs at the yearly Lebowskifest or as everyday recreational activities unquestionably also heightens its appeal.[37] The Dude's values, which his devotees liken to the wisdom of the Tao Te Ching, centre on anti-materialism, indifference to money and 24/7 time, a delight in simple pleasures such as bowling, and a firm belief in the integrity of personal space. In short, this is a slacker philosophy at odds not only with the German nihilists who plague the Dude ('he values *everything*, but no particular thing is supreme') but with conventional values, in which Zen mindfulness – with a nod to Jewish mysticism – allows for the modest triumph of an underdog heroically tending the flame of 1960s resistance to both nihilists and the Man.[38] Like Elliott Gould's Philip Marlowe in Altman's *The Long Goodbye*, with his refrain, 'It's all right with me', or the surfers in John Milius's *Big Wednesday* (1978), followers of Dudeism 'have said, each in their own way, "Fuck it" to the stressed-out square community and have chosen to follow their inner Dude's calling to find some kind of metaphorical Tibet or Tao or whatever you call it in their lives'.[39] It is worth noting that the Dude is not the only character in *The Big Lebowski* who lives by a chosen rather than culturally imposed philosophy: Walter Sobchak (John Goodman), a Jewish convert and Vietnam-vet, adheres passionately to the rules of both bowling ('This is not Nam, this is bowling. There are rules') and Orthodox Jewish practice, refusing, for example, to 'roll' on the Sabbath because he is *'shomer* fucking *shabbes'*.[40] Like the Dude, he has constructed, with a more uptight emphasis on adhering to codes and regulations, a performative identity for himself that is at odds with mainstream society and the meaningless chaos of the present day (it is set against the first Gulf War): 'Three thousand years of beautiful tradition from Moses to Sandy Koufax. You're goddam right I'm living in the past.' The Dude, therefore, confronts in the film several ways of living differently from his own hedonistic laziness, from nihilism to Walter's rule-following, and, as Douglass and Walls note, 'This does not imply, however, that dude-ism is vindicated.'[41] As they conclude, while laziness does bring happiness, it is more important that the film 'leads us to the ultimate questions: Is life *actually* purposeless and meaningless? And if so, is it up to each of us to find our own purpose?'[42]

As with Harry Dean Stanton's code-driven Repo Man in Alex Cox's film, the Dude has some relation to the figure of the cultist himself, who is a knowing but undemonstrative transgressor, with 'not so much an ethos as a style', holding himself apart from other people, and controlling his small space in the world through alternative cultural capital.[43] The cultist's favourite films, like the Dude's rug, are what make it all hang together, mapping out his territory and recreating the self as a living archive of cinematic knowledge. The cultist, Dude-like in his seemingly trivial attachments and nostalgia, carves out this personal niche to keep his identity afloat in a threatening and amorphous mass society.

Masculinity and Nostalgia

The central characters in the roll call of cult films are not always inspirational role models like The Dude, Maude, Cady in *Mean Girls*, Baby in *Dirty Dancing* and Andy Dufresne. It is hard to *identify* with Divine in *Pink Flamingos* or El Topo or Frank N. Furter, though it is easy to respond to their frustrations, desires and unhinged excesses as we watch them wide-eyed, captivated and from a safe distance. Quite a few of them are losers, or criminals, or antisocial at the very least, and their therapeutic value is as much like that of the protagonists in cult books, such as Holden Caulfield in *The Catcher in the Rye*, the fantasy sadists in Ayn Rand, or the dazed gonzo hero of *Fear and Loathing in Las Vegas*. Think also, for example, of J.D. (Christian Slater channelling a teenage Jack Nicholson) in *Heathers*, Alex in *A Clockwork Orange* or the lycanthropic Ginger in *Ginger Snaps* (2000); transgressive certainly, as well as thrillingly punkish and anarchic, but better to observe than to imitate and reincarnate in our own selves. We must not forget the pessimism of many cult films, whose heroes and heroines fail as often as triumph and, like cult rock stars, rarely get old.

In fact, cult films frequently showcase grandstanding male anti-heroism and psychosis, charismatically embodied in star performances of varying degrees of self-contained fascination; in performances that, as Justin Smith says, 'create an iconic mask which draws attention to its own charismatic artifice and reveals the hollowness behind it'.[44] Not all cult films centre on a star performance.

A Clockwork Orange and *The Rocky Horror Picture Show* do, and so too *Pink Flamingos*, *The Searchers*, *The Shining*, *Fight Club* and *Withnail and I*. But the charge that many cult films are fantasy projections of male self-pity and narcissism is not entirely off the mark. Nostalgia drives the emphasis on male resistance in a string of films such as *Get Carter*, *Withnail and I*, *Shaft*, *A Clockwork Orange*, *Repo Man* and *Scarface*, in which the cult of stylish outsiderdom or outright criminality is burnished by codified and imitable clothing (Withnail's coat, for example, Alex's droog uniform, Shaft's hip gear) and dialogue that is tending to the self-reflexive and self-dramatizing. There is a sense of the character trying to live up to a role he has opted for, a role that enables him to dominate the little stage of his world, even as the times leave him behind and his obsolescence or death approaches.[45] Thus Withnail (Richard E. Grant) (repeating the failure of his Uncle Monty, another aesthete outsider living in the past and destined never to play the Dane on stage) despairingly addresses caged wolves with a speech from *Hamlet* ('I have of late – but wherefore I know not – lost all my mirth'); and Montana (Al Pacino) in *Scarface*, in his monologue to shocked diners at a classy restaurant, displays a semi-tragic awareness that his pursuit of individualism has led to his embodying the necessary but abject social role of 'the bad guy'. Carter in *Get Carter* is an impressively hard hitman but his style of unreconstructed masculinity is already ending its usefulness, pastiching as it does the isolated killers and private eyes of pulp novels and film noir (he reads Raymond Chandler on the train at the start of the film). The idea of criminals living by a personal code is a familiar one in cult films, where it is invariably an homage to outlaw masculinities in old movies, as, for example, in Tarantino's *Reservoir Dogs* (1991) and *Pulp Fiction*, though it may also embrace an existentialist commitment to lighting out for the territory at high speed (*Zabriskie Point*, *Two Lane Blacktop*, *Vanishing Point* (1971)), or securing a unique niche (Divine as the filthiest person alive). In *Get Carter* the code that spurs Carter to revenge his niece's involvement in porn is what makes him outdated and guarantees his death. As in the American revisionist films noirs of the early 1970s, such as *Chinatown* (1974) and *Night Moves* (1975), this anti-hero is incapable because of his code to comprehend the depth of corruption around him. By a further twist, it seems to have been Carter's pristine hardman image that raised him to a cult icon in the 1990s, the period of British 'New Laddism', when the film was rereleased. Rather as the Bogart cult of the 1960s reclaimed a lost masculinity of romantic but cool assurance, Carter embodied unapologetic priapic machismo at a time of reaction against the feminization of society.[46] The cult of male anti-heroes, from *The Wild Bunch* (1969) and *Straw Dogs* (1971) to *Taxi Driver* to *Fight Club*, often seems to revolve around this kind of longing for an impossible masculinity that enables, through force of style and performance, to secure a sense of control in an incomprehensible or fragmented world.

The disconnection between style and morality in these films is crucial, even if the heroes' transgressions are minor and infantile, such as Withnail's drunken rants. Equally unintended by the same screenwriter, Oliver Stone, as Tony Montana's cool appeal was the satanic charisma of the corrupt junk bond dealer, Gordon Gekko, in *Wall Street* (1987), who, as depicted in *Boiler Room* (2000), became a cult hero for some traders who creatively misread the film's intentions and took Stone to be of Gekko's party without knowing it. The excitement of being with such characters enables the Faustian rise and fall structure to be ignored, with ethical consequences that can be disturbing – as with *The Wolf of Wall Street*, which some critics took for a celebration of Jordan Belfort's criminality rather than an ironic incitement to get caught up in it. One is reminded of Stanley Fish's argument, in *Surprised by Sin*, that *Paradise Lost* works by enacting in the reader the same seduction and fall as undergone by Adam and Eve.[47] The focus in these films is on white maleness and alienation (key, as we've seen, to cult novels too), and the importance of achieving an aesthetic way of living that allows you to live authentically in the moment. This is Hemingway-lite, you might say, and feeds off several traditions of white male representation, which in American films, are most obviously identified with the Western and its variations such as the gangster film and the film noir, where psychosis is never far away. A key moment is in *Taxi Driver* when Travis – De Niro improvising – says to his reflection, 'Here is a man who would not take it anymore' – a very historically specific act of summoning a resistant self. Travis is not recommended as a blueprint for everyday behaviour, any more than his world, the vividly depicted excremental Hell of pre-cleaned up New York, is a helpful documentary guide for tourists (though the shots of 42nd Street are now a time capsule for those nostalgic for 1970s sleaze). But you can imagine taking on, in bathetic imitation, elements of his self-help regime, with which he attempts to suture together his disintegrated self by transforming his body into some kind of cybernetic extension of his tank-like taxi.

Fight Club, reworking *Taxi Driver*, is fundamentally about identity, millennial masculinity and the psychosis of rebellion against ball-breaking consumerism, and, like *The Wicker Man*, *Quadrophenia* and *The Howling* (1981) (and *Eyes Wide Shut*, if you believe the conspiracists) is a cult film *about* a cult. In Tyler Durden (Brad Pitt), *Fight Club* has a central character who is charismatic but unreliable (spectacularly so, as he doesn't exist), observed by an apparently normal alter ego, who observes him as 'I' (Marwood) does Withnail. Like *Taxi Driver* the film depicts a hellish world (a soft and meaningless hell rather than the literal one of *Taxi Driver*) and is an instruction manual, or wake-up call, to live more authentically in it; which was imitated in real life by various fight clubs' being set up to initiate homoerotic encounters between the disaffected. And like *Taxi Driver* (and *Heathers*, in which Veronica (Winona Ryder) is drawn into J.D.'s rebel delirium, before she is liberated by his self-immolation into becoming 'the new sheriff in town'), *Fight Club* it is a trap, emotionally aligning receptive viewers with madness, culminating in the pre-9/11 fantasy of collapsing skyscrapers. These male anti-heroes of cult films live by private personal codes, despite their violence or aimlessness, in worlds isolated from women or troubled by them, and trying to live in their own anachronistic outsider style with enough energy and grace.

These films are available as cognitive maps of hostile worlds. They spin a different version of the underlying impulses in many American films, the lone protagonist on a journey, but the mythic drift is apocalyptic and closure is lacking. To that extent some cult films intersect with and sometimes subvert the lionization of male pathology in cinema generally. Justin Smith, seeing cult films as 'transitional objects in the process of subjective self-recognition with which we are all engaged', suggests that

> Cult films are the repositories of fears and longings in the negotiation of sexual difference and subjectivity. They endorse cultural marginality, reassuring their devotees that not 'fitting in' is fine, maybe even heroic. They offer alternative systems of order, symbolic rituals and rites of passage. They provide frameworks for alternative forms of belief.[48]

Take, for instance, *The Matrix* (1999). This was a popular film, reminiscent of *They Live* and *Society*, which gathered an immense cult following at the turn of the millennium, as well as inspiring a slew of philosophical readings. *The Matrix* itself is a near-perfect visual metaphor for ideology, not as a set of ideas but as a lived experience which distracts the exploited masses while their lives are siphoned off to feed the system. But while the film is Marxist, Situationist even, in its totalizing vision of the world as illusion and spectacle, its fascination with 'guns, lots of guns', valorization of a militia of the elect led by a white Messiah, and use of the iconography of contemporary conspiracy theory (such as state-sponsored 'men in black') smacks rather more of right-wing libertarianism. Pat Mellencamp argues that the appeal of the film is

> its message of self-empowerment through the auspices of a benevolent teacher represents the New Age philosophical paradigm – high-tech meets ancient Eastern discipline and practices … . The overriding message of the film is that if our belief in ourselves remains steadfast, there is nothing we cannot accomplish and become. Our thoughts, which we learn to focus and discipline, create and determine our world – a distinctly Eastern philosophical premise.[49]

The Matrix might be taken as plausible mapping of the world, a metaphorical description of political reality. Indeed, I suspect that one reason for the film's impact and popularity, quite apart from its substantial merits as an action movie, was that its systematic presentation of the world as a hoax and a prison was felt by audiences to be essentially true. *The Matrix* dredges up the nihilism, powerlessness, grandiosity and unfocused rage generated in us neophyte 'Last

Men' by the experience of capitalism. Like superhero movies, it offers the bold compensatory fantasy that we, unlike the drones around us, can see through the System and superheroically counter it, while simultaneously remaining cool, poised, very well dressed and sexily subversive.

The film is, of course, capable of appropriation by both the Right and the Left. Most films are. Hollywood films tend to build in ideological ambiguity in order to appeal to the fantasies of the widest possible audience. Certainly, *The Matrix* can be read as leftist in so far as its totalizing vision offers, as Marxism used to, a seamlessly paranoid negation of surface reality (there is an element of this in *Room 237*, of course, an urge to see the film and through the film to a wider truth unsuspected by ordinary viewers). Acquiescence requires all-encompassing conversion rather than a slight readjustment of one's view of things. We see democracy, but the reality – as in *They Live* – is fascism. We think we're free, but actually we're prisoners, ticking over on life supports. In short, this is the theory of false consciousness taken to a heuristic, barmy extreme. Only by the actions of a sort of Leninist groupuscule, a visionary avant-garde of technologically savvy white men, spiritually attuned black men and sexy leather-clad women, will humanity find salvation, whether it wants to or not. (I doubt I'm alone in sympathizing with the Judas-figure, who, while acknowledging that the steak he enjoys is a simulation, nevertheless opts for the inhabitable lie of the matrix over the wasteland it obscures.) As Andrew Roberts remarks, in a book on Fredric Jameson:

> [*The Matrix*] is surely one of the most Marxist films ever to have come out of Hollywood … . In other words, if we ask what the 'Matrix' is, then the answer is that it *is* ideology in the Marxist sense of a fiction obscuring the reality of exploitation. In fact, this film articulates a more thorough-going Althusserian or Jamesonian sense of what ideology is: 'the Matrix' is more than a set of false beliefs about reality (or false consciousness) – it is reality, it conditions and defines how the people caught up in themselves think and act.[50]

So you could see the film as a droll popularization of hard-core political theory as well as an exemplary 'awful warning' in the dystopian tradition of SF. Like *Fight Club*, it seems roughly leftist in its hostility to actually existing consumerism, and liberating in fantasizing the overthrow of oppressive reality.[51] But *Fight Club* (echoing *Taxi Driver*) has the good grace to admit that its hero's antisocial refusal of, essentially, everything is an index of his psychosis and that his revelation of the ubiquity of consumer ideology can have no other outlet than gratuitous acts of self-abusive violence and political vandalism. *The Matrix* walks a fine line between satirical left-wing consciousness raising and right-wing contempt for the Last Men of consumerism; it communicates a yearning for total revolution and for transcending banal reality through the pursuit of liberation for its own sake.

What such films revel in is not so much the promise of homogenous social order but an anarchistic trust in unbridled individualism acting on behalf of Family, Nation and the Law. As Sean French points out in his little book on *The Terminator* (1984), what in Britain often plays as subversive anti-authoritarianism, belongs more in the United States to America's libertarian tradition. Exemplified by the militia rather than by fascists *per se*, this tradition 'sees almost all forms of social organisation and control … as creeping forms of communism which are neutering the pioneering spirit that built America'.[52] A popular reading of it is as a vast metaphor which 'examines the idea of an individual searching for their true self while attempting to escape the box that we often make of our lives'.[53] It would be naive to read *The Matrix* literally as a call to antisocial violence; that is merely, from one perspective, the ostensible plot of the film. As we discussed in Chapter 3, modern society has been comprehensively seen through, debunked, made transparent by a cynicism available equally to the disenchanted intellectual and the dimmest nu-metal fan. For all the ideological blandishments, we *know* that the West is decadent, moribund, spiritually bereft and deserves all it gets.[54] It is indeed disquieting to think that consumerism is the end of history and the best to which humanity can now aspire. Like other turn-of-the-century movies, such as *American Beauty* (1999) and *Fight Club*, *The Matrix* articulates a distaste (a male one, especially, for these films are not without misogyny) for the banal values and relaxed softness of consumer culture, its emasculating secular ordinariness and fantasizes that the reality is more interesting, exciting and intoxicatingly worse and that by acts of doomed resistance one can proclaim, as the hero does in *American Beauty*, 'I rule!'. This links back, I think, to the cult interpretations of Kubrick films we discussed earlier, in which the desire for an overarching conspiratorial explanation of the film within an essentially paranoid understanding of the world expresses itself in satisfyingly dense esoteric readings.

Dionysus on the Sofa

It might seem odd to suggest that watching cult films such as *Taxi Driver*, let alone *Pink Flamingos*, *The Matrix* and *Fight Club*, might be regarded as therapeutic; cathartic perhaps, and intellectually challenging or emotionally wrenching in company or alone, but hardly cures for emotional problems. This is a different experience from *The Shawshank Redemption*, *Harold and Maude* and *The Big Lebowski*, though they also present ways of escaping the matrix of everyday reality; the erotic thrill of imagining the worst and oneself apart from it. But there is also the experience of the cult film to consider, as a space to enter and be changed or challenged by – a therapeutic jolt or reality check rather than balm for the soul, of course, is to take too restrictive a view of the films. For a start it is selective; not *all* cult films fit this masculinist template, as you can see with *Clueless* (1995), *The Princess Bride*, *Mean Girls* and *Fast Times at Ridgemont High* (1982), and watching them, like reading novels in a reading group, may be very different:

> It might be said that the reading group is a forum for the kind of talk associated with women: co-operation rather than competition, the model of 'emotional literacy' which values teamwork, listening, and sharing over self assertion and winning the argument. Reading groups could, then, be seen as part of the feminization of culture.[55]

Nevertheless, many cult films can, in their extremity, be a test – quite literally with some films, whose emetic shocks administer less than cosy rebuffs and challenge emotions as well as ideas. Gorehounds among you may recall *that* bit in *Bloodsucking Freaks* (1976) when a 'doctor' drills into a girl's head and sucks her brains out with a straw. One of those legendary moments of intimate violence, like the 'splinter in the eye' in *Zombie Flesh Eaters*, it ranks high in cult cinema's pantheon of misogynistic money-shots. An American 'grindhouse' movie shown on 42nd Street under the title *The Incredible Torture Show*, *Bloodsucking Freaks* was the original 'torture porn' film, in which an enterprising lunatic, Sardu (Seamus O'Brien), and his midget assistant, Ralphus (Luis De Jesus), run Theatre of the Macabre, an S&M show which tortures women in front of audiences who think it is staged. *Bloodsucking Freaks* acquired notoriety as one of the most uncompromising exploitation films of the 1970s and, now re-released on DVD and Blu-Ray by trash mavens Troma, has become a collectable cult item for thrill-seeking trash cinephiles.

I first saw *Bloodsucking Freaks* in the 1990s on a grainy umpteenth-generation dubbed video, whose grottiness complemented the film's sleazy amateurism. The film, borrowing from Herschell Gordon Lewis's *Wizard of Gore* (1970) and Roger Corman's *Little Shop of Horrors* (1960), plays with ideas about art as horror – 'It is not SM, it is art,' as Sardu insists. This saving element of self-reflexivity enables cultists and academics like me to read it as an intense statement about exploitation, the voyeurism of audiences and the instability of art and trash. What precisely was I getting from the experience of seeing that straw go in and the brains get sucked out? I don't mean watching horror in general, but watching and (I admit) enjoying such a comprehensively disreputable piece of cinema. After all, I could have been catching up with good cinema, for which, say, Tarkovsky might be taken as exemplary – serious, intense, spiritually elevating and now, thanks to DVD and online streaming, easily accessible. Yet, much as I love *Solaris* (1972) and *Stalker* (1979), they lack whatever it is that appeals in seeing brains get sucked out. *Bloodsucking Freaks* is a bad object if ever there was one, a toxic event from which nothing good could come. Picketed in the 1970s by the feminist group, Women Against Violence, it's the sort of film Patrick Bateman might rewatch with the same avidity and for much the same reason as *Body Double* (1984): 'I rerent *Body Double* because

I want to watch it again tonight even though I know I won't have enough time to masturbate over the scene where the woman is getting drilled to death by a power drill.'[56] Liking that kind of film raises key issues about the pleasures of exploitation and trash (after all, 'child pornography' has its cultists too). Yet, while scarcely an American psycho, I not only like such trash but prefer it in some ways; and loving trash – and loving *that* I love it – is part of who I am.

Bloodsucking Freaks combines most of the key elements in exemplary fashion – an exploitation film, low-budget, transgressive, overlooked and disregarded. It is without redeeming virtues beyond its extremity and shamelessness, which recommend it to cultists. Shabbily made, it deliberately sets out to offend, though its grindhouse audience presumably lapped it up and cultists later embraced it precisely because it was offensive. Trash does sometimes overlap with art house, as with *A Serbian Film* (2010), and, in fact, much trash is less transgressive than arty trash with pretentions. Low pleasures and erotic frissons have long been associated with art films, historically often marketed as sexy foreign fare.[57] The more extreme exploitation films come across as a sort of alternative avant-garde, with a similar battery of bourgeois-baiting effects to films designed for very different audiences, such as *L'age d'or* (1930), the films of the Vienna Actionists or Stan Brakhage's alarming autopsy footage epic, *The Act of Seeing with One's Own Eyes* (1971). Trash aesthetes habitually have a taste equally for the low and the high, both distant from the middlebrow; and a taste for trash exploitation and Tarkovsky, neither of them multiplex fodder, actually makes perfect sense. The trash aesthete, as a species of fan, is as exclusive as any other class of cultist, and it is the rarity of the experience of trash, or banned films generally, that often gives value to the experience of it.

In J. K. Huysmans's great Decadent novel *A Rebours*, published in 1884 and generally translated as *Against Nature*, the sickly aristocratic hero, Des Esseintes, isolates himself against the vulgar modern world in a private sanctum of exquisite tastes and erotic experiments. Although ultimately comic and a failure (he ends up reverting to Catholicism), Des Esseintes is nevertheless the unlikely begetter of a certain kind of connoisseur – the aesthete whose recoil from the everyday is an elite rejection of everything in modern culture, a culture that these days, even more so than in Huysmans's time, is omnipresent, commercialized and vulgar. Better to create a private world of rare, erotic, pretentious pleasures, which the bizarre field of trash offers, than to submit to the embrace and ennui of the ordinary. Des Esseintes is a complete and compulsive highbrow snob, but he provides a model too for his alter ego, the discerning trash aesthete. Instead of high culture – though he may feel at home among that as well – the trash aesthete inhabits a rarefied realm of the debased, pornographic, extreme and unredeemable, from which he is protected by irony, knowingness and – in the case of the academic trash aesthete – a forbidding carapace of cultural capital, including theory of the most abstruse kind that enables us to intellectualize rubbish without apparent bad faith.[58] At a time when even the most difficult and transgressive culture is commodified and tamed by the market place, this is a perversely highbrow gesture of subjective revolt that finds in trash the resources for a curious education of the self. Much cult assumes a social enterprise or some kind of homosocial bonding, but this is more an idiosyncratic and self-conscious negation of mainstream tastes (and political correctness), even if it is a negation quite widely shared: such is one of the recognized paradoxes of postmodern culture, in which so many endeavour, through appropriate consumption practices, to be different, just like everyone else and *in exactly the same way*.

The Other of trash cinema offers an escape from boredom into the sublimely indefensible. Every trash aesthete will have his or her own demons and hence reasons for loving trash and not all will like the same generally dislikeable films. But we can make a few guesses as to what impels immersion in very bad things such as *Bloodsucking Freaks*. The pleasures of trash are what it does to you, the levels of experience, arousal and intensity that distance one from the ordinary tedium of real life. Trash of an extreme sort – what the critic Mikita Brottman has called offensive films – may be a kind of 'body genre':

> The ultimate aim of offensive films is the arousal of strong emotions in the lower body – nausea, weakness, faintness, and a loosening of bowel and bladder control – normally by way of graphic scenes featuring the by-products of bodily detritus: vomit, excrement, viscera, brain tissue, and so on.[59]

This implies a phenomenology of trash that would relate the films to the Abject as the psychoanalyst and theorist Julia Kristeva defined it.[60] Films like *Bloodsucking Freaks* enable us to rehearse in mediated safety our reactions, both fascinated and repulsed to the point of nausea, to the traumatic experience of encountering something liminal and outside the social and cultural order. Although trash films may be grossly off-putting, they can also be seen, paradoxically, as a kind of security (or comfort) blanket – transitional objects that enable rehearsal of emotional and physical responses to the Abject. They also demonstrate an ability to survive extreme screen experiences outside the usual comfort zones. Exposing oneself to dangerous extremity is itself both challenging and sublime, allowing for what Mathijs and Sexton call 'self-reflexive modes of performative reception in the negotiation of the phenomenal experience of moments of abjection, impurity, and grotesquerie'.[61] Trash aesthetes' ritual return to the scene of the Abject is a way, both masterful and masochistic, of coping with threatening images and experiences and domesticating them through compulsive repetition. This is the pursuit, from the comfort of one's armchair in front of the TV, of the 'Dionysian', which is a feature of much cult practice and embodied in the panic-inducing Frank N. Furter, the Dionysus in drag of *The Rocky Horror Picture Show*.[62] Thus the trash aesthete carves out a little cultural space for himself, a psychogeographical flâneur both immersed in and safely distanced from contamination by the Other.[63]

Exploitation films are typically 'bad' films not just in terms of style but often ethically too in their perceived address to the Patrick Bateman repressed in all men. Decadent and amoral, the trash aesthete's sedentary hedonism at best allows for the articulation of an alternative set of aesthetic criteria; at worst, like that arch-aesthete Proust in his cork-lined bedroom enjoying the spectacle of starving rats goaded to fight with pins, it might suggest an antisocial, even psychotic suspension of morality – an unwitting symptom rather than ironic embrace of postmodern relativism and its ethical deliquescence.[64] But, while deliciously melodramatic, this is actually nonsense, and not only because most trash aesthetes you're likely to meet are as mild-mannered as the neurasthenic Des Esseintes, and more like the one-to-one communing with a film that we get in *Harold and Maude*. Their sedentary excursions into the perverse and extreme involve after all nothing more transgressive than watching and obsessing about bad movies. No rats, let alone women, are harmed by the trash aesthete's modest refusals of propriety and good taste. Nor are his brains sucked out by the likes of *Bloodsucking Freaks*. Indeed the pleasures, while viscerally bracing, of contemplating the unwatchable and monitoring one's quickened, pulsating awareness of the Abject in the midst of life can be sharply intellectual – a deliberate, though left-handed, attempt to grasp, as a different kind of aesthete put it in 1873, 'at any exquisite passion, or any contribution to knowledge that seems by a lifted horizon to set the spirit free for a moment, or any stirring of the senses, strange dyes, strange colours, and curious odours, or work of the artist's hands, or the face of one's friend'.[65] It just happens that, for some of us, such rare sublime intensities of ecstasy and experience are to found in the presence of trash. Less sociable than the Dude, who has his support structure and rituals to map out his day and guide him safely home, the trash aesthete's more rarefied slacker lifestyle finds compensation in trash for spiritual distance and the anomic desacralization of the world, replacing it with thrills, eroticism and hints of transcendence and poeticism. Thereby (Rorty again) to achieve 'the aim of a just and free society as letting its citizens be as privatistic, "irrationalist", and aestheticist as they please so long as they do it in their own time – causing no harm to others and using no resources needed by those less advantaged'.[66]

At this point we can return to the idea of the Dionysian, the dark forces of repressed vitality associated with Dionysus, the Greek god of wine and theatre, who embodies the ecstatic blurring of boundaries and transformation of the self. The Dionysian is a staple of cult criticism as Mathijs and Sexton remark – 'the most often-used metaphor for critics attempting to illustrate film cults'.[67] Dionysus was, according to Dean DeFino, the presiding God of the hippie counterculture, whose presence in cult films of the midnight movie period is embodied in the women of *Faster Pussycat! Kill! Kill!*, whose dangerous femaleness threatens male power. Cult film, he argues, is 'a mode of discourse that not only demands submission but embodies the Dionysian spirit in its ecstatic communal rituals'.[68]

The cult film, combining nostalgia and curdled utopianism in the counterculture, offered a space in which consumption could become psycho-sexual liberation; a fantasy space for erotic dreams of liberation and destruction, which can be alarming and disorientating as well as transformational – to be 'lost in time, and space, and meaning', as it is said at the end of *Rocky Horror*, and which might also describe the head-spinning semiotic bender of watching cult films. Ferris Bueller, for instance, like Frank N. Furter, is a Dionysian role model, the pampered host of the film, educating others in living for the moment and making the most of free time (like cultists he refuses to follow scheduled time, bunking off school and taking Chicago by storm). Through him his friend, Cameron, learns to stand up to his father by trashing his luxurious car and 'for the first time in his life he is going to be just fine' (in fact, Ferris seems to have planned the day with this aim ('You knew what you were doing when you woke this morning, didn't you?' his girlfriend Sloane accuses him)). I was delighted to find a blog, among the numerous websites detailing the 'lessons' of *Ferris Bueller*, summarizing the four mindfulness lessons to be learnt from the film's injunction to be 'totally disconnected from technology or your to-do lists and [take] time to fully be in your present moment'.[69] Ferris, God-like, offers change and transcendence if only for one day. 'The psychological fragmentation and manipulated homogeneity of our media-dominated consumerism may create an intense need for some kind of transcendence,' Richard Seaford comments:[70]

> Humanity emerges from nature and aspires to divinity. Dionysos [*sic*], by transcending these fundamental divisions, may *transform the identity* of an individual into animal and god. And it is by his presence that he liberates the individual from the circumstances of his life.[71]

These therapeutic uses of film as spiritual self-help could be redescribed as securing a closer fit to the stresses and iniquities of everyday life; learning to chill out about them and dampening down the urge to scream, 'I'm mad as hell and won't take it anymore' by watching *Network* (1976) instead and practising more proportionate emotional responses. It is about coping with what Wizard

Figure 24 Ferris (Matthew Broderick) offers invaluable advice in *Ferris Bueller's Day Off*.

tells Travis is the optimum solution to his ills in *Taxi Driver*: 'Go out and get laid. Get drunk, you know, do anything. Cos you got no choice anyway. I mean we're all fucked, more or less you know.' To which Travis replies, 'Yeah, I don't know. That's about the dumbest thing I ever heard.'

Envoi

In the history of cinema there is one perfect moment of salvation through cult film and that is in Woody Allen's *Hannah and Her Sisters* (1986). The effect works best if you watch clips of it on YouTube and ignore the rest of the film.

In one of the film's narrative threads Allen plays Mickey, a hypochondriac, who discovers that that not having a brain tumour is even more troubling than the disease itself. Thrown into despair by the meaninglessness of life and the inevitability of death, he goes in search of answers. Having worked his way through a selection of the world's religions, he is close to what Nietzsche called 'the abyss' and concludes that 'I just felt that in a Godless universe, I didn't want to go on living.' After a botched suicide attempt, he wanders the street disconsolately before deciding that 'I just, I just needed a moment to gather my thoughts and, and be logical and put the world back into rational perspective' and finding himself at a screening of the cult classic, *Duck Soup* (1933). Caught up in the Marx Brothers's crazy antics, he accepts the absurdity, contingency and quotidian pleasures of the world as it is, and the possibilities of comedy as redemption:

> And I went upstairs to the balcony, and I sat down, and, you know, the movie was a-a-a film that I'd seen many times in my life since I was a kid, and-and I always, uh, loved it. And, you know, I'm, I'm watching these people up on the screen and I started getting hooked on the film, you know. And I started to feel, how can you even think of killing yourself? I mean isn't it so stupid? I mean, look at all the people up there on the screen. You know, they're real funny, and what if the worst is true. What if there's no God, and you only go around once and that's it. Well, you know, don't you want to be part of the experience? You know, what the hell, it's, it's not all a drag. And I'm thinking to myself, geez, I should stop ruining my life – searching for answers I'm never gonna get, and just enjoy it while it lasts. And, you know, after, who knows? I mean, you know, maybe there is something. Nobody really knows. I know, I know 'maybe' is a very slim reed to hang your whole life on, but that's the best we have. And then, I started to sit back, and I actually began to enjoy myself.

Now, you can say many things about that scene: that Mickey opts for acceptance as abruptly as he gave into despair; that his epiphany is undermined by his

Figure 25 Putting the world back into rational perspective in *Hannah and Her Sisters*.

hypochondria; that *Duck Soup* is a film of chaos and political satire; that it is all far too pat, especially when, in a sentimental, an almost parodically sentimental ending, Mickey and his new wife, find they are having a baby; that the film as a whole is much darker and ironic; that subsequent events in Allen's life and allegations against him speak against taking his films as a guide to anything. That is why I say, watch it on YouTube and ignore the bits that don't fit. After all, if Mickey had wandered into *The Sorrow and the Pity* (1972), Alvy Singer's standby for dates in *Annie Hall*, or *Shoah* (1985) (the film event for Jews in the year before *Hannah and Her Sisters* was released) he might not have ended up so cheerful and resigned to ordinary unhappiness. It is doubtless significant that *Duck Soup* was made before the war and the Holocaust, so that it is an escape into a less existentially troubling period. The Holocaust is a presence in the rest of the film, announced directly and not in code as it allegedly is in *The Shining*: 'I had a great evening; it was like the Nuremberg Trials,' and in this speech by Harry (Max von Sydow), a tortured European intellectual is unable to achieve Mickey's calm acceptance (he's too invested in high culture, perhaps, like Bergman films):

> You missed a very dull TV show on Auschwitz. More gruesome film clips, and more puzzled intellectuals declaring their mystification over the systematic murder of millions. The reason they can never answer the question, 'How could it possibly happen?,' is that it's the wrong question. Given what people are, the question is 'Why doesn't it happen more often?'

So, as I say, we must take our lesson selectively from the film to make it 'guide-like' and, for the receptive cinephile, inspiring. And not put it alongside the more caustic *The Purple Rose of Cairo* (1985), in which addiction to cinema is portrayed as a housewife's escape from a loutish husband: life-saving, of course, but at the price of reality.[72] But you could compare it with the final scene in *Manhattan* when Isaac Davis (Woody Allen), having lost Tracy (Mariel

Hemingway), his much younger but emotionally more mature love, makes a list of things, including Groucho Marx, that render life worth living (not including children, oddly, perhaps because at this point Allen wasn't a father):

> Why is life worth living? It's a very good question. Um ... Well, there are certain things I guess that make it worthwhile. Like what ... okay ... um ... . For me, uh ... ooh ... I would say ... what, Groucho Marx, to name one thing ... uh ... um ... and Willie Mays ... and um ... the 2nd movement of the Jupiter Symphony ... and um ... Louis Armstrong, recording of 'Potato Head Blues' ... um ... Swedish movies, naturally ... *Sentimental Education* by Flaubert ... uh ... Marlon Brando, Frank Sinatra ... um ... those incredible apples and pears by Cezanne ... uh ... the crabs at Sam Wo's ... uh ... Tracy's face.[73]

Hannah and Her Sisters was, according to Fuat Ulus, who uses clips of it in his therapeutic analyses, 'the first film in which the movie therapy concept has ever been processed', and Mickey's 'mini catharsis' is recommended for 'existential, support and empowerment groups'.[74] Few directors have so openly presented a philosophical aspect as Woody Allen; a world in an old-fashioned auteurist sense, inspired by the large existential visions of Bergman and Fellini, with a resilient comic vision, and a focus on absurdity and repetition, art and love (represented especially in his later films by magic). Let's take the *Duck Soup* scene as the definitive model of therapeutic viewing – a tutelary symbolic moment, an epiphany, in fact, which suggests how the experience of watching the right film, a cult film in this case, can in a seemingly banal way make life more bearable.[75]

What would a guide to life look like, stripped down to a Buzzfeed-style listicle of cult quotations? 'Always look on the bright side of life', of course, 'Be cool, but care' (*Bill & Ted's Excellent Adventure*), 'Life moves pretty fast.' 'Get busy livin' or get busy dyin'' 'Don't dream it, be it'. That whole *Duck Soup* speech from *Hannah and Her Sisters*. *Harold and Maude* supplies enough high-concept zingers, by turns cloying, wise and amoral, to bulk out a *Little Book of Cult Wisdom* like one of those stocking-filler books of calm and happiness: 'Vice, virtue. It's best not to be too moral. You cheat yourself out of too much life. Aim above morality. If you apply that to life, then you're bound to live life fully.' 'Harold, everyone has the right to make an ass out of themselves. You just can't let the world judge you too much.' On the other hand, you might plump for the minimal creed offhandedly announced, as if it were an Oscar nomination, by a dragged up Michael Palin at the end of *Monty Python's The Meaning of Life*:

> Well, it's nothing very special. Try to be nice to people, avoid eating fat, read a good book every now and then, get some walking in, and try and live together in peace and harmony with people of all creeds and nations.

Figure 26 Michael Palin helpfully reveals the meaning of life at the end of *Monty Python's The Meaning of Life.*

I could live with that. Perhaps, with cult films we are dealing with a philosophy of life that melds whistling in the dark with a sense of the necessity of doing *something* (even if forced to, like the Dude, against his better, lazier nature), against a shadowed background of life's essential meaninglessness and an understanding of what Tarkovsky said in this passage from his diary: 'Of course life has no point. If it had man would not be free, he'd become a slave to that point and his life would be governed by completely new criteria: the criteria of slavery.'[76] This hardly covers everything, but as Wizard says to Travis after his garbled attempt to sum up what life is all about, 'I'm not Bertrand Russell. Well, what do you want?' I'm in way over my head already with this 'meaning of life' malarkey, and to try to do any more I would need a *much* bigger book.

NOTES

Preface

1 My mother, bless her, disputes this. My parents also banned me from reading
Action comic, which I cherished for its 'Hookjaw' strip about a vengeful shark.

Chapter 1

1 The foundational books on cult film, which established the canon for the 'midnight
movie' period, were Danny Peary's trilogy, *Cult Movies* (London: Vermilion,
1982), *Cult Movies 2* (London: Vermilion, 1983) and *Cult Movies 3* (London:
Sidgwick & Jackson, 1989); Michael Weldon, *The Psychotronic Encyclopedia of Film*
(New York: Ballantine, 1983); J. Hoberman and Jonathan Rosenbaum, *Midnight
Movies* (New York: Harper, 1983); Stuart Samuels, *Midnight Movies* (New York:
Macmillan, 1983); V. Vale, Andrea Juno, and Jim Morton (eds), *Incredibly Strange
Films* (San Francisco: RE/Search Publications, 1986). Recent popular guides
include Alain Riou, *Les films cultes* (Paris: Éditions du Chêne, 1998); Karl French
and Philip French, *Cult Movies* (London: Pavilion, 1999); *The Rough Guide to
Cult Movies* (London: Penguin, 2001); Ali Catterall and Simon Wells, *Your Face
Here: British Cult Movies since the Sixties* (London: Fourth Estate, 2002); Soren
McCarthy, *Cult Movies in Sixty Seconds: The Best Films in The World in Less Than a
Minute* (London: Fusion, 2003); Ernest Mathijs and Xavier Mendik, *100 Cult Films*
(London BFI/Palgrave Macmillan, 2011); and Steven J. Schneider (ed.), *101 Cult
Movies You Must See Before You Die* (London: Apple, 2015).
2 Jonathan Lethem, *They Live* (Berkeley: Soft Skull, 2010); and D. Harlan Wilson,
They Live (London and New York: Wallflower, 2015).
3 This is the probably the best place for a guide to 'further reading' in academic
cult studies. The development of cult film as a field of scholarship in the English
language started with J. P. Telotte (ed.), *The Cult Film Experience: Beyond All Reason*
(Austin: University of Texas Press, 1991). The second wave of cult criticism was
kicked off by Xavier Mendik and Graeme Harper (eds), *Unruly Pleasures: The Cult
Film and Its Critics* (Guildford: FAB Press, 2000); and Mark Jancovich, Antonio
Lazaro Reboll, Julian Stringer and Amy Willis (eds), *Defining Cult Movies: The
Cultural Politics of Oppositional Taste* (Manchester and New York: Manchester
University Press, 2003). The current richness and diversity of the field is represented
by Justin Smith, *Withnail and Us: Cult Films and Film Cults in British Cinema*
(London: I.B. Tauris, 2010); Kate Egan and Sarah Thomas (eds), *Cult Film Stardom:
Offbeat Attractions and Processes of Cultification* (London: Palgrave Macmillan,
2013); J. P. Telotte and Gerald Duchovnav (eds), *Science Fiction Double Feature: The
Science Fiction Film as Cult Text* (Liverpool: Liverpool University Press, 2015); and

two ongoing series of short books, Wallflower Press's *Cultographies* and Auteur's *Devil's Advocates*. The essential articles and chapters are collected in Ernest Mathijs and Xavier Mendik (eds), *The Cult Film Reader* (Maidenhead: Open University Press, 2007), while Ernest Mathijs and Jamie Sexton, *Cult Cinema* (Chichester: Wiley-Blackwell, 2011) is the standard textbook. On cult's problematic relationship with fan studies, see Matt Hills, *Fan Cultures* (London: Routledge, 2002); and Mark Duffett, *Understanding Fandom: An Introduction to the Study of Media Fan Culture* (New York and London: Bloomsbury, 2015).

4   Mikita Brottman, 'Star Cults/Cult Stars', in *Unruly Pleasures*, 108.

5   J. P. Telotte, 'Beyond All Reason: The Nature of Cult', in *The Cult Experience*.

6   Dan Bentley-Baker, 'What is Cult Cinema? A Checklist', *Bright Lights Film Journal*, 31 July 2010. Available online: http://brightlightsfilm.com/what-is-cult-cinema-a-checklist/#.VkTiQfnhDIU (accessed 23 November 2015).

7   Jonathan Eig, 'A Beautiful Mind(fuck): Hollywood Structures of Identity', *Jump Cut: A Review of Contemporary Media* 46 (2003). Available online: http://www.ejumpcut.org/archive/jc46.2003/eig.mindfilms/index.html (accessed 16 November 2015).

8   Bentley-Baker, 'What is Cult Cinema?'.

9   See Joan Hawkins, *Cutting Edge: Art-Horror and the Horrific Avant-Garde* (Minneapolis: University of Minnesota Press, 2000), 37–8; and I. Q. Hunter, *British Trash Cinema* (London: BFI/Palgrave, 2013), 92–4.

10 Mathijs and Sexton, *Cult Cinema*, 52.

11 Christian Keathley, *Cinephilia and History, or The Wind in the Trees* (Bloomington: Indiana University Press, 2005), 7.

12 Jamie Sexton, 'From Bad to Good and Back Again? Cult Cinema and Its Unstable Directory', in *B is for Bad Cinema: Aesthetics, Politics, and Cultural Value*, ed. Claire Perkins and Constantine Verevis (Albany: State University of New York Press, 2014), 136.

13 Andrew Sarris, *Confessions of a Cultist: On the Cinema 1955–1969* (New York: Simon & Schuster, 1970); Manny Farber, 'White Elephant Art vs. Termite Art', in *Movies* [originally published as *Negative Space*], ed. Farber (New York: Hillstone, 1971), 134–44.

14 Parker Tyler, see also Greg Taylor.

15 Greg Taylor, *Artists in the Audience: Cults, Camp and American Film Criticism* (Princeton: Princeton University Press, 1999), 14.

16 Taylor, *Artists*, 15.

17 Telotte, 'Beyond All Reason', 8–11.

18 Peary, *Cult Movies*, 47.

19 Aljean Harmetz, *Round Up the Usual Suspects: The Making of* Casablanca – *Bogart, Bergman and World War II* (New York: Hyperion, 1992), 343.

20 Telotte, 'Beyond All Reason', 9.

21 Ibid., 11.

22 Umberto Eco, '*Casablanca*: Cult Movies and Intertextual Collage', in *Travels in Hyperreality*, ed. Eco, trans. William Weaver (1986; London: Picador, 1987), 198.

23 Ibid.

24 James Card, 'Confessions of a *Casablanca* Cultist: An Enthusiast Meets the Myth and Its Flaws', in *Beyond All Reason*, 7.

25 Eco, '*Casablanca*', 2010. On this, see Robert B. Ray, *A Certain Tendency of the Hollywood Cinema, 1930–1980* (Princeton: Princeton University Press, 1985), 138–40.

26 Eco, '*Casablanca*', 209.

27 Ray, *A Certain Tendency*, 89.

28 Peary, *Cult Movies*, 47–8.

29 Ray, *A Certain Tendency*, 110.

30 The poll was carried out for *Sight and Sound*'s September 2012 issue. It is available online here: http://www.bfi.org.uk/news/50-greatest-films-all-time (accessed 23 November 2015).

31 Samuels, *Midnight Movies*, 27.

32 Ibid., 10.

33 Hoberman and Rosenbaum, *Midnight Movies*, 99.

34 Samuels, *Midnight Movies*, 60–1.

35 Justin Smith, 'British Cult Cinema', in *The British Cinema Book*, ed. Robert Murphy, 3rd edn (BFI/Palgrave Macmillan, 2009), 59. For an in-depth discussion of British cult films, see Smith, *Withnail and Us*; Kate Egan, 'Cult Films in British Cinema and Film Culture', in *The Routledge History of British Cinema*, ed. I. Q. Hunter, Laraine Porter and Justin Smith (London and New York: Routledge, 2017 forthcoming); and my own *British Trash Cinema*, 20–31.

36 Harry Medved and Michael Medved, *The Golden Turkey Awards* (London: Angus & Robinson, 1980), 204–8.

37 Jeffrey Sconce, 'Trashing the Academy: Taste, Excess and an Emerging Politics of Cinematic Style', *Screen* 36, no. 4 (1995): 372.

38 Scott Michaels and David Evans, *Rocky Horror: From Concept to Cult* (London: Sanctuary, 2002), 331.

39 Michaels and Evans, *Rocky Horror*, 332.

40 Bruce Austin, 'Portrait of a Cult Film Audience', *Journal of Communications* 31 (Spring 1981): 43–9.

41 Janet Staiger, *Perverse Spectators: The Practices of Film Reception* (New York: New York University Press, 2000), 45–46.

42 Patrick T. Kinkade and Michael A. Katovich, 'Toward a Sociology of Cult Films: Reading *Rocky Horror*', *Sociological Quarterly* 33, no. 2 (Summer 1992): 203.

43 Dean J. DeFino, *Faster, Pussycat! Kill! Kill!* (London and New York: Wallflower, 2014), 93.

44 Telotte, 'Beyond All Reason', 11.

45 Gregory A. Waller, 'Midnight Movies, 1980–85: A Market Study', in *Beyond All Reason*, 167–86.

46 Smith, 'British Cult Cinema', 62.

47 The term 'subcultural capital' is inspired by Pierre Bourdieu's use of 'cultural capital' – cultural and educational resources that effect social status and mobility – in his *Distinction: A Social Critique of the Judgement of Taste*, trans. Richard Nice (Cambridge, MA: Harvard University Press, 1984).

48 Nathan Hunt, 'The Importance of Trivia: Ownership, Exclusion and Authority in Science Fiction Fandom', in *Defining Cult Movies*, 186.

49 *Time Out, 100 Films to Change Your Life* (London: Ebury, 2006), 126.

50 On cult and collecting, see Charles Tashiro, 'The Contradictions of Video Collecting', *Film Quarterly* 50, no. 2 (1996): 11–18; Barbara Klinger, 'The Contemporary Cinephile: Film Collecting in the Post-Video Era', in *Hollywood Spectatorship: Changing Perceptions of Cinema Audiences*, ed. Melvyn Stokes and Richard Maltby (London: BFI, 2001), 132–51; and Kate Egan, 'The Amateur

Historian and the Electronic Archive: Power and the Function of Lists, Facts and Memories on "Video Nasty"-Themed Websites', *Intensities: The Journal of Cult Media, 3, Special Horror Issue* (Spring 2003). Available online: http://www.cultmedia.com/issue3/Aegan.htm (accessed 13 July 2015); and Lincoln Geraghty.

51 On cult tourism and *The Wicker Man*, see Benjamin Franks, Stephen Harper, Jonathan Murray, and Lesley Stevenson (eds), *The Quest for* The Wicker Man: *Historical, Folklore and Pagan Perspectives* (Edinburgh: Luath, 2005); and Jonathan Murray, Lesley Stevenson, Stephen Harper and Benjamin Franks (eds), *Constructing* The Wicker Man: *Film and Cultural Studies Perspectives* (Dumfries: University of Glasgow, Crichton Publications, 2005).

52 Lincoln Geraghty, *Cult Collectors: Nostalgia, Fandom and Collecting Popular Culture* (London and New York: Routledge, 2014), 181.

53 Hadley Freeman, *Life Moves Pretty Fast: The Lessons We Learned from Eighties Movies (and Why We Don't Learn Them from Movies Any More)* (London: Fourth Estate, 2015 EBook), loc. 578.

54 Quoted in Jami Bernard, *Quentin Tarantino: The Man and His Movies* (London: HarperCollins, 1995), 207.

55 French and French, *Cult Movies*, 123–4.

56 Geoff King, *Donnie Darko* (New York and London: Wallflower, 2007), 6.

57 Smith, *Withnail and Us*, 215.

58 Sexton, 'From Bad to Good', 141.

59 Gillian Orr, '10 years of *Mean Girls*: how the film defined a generation – and gave it a new language', *The Independent*, 1 May 2014. Available online: http://www.independent.co.uk/arts-entertainment/films/features/10-years-of-mean-girls-how-the-film-defined-a-generation-and-gave-it-a-new-language-9308410.html (accessed 23 November 2015).

60 Scott Mendelson, 'Why "Mean Girls" Still Matters, 10 Years Later', *Forbes*, 30 April 2014. Available online: http://www.forbes.com/sites/scottmendelson/2014/04/30/why-mean-girls-still-matters-10-years-later/ (accessed 23 November 2015).

61 Barbara Klinger, Barbara, *Beyond the Mutliplex: Cinema, Technologies, and the Home* (Berkeley: University of California Press, 2006), 188.

62 I'll pick up this point again in the next chapter, but see Joanne Hollows, 'The Masculinity of Cult', in *Defining Cult Movies*, 35–53.

63 The role of contemporary critics in all this intrigues me. Many films that turn up on their 'Top Ten' lists are decidedly obscure and 'culty' as well as box-office failures, rather as if critics have become cult gatekeepers, who judge films by their immanent cult qualities in order to differentiate their cinephile preferences from those of mass audiences. It was ever thus, I suspect, and an inevitable by-product of the endless tussles over cultural capital and aesthetic authority between insecure, supposedly vanguard elites and the popular audiences whom they serve but who are mostly indifferent to them. The critic as elite/semi-official cultist is a large and complex topic, which I haven't begun to think through fully, but I'll tentatively address it again in Chapter 4 with regard to the dreadful but critically lauded *Inherent Vice* (2015). It's touched on in my *British Trash Cinema*, 176–7.

64 Sarah Atkinson and Helen W. Kennedy, 'Secret, immersive cinema is likely to change the future of film', *The Conversation* 1 December 2015, available online: https://theconversation.com/secret-immersive-cinema-is-likely-to-change-the-future-of-film-50034 (accessed 7 December 2015).

65 Atkinson and Kennedy, 'Secret, immersive cinema'.

66 On *TV* binging, see Debra Ramsay, 'Confessions of a Binge Watcher', *CST Online*, available online: http://cstonline.tv/confessions-of-a-binge-watcher and Jason Mittell, 'Notes on Rewatching', *Just TV* (27 January 2011), available online: http://justtv.wordpress.com/2011/01/27/notes-on-rewatching/ (both accessed 25 November 2015).

67 See Henry Jenkins's entries on *Snakes on a Plane* on his blog 'Confessions of an Aca-Fan': 'The Snakes on a Plane Phenomenon' (21 July 2006), available online: http://www.henryjenkins.org/2006/06/the_snakes_on_a_plane_phenomen.html, and 'Snake Eyes' (24 August 2006), available online: http://www.henryjenkins. org/2006/08/snake_eyes.html (both accessed 23 November 2015).

68 Barbara Klinger, 'Becoming Cult: *The Big Lebowski*, Replay Culture and Male Fans', *Screen* 51, no. 1 (2010): 19.

69 See Iain Robert Smith, *The Hollywood Meme: Transnational Adaptations of American Film and Television* (Edinburgh: Edinburgh University Press, 2016).

70 Tantalizingly, according to Ernest Mathijs, in Schneider (ed.), *101 Cult Movies*, 42, 'teen audiences of the time reported being "roused"' by *Plan Nine from Outer Space*.

71 Richard Maltby, 'New Cinema Histories', in *Explorations in New Cinema Histories: Approaches and Case Studies*, ed. Richard Maltby, Daniel Biltereyst and Philippe Meers (Chichester: Wiley-Blackwell, 2011), 11.

72 Unkrich's website is: http://www.theoverlookhotel.com/ (accessed 12 December 2015).

Chapter 2

1   Raymond Durgnat, *Durgnat on Film* (London: Faber and Faber, 1976), 179.

2   Rob van Scheers, *Paul Verhoeven*, trans. Aletta Stevens (London: Faber and Faber, 1997), 271.

3   Leslie Halliwell, *Halliwell's Film & Video Guide 1997 Edition*, revised and updated 12th edition, ed. John Walker (London: HarperCollins, 1996), 678.

4   Anne Thompson, 'Is Bigger Better? The 21st Annual "Grosses Gloss"', *Film Comment*, March–April 1996, 63.

5   *The Razzie Reporter* 15, no. 1 (Summer 1996), http://www.razzies.com/ Reporter796.html/ (accessed 31 March 1999).

6   Mim Udovitch, 'What Do You Mean, You Liked *Showgirls*? Tarantino & Juliette', *Premiere* UK Edition June 1996, 60.

7   See Linda Ruth Williams, 'Nothing to Find', *Sight and Sound* 6, no. 1 (January 1996): 28–30; and Claire Monk, '*Showgirls*', *Sight and Sound* 6, no. 1 (January 1996): 51–2.

8   http://www.filmzone.com/Showgirls/shinfo.html/ (accessed 6 February 1997).

9   Williams, 'Nothing to Find', 28–30; Yvonne Tasker, *Working Girls: Gender and Sexuality in Popular Cinema* (London and New York: Routledge, 1998), 156–7.

10 Monk, '*Showgirls*', 52.

11 Larissa MacFarquhar, 'Start the Lava!', *Premiere* US Edition, October 1995, 82.

12 MacFarquhar, 'Start the Lava!', 80.

13 *Showgirls*'s bitter celebration of the 'End of History', the simultaneous triumphs of capitalism and trash culture, links it to 'Dumb White Guy' movies like *Bill &*

Ted's Excellent Adventure (1988), *Forrest Gump* (1994) and *Beavis and Butthead Do America* (1996). See I. Q. Hunter, 'Capitalism Most Triumphant: Bill & Ted's Excellent History Lesson', in *Pulping Fictions: Consuming Culture Across the Literature/Media Divide*, ed. Deborah Cartmell, I. Q. Hunter, Heidi Kaye and Imelda Whelehan (London: Pluto, 1996), 111–24.

14 Steve Chibnall, 'Double Exposures: Observations on *The Flesh and Blood Show*', in *Trash Aesthetics: Popular Culture and Its Audiences*, ed. Deborah Cartmell, I. Q. Hunter, Heidi Kaye and Imelda Whelehan (London: Pluto, 1997), 88.

15 Lisa A. Lewis, 'Introduction', in *The Adoring Audience: Fan Culture and Popular Media*, ed. Lewis (London: Routledge, 1992), 2. See also Joli Jensen, 'Fandom as Pathology: The Consequences of Characterisation' in Lewis, 9–29.

16 David Thomson, *A Biographical Dictionary of Film*, revised and enlarged edition (London: André Deutsch, 1994), 771.

17 On Verhoeven's irony and outsider's sensibility, see R. J. Ellis, ' "Are You a Fucking Mutant?": *Total Recall's* Fantastic Hesitations', *Foundation: The Review of Science Fiction* 65 (Autumn 1995): 81–97; and I. Q. Hunter, 'From SF to Sci-Fi: Paul Verhoeven's *Starship Troopers*', in *Writing and Cinema*, ed. Jonathan Bignell (London: Longman, 1999), 179–92.

18 See Scott Lash, *The Sociology of Postmodernism* (London: Routledge, 1990).

19 Chibnall, 'Double Exposures', 88.

20 Laura Mulvey, *Citizen Kane* (London: British Film Institute, 1992), 72.

21 Mulvey, *Citizen Kane,* 71.

22 Richard Rorty, *Contingency, Irony and Solidarity* (Cambridge: Cambridge University Press, 1989), 134.

23 Richard Rorty, 'The Pragmatist's Progress', in Umberto Eco with Richard Rorty, Jonathan Culler and Christine Brooke-Rose, *Interpretation and Overinterpretation*, ed. Stefan Collini (Cambridge: Cambridge University Press, 1992), 106.

24 Rorty, 'The Pragmatist's Progress', 97–8.

25 Ibid., 107.

26 Ibid.

27 Rorty, *Contingency, Irony and Solidarity*, 73.

28 Charles Taylor, 'Alive and Kicking', *Salon*, 31 March 2004. Available online: http://www.salon.com/2004/03/31/showgirls_2/ (accessed 26 November 2015).

29 Frédéric Bonnaud, 'The Captive Lover: An Interview with Jacques Rivette', *Senses of Cinema* 16 (September 2001). Available online: http://sensesofcinema.com/2001/16/rivette-2/ (accessed 26 November 2015).

30 Noël Burch, '*Showgirls* Round Table: Embarrassing *Showgirls*', *Film Quarterly* 56, no. 3 (2003): 36.

31 Ernest Mathijs and Xavier Mendik, *100 Cult Movies* (London: BFI/Palgrave Macmillan, 2011), 181. http://www.theatlantic.com/entertainment/archive/2014/04/its-still-ok-to-hate-em-showgirls-em/360644/; http://www.vanityfair.com/culture/2015/05/showgirls-20-anniversary-las-vegas.

32 Adam Nayman, *It Doesn't Suck: Showgirls* (Ontario: ECW Press, 2014).

33 Nayman, *It Doesn't Suck*, 97. On *Starship Troopers'* equally complex invitation to the audience to occupy 'radically different generic positions' (133), see Martin Barker, with Thomas Austin, *From* Antz *to* Titanic (London: Pluto, 2000), 120–33.

34 John Thornton Caldwell, 'Prefiguring DVD Bonus Tracks: Making-ofs and Behind-theScenes as Historic Television Programming Strategies Prototypes', in

Film and Television After DVD, ed. James Bennett and Tom Brown (New York: Routledge, 2008), 149–71.

35 Linda Ruth Williams, 'No Sex Please We're American', *Sight and Sound*, 6 June 2012. Available online: http://old.bfi.org.uk/sightandsound/feature/70 (accessed 26 November 2015).

36 There is also a sixty-minute German film, *Showgirls: Exposed* (2010), which has been touted as a sequel to *Showgirls*: http://www.screenjunkies.com/video/showgirls-exposed-trailer-2-delivers-neon-lights-and-booty/ (accessed 26 November 2015). A musical version of *Showgirls* played in New York in 2013: http://www.showgirlsthemusical.com/ (accessed 26 November 2016).

37 Nayman, *It Doesn't Suck*, 106–8. Jason Adams, 'Awfully Good: *Showgirls 2: Penny's from Heaven*, *JoBlo*' 25 September 2013. Available online: http://www.joblo.com/movie-news/awfully-good-showgirls-2-pennys-from-heaven (accessed 26 November 2015).

38 Rich Juzwiak, 'So Weird It's Weird: *Showgirls 2 Doesn't Suck*', *Gawker* 12 April 2012. Available online: http://gawker.com/5901364/so-weird-its-weird-showgirls-2-doesnt-suck (accessed 26 November 2015).

39 I. Q. Hunter, 'Beaver Las Vegas!: A fan-boy's defence of *Showgirls*', in *Unruly Pleasures: The Cult Film and Its Critics*, ed. Xavier Mendik and Graham Harper (Guildford: FAB Press, 2000), 187–201.

40 Deborah Cartmell, I. Q. Hunter, Heidi Kaye and Imelda Whelehan (eds), *Sisterhoods: Across the Literature/Media Divide* (London: Pluto, 1998).

41 Jacinda Read, 'The Cult of Masculinity: From Fan-Boys to Academic Bad-Boys', in *Defining Cult Movies: The Cultural Politics of Oppositional Taste*, ed. Mark Jancovich, Mark, Antonio Lazaro Reboll, Julian Stringer, and Any Willis (Manchester and New York: Manchester University Press, 2003), 54–70. Joanne Hollows, 'The Masculinity of Cult', in the same book, 35–53.

42 Rorty was a provocative choice, since his postmodern bourgeois liberalism, as he called it, as much as his cool relativism and accessible prose, was a red rag to radical theorists, cf. Christopher Norris, *Uncritical Theory: Post-Modernism, Intellectuals and the Gulf War* (London: Lawrence and Wishart, 1992). This was at a time when every article I sent off to a journal came back with at least one peer reviewer commenting that I should 'add more theory'.

43 I failed. The chapter wasn't entered into the RAE, as it was called then.

44 On the tribulations of aca-fans and fan scholars, see Mark Duffett, *Understanding Fandom: An Introduction to the Study of Media Fan Culture* (London and New York: Bloomsbury, 2013), 267–9.

45 Jonathan Gray, Cornel Sandvoss, and C. Lee Harrington (eds), *Fandom: Identities and Communities in a Mediated World* (New York and London: New York University Press, 2007), 3–4.

46 Melvyn Stokes and Matthew Jones, 'Windows on the World: Memories of European Cinemas in 1960s Britain', *Memory Studies* (forthcoming, 2016); Matthew Jones, 'Far from Swinging London: Memories of Non-urban Cinema-going in 1960s Britain', in *Cinema Beyond the City: Small-Town and Rural Film Culture in Europe*, ed. Judith Thissen and Clemens Zimmerman (London: BFI, forthcoming 2016).

47 On the *different* kinds of 'committed audiences' 'who work hardest to remember, make sense, make comparisons and connections across films, and examine their

own reactions to [films]' and for whom 'this kind of deliberation is ordinary, and pleasurable', see Martin Barker, Kate Egan, Tom Phillips and Sarah Relph, *Alien Audiences: Remembering and Evaluating a Classic Movie* (London: Palgrave Pivot: 2015 Ebook).

48 For what it's worth, I liked *Fifty Shades of Grey* (2015) for the same reasons as I did *Showgirls*. My response is summed up for me in an excellent article by Richard McCulloch, who writes that *Fifty Shades* is 'a really sophisticated piece of filmmaking. I admit I went in expecting a load of trashy nonsense that I could laugh at. What I didn't expect was a film that was in on the joke, but also smart enough to slowly reel me into the narrative without realising it,' 'Tied Up in Knots: A Defence of *Fifty Shades of Grey*', *Auteuse Theory: A Blog on Women's Cinema* (26 April 2015), online: auteusetheory.blogspot.co.uk/2015/04/tied-up-in-knots-in-defence-of-fifty.html (accessed 18 December 2015). What intrigues me, however, is what 'ordinary audiences' (*not* fans) made of the film, based as it was on a much despised but enormously popular novel. I attempt to make sense of the book's appeal in 'Pre-reading and Failing to read *Fifty Shades of Grey*', *Sexualities* 16, no. 8 (2013): 969–73, and recommend the entire issue, which is devoted to the book, for insights into its readership.

Chapter 3

1 This aperçu is a meme across a number of films, initially in *Lawrence of Arabia* (1962), when Lawrence extinguishes a match with his fingers, and then repeated in *All the President's Men* (1976) (conspiracy film), when Deep Throat tells an anecdote: 'The trick is not caring that it hurts.'

2 Deborah Yaffe, *Among the Janeites: A Journey through the World of Jane Austen Fandom* (Boston and New York: Mariner Books, 2013), 158.

3 Rorty, *Contingency, Irony and Solidarity*, 118.

4 Danny Peary, *Cult Movies: A Hundred Ways to Find the Reel Thing* (London: Vermillion, 1982), 170.

5 Peary, *Cult Movies*, 170.

6 Geoffrey Cocks, *The Wolf at the Door: Stanley Kubrick, History & the Holocaust* (New York: Peter Lang, 2004), 171.

7 A film on YouTube by JMC and MW, *The Shining Code 2.0* (2012) lays out the basic theory: https://www.youtube.com/watch?v=b0hOiasRsrA (accessed 30 December 2015).

8 Joe Martino, 'Stanley Kubrick Admits He Helped NASA Fake Moon Landings In New Film?', Collective Evolution 10 December 2015, http://www.collective-evolution.com/2015/12/10/stanley-kubrick-allegedly-admits-moon-landings-faked-in-new-film/ (accessed 30 December 2015). This appears to be a hoax, as the purported interview with Kubrick is with someone who looks nothing like him. The Moon theories emerge from long-standing conspiracies that are politically unstable, involving complete disbelief in the government.

9 John Brown, 'The Impossible Object: Reflections on *The Shining*', in *Cinema and Fiction: New Modes of Adapting 1950–1980*, ed. John Orr and Colin Nicholson (Edinburgh: Edinburgh University Press, 1992), 104–21.

10 Dennis Bingham, 'The Displaced Auteur: A Reception History of *The Shining*', in *Perspectives on Stanley Kubrick*, ed. Mario Falsetto (New York: GK Hall, 1996), 285–306.

11 Paul Mayersberg, 'The Overlook Hotel', *Sight and Sound* Winter 1980–81, available online: http://www.visual-memory.co.uk/sk/ss/theshining.htm (accessed 30 December 2015).

12 P. L. Titterington, 'Kubrick and *The Shining*', *Sight and Sound* 50, no. 2 (Spring 1981): 120–1.

13 Dan Nosowitz, 'Why Every Horror Film of the 1980s Was Built on "Indian Burial Grounds"', *Atlas Obscura* 22 October 2015, online: http://www.atlasobscura.com/articles/why-every-horror-film-of-1980s-was-built-on-indian-burial-grounds (accessed 30 December 2015).

14 Fredric Jameson, 'Historicism in *The Shining*', *Signatures of the Visible* (London and New York: Routledge, 1992), 82–99, available online: http://www.visual-memory.co.uk/amk/doc/0098.html (accessed 30 December 2015).

15 Jameson, 'Historicism in *The Shining*'.

16 A recut trailer by Robobos online wittily reimagines *The Shining* as a romantic comedy, riffing on the idea that it is essentially about fathers and sons: https://www.youtube.com/watch?v=sfout_rgPSA.

17 Roger Luckhurst, *The Shining* (British Film Institute/Palgrave Macmillan, 2013); Daniel Olson, Stanley Kubrick's The Shining: *Studies in the Horror Film* (Lakewood: Centipede Press, 2015); and Laura Mee, *The Shining* (Leighton Buzzard: Auteur, forthcoming).

18 On fans' interest in paratexts as ways of getting closer to the mysterious director, see Kate Egan, 'Precious Footage of the Auteur at Work: Framing, Accessing, Using, and Cultifying Vivian Kubrick's *Making the Shining*', *New Review of Film and Television Studies* 13, no. 1 (2015): 1–20.

19 Cocks, *The Wolf at the Door*, 219.

20 Mary Katherine Ham, "Frozen" is just Disney's "The Shining", online: https://mkhammer.squarespace.com/blog/2014/10/27/frozen-is-just-disneys-the-shining (30 October 2014) (accessed 30 December 2015).

21 Nathan Abrams, ' "A Double Set of Glasses": Stanley Kubrick and the Midrashic Mode of Interpretation', *De-Westernizing Film Studies*, ed. Saer Maty Ba and Will Higbee (London and New York: Routledge, 2012), 141; Nathan Abrams, 'Room for a Jewish Disaster?', *Jewish Quarterly* 61, no. 1 (2014): 58–60. Abrams latches on to *The Room* precisely 'because there is nothing explicitly Jewish about the film, or its creator, whatsoever' (58).

22 Abrams, ' "A Double Set" ', 148.

23 Mathijs and Sexton, *Cult Cinema*, 133: on Gnosticism and cult – 'an escape from this world through the acquisition of esoteric knowledge'.

24 Rita Felski, *The Limits of Critique* (Chicago and London: The University of Chicago Press, 2015 EBook), loc. 1236.

25 Graham Allen, 'The Unempty Wasps' Nest: Kubrick's *The Shining*, Adaptation, Chance, Interpretation', *Adaptation* 8, no. 3 (2015): 361.

26 Allen, 'The Unempty', 370.

27 This and other Kubrick conspiracies are gathered here: M. Morris, '10 Insane Conspiracy Theories About Stanley Kubrick', *Listverse*, 17 January 2014, online: http://listverse.com/2014/01/17/10-insane-conspiracy-theories-about-stanley-kubrick/ (accessed 30 December 2015). They are also discussed in a very sensible article in the British magazine: Dean Ballinger, 'The Kubrick Conspiracies', *Fortean Times* 332 (October 2015): 32–6. Some theories even relate *Eyes Wide Shut* to the faked Moon Landing, as Kubrick

allegedly wanted the film to be released thirty years to the day after the Apollo 11 launch.

28 IlluminatiWatcher, 'Illuminati Symbolism and Analysis of *Eyes Wide Shut*', 25 March 2015, online: http://illuminatiwatcher.com/illuminati-symbolism-and-analysis-of-eyes-wide-shut/ (accessed 30 December 2015).

29 Laurent Vachaud, '*Le secret de la pyramide*', *Positif* 623 (January 2013). It is covered in Damien LeBlanc, 'Is *Eyes Wide Shut* a Requiem for Stanley Kubrick's Estranged Scientologist Daughter?', *BLOUIN ARTINFO*, 9 August 2013, online: http://uk.blouinartinfo.com/news/story/943848/is-eyes-wide-shut-a-requiem-for-stanley-kubricks-estranged (accessed 30 December 2015).

30 Eve Kosofsky Sedgwick, *Touching Feeling: Affect, Pedagogy, Performativity* (Durham: Duke University Press, 2003), 139.

31 Nathan Abrams, *The New Jew in Film: Exploring Jewishness and Judaism in Contemporary Cinema* (London: I.B. Tauris, 2012), 71. See also 202–4.

32 On *Rosemary's Baby* as a post-Holocaust horror film, suffused with Jewish paranoia, see Nathan Abrams, 'The Banalities of Evil: Polanski, Kubrick, and the Reinvention of Horror', in *Religion in Contemporary European Cinema: The Postsecular Constellation*, ed. Costica Bradatan and Camil Ungureanu (New York and Abingdon: Routledge, 2014), 145–65.

33 Justin Smith, 'British Cult Cinema', in *The British Cinema Book*, ed. Robert Murphy, 3rd edn (BFI/Palgrave Macmillan, 2009), 59.

34 Jack Z. Bratich, *Conspiracy Panics: Political Rationality and Popular Culture* (Albany: State University of New York Press, 2008) 'consider constituent conspiratological skepticism as the anonymous murmurings of creative power, a realm of popular tactics located in the "interstices" of structured power' (169).

35 Gordon B. Arnold, *Conspiracy Theory in Film, Television and Politics* (Westport, CT: Praeger, 2008), 82–3.

36 David Bordwell, 'All Play and No Work? *Room 237*', *Observations on Film Art*, 7 April 2013, http://www.davidbordwell.net/blog/2013/04/07/all-play-and-no-work-room-237/.

37 Donato Totaro, '*Room 237*: Experimenting with documentary and film criticism', Offscreen 16, no. 9 (June 2015), online: http://offscreen.com/view/room-237-documentary-and-criticism (accessed 30 December 2015).

38 Chuck Klosterman, '*The Shining*, Immersion Criticism, and what might be the documentary of the year', *Grantland* (29 March 2013), online: http://grantland.com/features/documentary-year/ (accessed 30 December 2015).

39 Ernest Mathijs, 'Time Wasted', *Flow* 11, no. 10 (March 2010), online: http://flowtv.org/2010/03/time-wasted-ernest-mathijs-the-university-of-british-columbia/ (accessed 17 December 2012).

40 Girish Shambu, 'On *Room 237*, Criticism and Theory', 10 October 2012, http://girishshambu.blogspot.co.uk/2012/10/on-room-237-criticism-and-theory.html (accessed 30 December 2015). According to another irritated professional critic, Jonathan Rosenbaum, Ascher 'refuses to make any distinctions between interpretations that are semi-plausible or psychotic, conceivable or ridiculous, implying that they're all just "film criticism" and because everyone is a film critic nowadays, they all deserve to be treated with equal amounts of respect and/or mockery'. This is quoted in a highly amusing article on the film as 'an act of revenge from a filmmaker upon the critics' and the thin line between

interpretation and paranoia by Robert Greene, '*Room 237* and the Attack of the Id Critic', *Press Play* (9 April 2013), online: http://blogs.indiewire.com/pressplay/room-237-and-the-attack-of-the-id-critic (accessed 30 December 2015).

41 Check out: http://fantheories.wikia.com/wiki/FanTheories_Wiki. Theories range from *Taxi Driver* ending with a dream, the Harry Potter films taking place in Harry's head, to Disney films sharing the same universe.

42 For a wider conservative, and Christian, take on Hollywood as propaganda for liberalism, see the epic documentary from The Apologetics Group, *Pandora's Box Office: Hollywood's War on Traditional Family Values* (2010). Michael Medved, *Hollywood vs. America: Popular Culture and the War on American Values* (New York: HarperCollins, 1992) is the ur-text for what is essentially a conspiratorial intervention in America's ongoing culture wars.

43 'Paranoid Reading and Reparative Reading, or, You're So Paranoid, You Probably Think This Essay is about You', in *Touching Feeling*, 123–51.

44 Sedgwick, *Touching Feeling*, 143. The reparative criticism, which she offers as an alternative to the purely negative paranoia of repeatedly seeing through things, 'wants to assemble and confer plenitude on an object that will then have resources to offer to an inchoate self' (149). Her example is camp, which, though 'understood mainly as the degree of its self-hating complicity with an oppressive status quo' (149), could be reparatively rethought instead in terms of its more positive contingent and Bakhtinian features such as its '"over"-attachment to fragmentary, marginal, waste or leftover products'(150), a formulation that relates it to cult's fetishization of waste. IlliminatiWatcher's thoroughly paranoid article is reparative in a certain sense, insofar as while it is, in Sedgwick's phrase, an 'interpretive project of unveiling hidden violence' everywhere, it is also buzzing with surplus gleeful energy in its happy paranoia. The 'facts' may depress him, but enumerating them is clearly a life-enhancing pleasure.

45 See David Bordwell, *Making Meaning: Inference and Rhetoric in the Interpretation of Cinema* (Cambridge, MA: Harvard University Press, 1989), 249–74. I've echoed the argument of Bordwell's classic demolition job on rote film interpretation throughout this chapter, though I retain sympathy for the aesthetic, emotional and pragmatic uses of interpretation, however bizarre the results.

46 Felski, *The Limits of Critique*, loc. 857. I'll return to this in Chapter 10 with reference to *The Matrix*.

47 Richard Maltby, Daniel Biltereyst and Philippe Meers (eds), *Explorations in New Cinema Histories: Approaches and Case Studies* (Chichester: Wiley-Blackwell, 2011). There has indeed been such a 'turn' in Kubrick studies, with the opening of the Stanley Kubrick Archive at the University of Arts, London. Recent books and journal issues devoted to Kubrick, while hardly elbowing interpretation aside, have tended towards exploring the films' production and reception contexts and their process of adaptation via interviews and archival immersion. See the special issue on 'Kubrick and Adaptation' of *Adaptation* 8, no. 3 (2015); and Tatjana Ljujic, Peter Krämer, and Richard Daniels (eds), *Stanley Kubrick: New Perspectives* (London: Black Dog, 2015).

48 On 'reading formations' see Barbara Klinger, *Melodrama and Meaning: History, Culture, and the Films of Douglas Sirk* (Bloomington: Indiana University Press, 1994), xvi.

49 Totaro, '*Room 237*'.

50   Fan studies, of course, is all about how audiences interpret differently and make
     even the simplest film persuadably multi-readable. As Yoda, the acme of cult
     philosophers, once said, 'Many of the truths that we cling to depend on our
     point of view.' But seeing texts as polysemic, even if within set boundaries or
     curtailed by hierarchies of dominant and oppositional readings, doesn't give the
     satisfaction of a single definitive interpretation, whose truth is guaranteed by the
     social location of the reader and their emotional investment. The postmodern
     free-for-all (or nihilism) that my approach risks is strongly countered by identity-
     based interpretations, where the validity of an interpretation is commensurate
     with the identity of the interpreter. The obvious retort to this chapter is that for
     many people, who aren't comfortably ensconced in white privilege, interpretation
     is extremely important indeed and uncovering the hidden determinations of
     films (racism, homophobia, sexism, etc.) is an urgent political priority that can
     withstand endless repetition and the law of diminishing returns.

51   On the other hand, Deleuze's much-quoted remark in *Cinema 2: The Time Image*,
     trans. Hugh Tomlinson and Robert Galeta (New York: Athlone Press, 1985), that
     Kubrick's is a cinema of the brain is worth considering:

>   If we look at Kubrick's work, we see the degree to which it is the brain which
>   is mise-en-scene. Attitudes of body achieve a maximum level of violence, but
>   they depend on the brain. For, in Kubrick, the world itself is a brain, there
>   is identity of brain and world, as in the great circular and luminous table in
>   *Doctor Strangelove*, the giant computer in *2001 A Space Odyssey*, the Overlook
>   hotel in *The Shining*. Available online: http://www.visual-memory.co.uk/amk/
>   doc/0105.html (accessed 28 January 2016).

52   The classic work is Susan Sontag, 'Against Interpretation', in *Against Interpretation
     and Other Essays* (1966; New York: Dell, 1969), 13–23.

53   Klosterman, 'The Shining'.

54   Jonathan Crary, *24/7: Late Capitalism and the Ends of Sleep* (London: Verso, 2013).
     A somewhat paranoid and apocalyptic book itself, it declares that '24/7 is part of
     an immense incapacitation of visual experience' and that 'the contingency and
     variability of the visible world are no longer accessible'.

55   Crary, *24/7* EBook, loc 1018–28.

56   Mathijs and Sexton, *Cult Cinema*, 134.

57   Robert B. Ray in *The Avant-Garde Finds Andy Hardy* (Cambridge, MA, and
     London: Harvard University Press, 1995) has suggested certain cinephiliac
     procedures taken from Surrealism among other avant-garde research strategies
     that enable rich ideological readings not of cult films but of completely ordinary
     programmers like the *Andy Hardy* movies. The call for a more aestheticized and
     less theoretically driven kind of interpretation recurs in literary and film studies,
     whether it is Sontag's 'erotics of interpretation', Bordwell's formalist 'post-theory'
     or Felski's reparative readings based on Bruno Latour's actor-network theory,
     which is an aesthetic and affirmative 'creative remaking' (*The Limits of Critique*,
     loc. 3334) 'that leaves room for the aleatory and the unexpected, the chancy and
     the contingent' (loc 2776). See Felski, *The Limits of Critique*, loc. 2766–3368.
     Rónán McDonald, *The Death of the Critic* (London and New York: Continuum,
     2007), 143–9, covers the 'new aestheticism' in literary studies, including 'a new
     rapport between theories of criticism and questions of value' and 'ententes between
     academe and journalism' in the 2000s. Like Bordwell in *Making Meaning*, Greg

Taylor suggests reviving some of the tradition of 'critical disinterestedness – seeing the movie "as it really is" [as] a useful corrective to the impulse for oppositional fandom'. Taylor, *Artists*, 157. As I've suggested that impulse is not wholly to be expunged as it is an incitement to do new things with films, to use them creatively, at a time when academic interpretation can be somewhat dispiritingly predictable and repetitive. For an intriguing discussion of how academic writing might avoid a rise in 'aesthetic subjectivism' and instead pursue a 'reflexive approach to scholars' aesthetic judgements as hermeneutic constructions of self-identity', see Matt Hills, 'Media Academics as Media Audiences: Aesthetic Judgements in Media and Cultural Studies', in *Fandom: Identities and Communities in a Mediated World*, ed. Jonathan Gray, Cornel Sandvoss, and C. Lee Harrington (New York and London: New York University Press, 2007), 33–47.

On ways of risking interpretation without 'the safety of textual analysis' (188) and linking (sensible, testable) interpretations to studies of real and implied audiences and their conscious participation in activating meanings (and ideologies) in films, see Martin Barker, with Thomas Austin, *From* Antz *to* Titanic (London: Pluto, 2000). Cult audiences are intriguing here, as they are both *more* willing to enter the implied audience role of a film, especially one requiring specific skills and emotional attachments, and therefore get involved and enjoy it, and also *more* willing to reject a film's implied audience and get involved in counter-interpretations and uses of it, for example, as reading it as camp. Over time these counter-interpretations may become the dominant ones.

58 A first-rate reparative reading, which I came across just as I was finishing this chapter, is Steven W. Thrasher, '*Star Wars: The Force Awakens* – Black Lives Matter's First Science Fiction Film', *The Guardian* (2 January 2015), online: http://www.theguardian.com/film/2015/dec/29/star-wars-the-force-awakens-black-lives-matters-first-science-fiction-film (accessed 2 January 2016). Basing his reading on one storm trooper in *Star Wars: The Force Awakens* being black (John Boyega) Thrasher is 'led to picture an Afrofuturist army of black skins living under white masks' and argue that 'if all the stormtroopers are black, *The Force Awakens* can be read as a tale specifically rooted in black oppression and, more importantly, black awakening and rebellion; indeed, it could be read as the first science fiction film of the Black Lives Matter era'.

59 Mathijs and Mendik, *100 Cult Films*, 1.

60 Jason Mittell, '*Lost* in a Great Story: Evaluation in Narrative Television (and Television Studies)', in *Reading* Lost, ed. Roberta Pearson (London: I. B. Tauris, 2009), 119–38.

Chapter 4

1 Sol Yurick, *The Warriors* (1965; London: Panther, 1972), 181.

2 Danny Peary, *Cult Movies: A Hundred Ways to Find the Reel Thing* (London: Vermilion, 1982), 379–80.

3 Simone Murray, *The Adaptation Industry: The Cultural Economy of Contemporary Literary Adaptation* (New York and London: Routledge), 146.

4 Andrew Calcutt and Richard Shepherd, *Cult Fiction: A Reader's Guide* (London: Prion Books, 1998), x.

5 Calcutt and Shepherd, *Cult Fiction*, xii.
6 Clive Bloom, *Cult Fiction: Popular Reading and Pulp Theory* (Basingstoke: Macmillan 1996).
7 Thomas Reed Whissen, *Classic Cult Fiction: A Companion to Popular Cult Literature* (Westport, CT: Greenwood Press, 1992), x.
8 Whissen, *Classic Cult Fiction*, xxiii.
9 Ibid., xxx.
10 Ibid., x.
11 Needless to emphasize perhaps, there is little mention of books that have massive fandoms such as *Harry Potter*, or indeed genres sustained by long-standing and committed readerships such as that for Catherine Cookson and Barbara Taylor Bradford, Shirley Conran or Jackie Collins. Their cult, if that is what it is, is defined by lack of literary respect, and in short invisibility except on the bestsellers list, though Jacqueline Susann's *Valley of the Dolls* has been reissued as a cult novel, not so much for its success in the 1960s, when it spawned two cult films, but as providing a template for the sex and shopping novel. Its feminist potential was overlooked by contemporary critics blinded by its trashiness. Just as we might like to expand the category of cult film to embrace *Dirty Dancing* and *Titanic*, at the risk of diluting the term, so we might consider whether less obviously transgressive books like *Valley of the Dolls* and *Lace* are cult fictions too.
12 Sarah Martín Alegre, 'Cult Novels on the Screen: *Dune* and *The Naked Lunch*', *Actas Del XXI Congreso Internacional AEDEAN*, ed. Fernando Toda Iglesia, Juan A. Prieto Pablos, María José Mora, and Teresa López Soto (Seville: Secretariado de Publicationes de la Universidad de Sevilla, 1999), 141.
13 Linda Hutcheon, *A Theory of Adaptation* (New York and London: Routledge, 2006), 170.
14 Sarah Cardwell, *Adaptation Revisited: Television and the Classic Novel* (Manchester: Manchester University Press, 2001), 25.
15 George Bluestone, *Novels into Film* (Berkeley: University of California Press, 1966), 2.
16 Cardwell, *Adaptation Revisited*, 21.
17 I. Q. Hunter, 'Post-classical Fantasy Cinema: *The Lord of the Rings*', in *The Cambridge Guide to Literature on Screen*, ed. Deborah Cartmell and Imelda Whelehan (Cambridge: Cambridge University Press, 2007), 154–66.
18 Murray, *The Adaptation Industry*, 171.
19 Timothy Corrigan, 'Film and the Culture of Cult', in *The Cult Film Experience: Beyond All Reason*, ed. J. P. Telotte (Austin: University of Texas, 1991), 28.
20 On cult novelizations and remakes, see I. Q. Hunter, 'Cult and Adaptation', in *The Routledge Companion to Cult Cinema*, ed. Jamie Sexton and Ernest Mathijs (New York and Abingdon: Routledge, 2017 forthcoming).
21 Brian McFarlane, *Novel to Film: An Introduction to the Theory of Adaptation* (Oxford: Clarendon Press, 1996).
22 Simon Braund (ed.), *The Greatest Movies You'll Never See* (London: Cassell Illustrated, 2013), 144–7.
23 Braund, *The Greatest Movies*, 100–1.
24 Ralph Freedman, *Hermann Hesse: Pilgrim of Crisis A Biography* (1978; London: Abacus, 1981), 9.
25 Freedman, *Hermann Hesse*, 12.
26 Murray, *The Adaptation Industry*, 158.

27 Sarah Martín Alegre, 'Cult Novels', 144.

28 Ernest Mathijs, *The Cinema of David Cronenberg: From Baron of Blood to Cultural Hero* (London and New York: Wallflower, 2008), 163.

29 Dudley Andrew, 'From Concepts in Film Theory', in *Film Theory and Criticism*, ed. Leo Braudy and M. Cohen, 6th edn (Oxford: Oxford University Press, 2004), 463.

30 Mathijs, *The Cinema*, 171.

31 See I. Q. Hunter, 'Spielberg and Adaptation', in *The Blackwell Companion to Steven Spielberg*, ed. Nigel Morris (Chichester: Wiley-Blackwell, 2017 forthcoming).

32 As one who found it, for all its technical brio, almost as unwatchable as *The Master*, I'm struck by why critics tended to like it. How on earth do these judgements get made? What is wrong with these people?

Chapter 5

1 See Cynthia Erb, *Tracking King Kong: A Hollywood Icon in World Culture* (Detroit: Wayne University Press, 1998).

2 Thomas Doherty, *Teenagers and Teenpics: The Juvenilization of American Movies in the 1950s* (Philadelphia: Temple University Press, 2002), 2–36.

3 Jim Hillier and Aaron Lipstadt, *BFI Dossier Number 7: Roger Corman's New World* (London: British Film Institute, 1981), 12–20.

4 Joao Luiz Vieira and Robert Stam, 'Parody and Marginality: The Case of Brazilian Cinema' *Framework* 28 (1985): 37.

5 On sexploitation and porn versions, see Bethan Jones, 'Slow Evolution: "First time Fics" and *The X-Files* Porn Parody', *Journal of Adaptation in Film & Performance* 6, no. 3 (2013): 369–85; and Iain R Smith, 'When Spiderman became Spiderbabe: Pornographic Appropriation and the Political Economy of the "Soft-Core Spoof" Genre', in *Peep Shows. Cult Film and the Cine-Erotic*, ed. Xavier Mendik (London: Wallflower Press, 2012), 109–18.

6 On remakes, see Constantine Verevis, *Film Remakes* (Edinburgh: Edinburgh University Press, 2006), 3–30.

7 Robert Stam, 'Beyond Fidelity: The Dialogics of Adaptation', in *Film Adaptation*, ed. James Naremore (New Brunswick, NJ: Rutgers University Press, 2000), 66.

8 I. Q. Hunter, 'The Irrational Enlargement of *Queen Kong*', *Film International* 15, no. 3 (2005): 42–9.

9 Howard Sounes, *Seventies: The Sights, Sounds and Ideas of a Brilliant Decade* (New York: Simon and Schuster, 2006), 223.

10 Ted Morgan, 'Sharks: The Making of a Best Seller', in *American Mass Media: Industries and Issues*, ed. Robert Atwan, Barry Orton and William Vesterman (New York: Random House, 1978), 140–50.

11 Martin Barker, 'News, Reviews, Clues, Interviews and Other Ancillary Materials – A Critique and Research Proposal', *Scope: An Online Journal of Film & TV Studies* February (2004), online: http://www.scope.nottingham.ac.uk/issue.php?issue=feb2 004&section=article (accessed 10 March 2009).

12 See Verevis, *Film Remakes*, 130–1, for a discussion of this in relation to remakes.

13 See Thomas Leitch, 'Adaptation: The Genre', *Adaptation* 1, no. 2 (2008): 106–20 for an analysis of adaptation as a genre.

14 Catherine Grant, 'Recognising *Billy Budd* in *Beau Travail*: Epistemology and Hermeneutics of Auteurist "Free" Adaptation', *Screen* 43, no. 1 (2002): 57.

15 I argue this with reference to Jackson's *The Lord of the Rings* trilogy in I. Q. Hunter, 'Post-Classical Fantasy Cinema: *The Lord of the Rings*', in *The Cambridge Guide to Literature on Screen*, ed. Deborah Cartmell and Imelda Whelehan (Cambridge: Cambridge University Press, 2007), 154–66.

16 Sarah Cardwell, *Adaptation Revisited: Television and the Classic Novel* (Manchester: Manchester University Press, 2002), 62.

17 For a discussion of intertextuality and transtextuality in Spielberg and especially *1941*, see Nigel Morris, *The Cinema of Steven Spielberg: Empire of Light* (London and New York: Wallflower Press, 2007), 66–9.

18 Among the most comprehensive and persuasive are Gérard Genette (1997 [1982]) *Palimpsests: Literature in the Second Degree*, trans. Channa Newman and Claude Doubinsky (Lincoln: University of Nebraska Press, 2007), and Stam, 'Beyond Fidelity'.

19 John Baxter, *Steven Spielberg: The Unauthorised Biography* (London: HarperCollins, 1997), 120–1.

20 Dean Crawford, *Shark* (London: Reaktion, 2008), 77.

21 Herman Melville, *Moby-Dick or, The Whale*, (London: Penguin, [1851] 1992), 187.

22 For an extended Jungian comparison of *Moby-Dick* and *Jaws*, see Janice Hocker Rushing and Thomas S. Frentz, *Projecting the Shadow: The Cyborg Hero in American Film* (Chicago and London: University of Chicago Press, 1995), 78–99; and for a discussion of how *The Life Aquatic with Steve Zissou* also shares 'some striking similarities' with *Moby-Dick*, see Dyalan Govender, Wes Anderson's *The Life Aquatic with Steve Zissou* and Melville's *Moby Dick*: A Comparative Study, *Literature/Film Quarterly* 36, no. 1 (2008): 61–7.

23 Christine Geraghty, *Now a Major Motion Picture: Film Adaptations of Literature and Drama* (Lanham, MD: Rowman & Littlefield, 2008), 197.

24 A summary of some of these films is provided in Jay Slater, 'The Tooth Hurts!', *The Dark Side* 126 (2007): 40–3; Patrick Jankiewicz, *Just When You Thought It Was Safe: A* Jaws *Companion* (Albany: BearManor Media, 2009), 199–206. See also Crawford, *Shark*, 82–4. Vieira and Stam, 'Parody and Marginality' offers a politically sophisticated analysis of *Bacalhau* as a self-denigrating admission of Brazilian cinema's inferiority to dominant cinema.

25 C. P. Lee and Andy Willis, *The Lost World of Cliff Twemlow: The King of Manchester Exploitation Movies* (Manchester: Hotun Press, 2009), 214–17.

26 Donato Totaro, 'A Genealogy of Italian Popular Cinema: The Filone', *Off Screen* 15, no. 11 (November 2011), online: http://offscreen.com/view/genealogy_filone (accessed 17 December 2015).

27 J. Hoberman, *The Magic Hour: Film at Fin de Siècle* (Philadelphia: Temple University Press, 2003), 147.

28 'Mother Nature goes ape-shit kind of movie' is how Quentin Tarantino describes *Lost Weekend* in the documentary, *Not Quite Hollywood: The Wild, Untold Story of Ozploitation* (2008).

29 Noel Carroll, 'Nightmare and the Horror Film: The Symbolic Biology of Fantastic Beings', *Film Quarterly* 34, no. 3 (1981): 23.

30 Hillier and Lipstadt, *BFI Dossier*, 41.

31 Dante confirmed the story about Universal dropping the plagiarism suit when I asked him at the *Cine Excess IV* Conference in London on 31 April 2010.

32 Hillier and Lipstadt, *BFI Dossier*, 45.

33 Ibid., 45.

34 Jane Caputi, *The Age of Sex Crime* (London: The Women's Press, 1988), 147.

35 See John Izod, *Hollywood and the Box Office, 1895-1986* (New York: Columbia University Press, 1988), 184–5.

36 Peter Guber, with Barbara Witus, *Inside The Deep* (New York: Bantam, 1977), 2.

37 Peter Benchley, 'Oceans in Peril' (1995), available online: http://seawifs.gsfc.nasa. gov/OCEAN_PLANET/HTML/ocean_planet_book_peril_intro.html (accessed 6 June 2009). The exploitation versions do not, however, experiment with turning the shark into the outright hero of the narrative, a twist accomplished only in the 'Hookjaw' strip in *Action* comic, and the 2006 videogame, *Jaws Unleashed*. On Hookjaw, see Martin Barker, *Action: The Story of a Violent Comic* (London: Titan Books, 1990), 13.

38 Crawford, *Shark*, 83.

39 Steve Alten, *Meg: A Novel of Deep Terror* (London: Doubleday, 2007).

40 For a striking interpretation of *Open Water* as an 'anti-porn film' challenging what he sees as *Jaws*'s pornographic sexism, see Walter C. Metz, 'Shark Porn: Film Genre, Reception Studies, and Chris Kentis' *Open Water*', *Film Criticism* 31, no. 3 (2007): 36–58.

41 *Frozen* (2010), a reworking of *Open Water* in which tourists trapped on a stalled ski lift are menaced by wolves, directly references *Jaws* in a discussion of the worst ways to die. The film was made by Bigger Boat productions.

42 Online: http://www.imdb.com/title/tt0470055/usercomments?start=0 (accessed 10 March 2009).

43 Filming murders from the killer's point of view was revitalized by *Jaws*, but it was not of course a new cinematic trope. It was a device used in *Dr Jekyll and Mr Hyde* (1932), for example, and to depict Jack the Ripper's killings in *A Study in Terror* (1965).

44 Quoted in Nigel Andrews, *Jaws* (London: Bloomsbury, 1999), 117.

45 Roger Corman, with Jim Jerome, *How I Made a Hundred Movies in Hollywood and Never Lost a Dime* (Cambridge, MA: Da Capo Press, 1998), xi.

46 Carol Clover, *Men, Women and Chain Saws: Gender in the Modern Horror Film* (London: British Film Institute, 1992), 20.

47 The wildly differing interpretations are comprehensively summarized in Lester D. Friedman, *Citizen Spielberg* (Urbana and Chicago: University of Illinois Press, 2006), 163–4.

48 Andrews, *Jaws*, 25.

49 Dan Rubey, 'The *Jaws* in the Mirror', *Jump Cut: A Review of Contemporary Media* 10–11 (1976): 20–3, online: http://www.ejumpcut.org/archive/onlinessays/JC10-11folder/JawsRubey.html (accessed 5 September 2008).

50 Walter C. Metz, 'The Cold War's "Undigested Apple-Dumpling": Imaging *Moby-Dick* in 1956 and 2001', *Literature/Film Quarterly* 32, no. 3 (2004): 228.

51 Metz, 'The Cold War's', 228.

52 See Andrews, *Jaws*, 143–50 on the 'feeding frenzy for semioticians' (143) that followed the film's release.

53 For an analysis of *Jaws* as a submarine film in the tradition of *The Enemy Below* (1957) and *Run Silent, Run Deep* (1958), see Robert Willson, '*Jaws* as Submarine Movie', *Jump Cut: A Review of Contemporary Media* 15 (1977): 32–3, online: http://www.ejumpcut.org/archive/onlinessays/JC15folder/JawsSubmarine.html (accessed

5 September 2008). See also Linda Maria Koldau, 'Submarines and Sharks: Musical Settings of a Silent Menace', *Horror Studies* 1, no. 1 (2010): 89–100.

54 Antonia Quirke, *Jaws* (London: British Film Institute, 2002), 49.

55 Richard Dawkins, *The Selfish Gene* (Oxford: Oxford University Press, 1976).

56 Linda Hutcheon, *A Theory of Adaptation* (New York and London: Routledge, 2006), 117.

57 Two accessible introductions to memetic are Daniel Dennett, *Darwin's Dangerous Idea: Evolution and the Meanings of Life* (London: Allen Lane The Penguin Press, 1995), 335–69; and Susan Blackmore, *The Meme Machine* (Oxford: Oxford University Press, 1999).

58 James Delingpole, *Fin* (London: Picador, 2000); Steven Hall, *The Raw Shark Texts* (Edinburgh: Canongate, 2007); Will Self, *Shark* (London: Penguin, 2015); and Ellen Connolly and Stephen Bates, 'Monster Munch: Three Shark Attacks in 24 Hours Throw Australian into Jaws Panic', *Guardian*, 13 January 2009, online: http://www.guardian.co.uk/world/2009/jan/13/australia-shark-attacks (accessed 6 June 2009).

59 See HouseKeeper13, 'Working Out the Kinks' (2008), online: http://www.fanfiction.net/s/4652160/1/Working_out_the_Kinks (accessed 8 March 2009).

60 Damien Hirst, *ABC* (London: Other Criteria/White Cube, 2013).

61 John Ellis, 'The Literary Adaptation: An Introduction', *Screen* 23, no. 1 (1982): 4–5.

Chapter 6

1 Nostalgia has inspired some recent cult and academic interest in British sexploitation films. The first books on sexploitation were David McGillivray, *Doing Rude Things: A History of the British Sex Film* (London: Sun Tavern Fields, 1992), (later adapted into a TV documentary) and the most comprehensive, Simon Sheridan, *Keeping the British End Up: Four Decades of Saucy Cinema* 4th rev. edn (London: Titan Books, 2011). See also Leon Hunt, *British Low Culture: From Safari Suits to Sexploitation* (London: Routledge, 1998); Sian Barber, 'The Pinnacle of Popular Taste?: The Importance of *Confessions of a Window Cleaner*', *Scope: An Online Journal of Film and Television Studies* 18 (October 2010), available http://www.scope.nottingham.ac.uk/article.php?issue=18&id=1246 (accessed 30 December 2015); and my *British Trash Cinema* (London: Palgrave Macmillan/British Film Institute, 2013), 101–38. My 'From Window Cleaner to Potato Man: Confessions of a Working Class Stereotype', in *British Comedy Cinema*, ed. I. Q. Hunter and Laraine Porter (London and New York: Routledge, 2012), 154–70, looks at the recent revival of the genre.

2 One of the most effective dramatic exploitations of the thrill and dangers of sex was actually in the horror genre, notably *Virgin Witch* (1970) and *Vampyres* (1974) and the 'lesbian vampire' films made by Hammer such as 'the Karnstein trilogy', *The Vampire Lovers* (1970), *Lust for a Vampire* (1971) and *Twins of Evil* (1972), and *Countess Dracula* (1971).

3 In Gillian Freeman's *The Undergrowth of Literature* (London: Thomas Nelson, 1967), it is claimed that 'Ninety per cent of pornographic books imported into England are sado-masochistic. Obviously the market is geared to demand and the demand is for sadistic sex' (56).

4   On Sade adaptations generally, see Jack Hunter (ed.), *Sadomania: Sinema de Sade* (London: Glitter Books, 2012), in which he describes *Cruel Passion* as 'predictably tame' (30).

5   Tanya Krzywinska, *Sex and the Cinema* (London and New York: Wallflower, 2006), 203.

6   Sheridan, *Keeping the British End Up*, 183

7   Krzywinska, *Sex and the Cinema*, 201.

8   Ibid., 204.

9   Ibid., 200.

10 On *Killer's Moon*, see Hunter, *British Trash Cinema*, 68–70.

11 The 80m BBFC cut was issued in a longer 86m version on the UK 1980 Hokushin video release, which is the version referred to here. See the unusually authoritative entry in Wikipedia for the differences between this pre-BBFC cut, the video version and the American video cut, *Adam and Nicole*. Sen had previously produced a Swedish-British film, *The Intruders* [*Swedish Sex Games*] (1974), also with Chris Chittell, which apparently has a similarly dark tone; see http://www.pre-cert.co.uk/display.php?vId=UK00172 (accessed 30 December 2015).

12 Sheridan, *Keeping the British End Up*, 138

13 Ibid.

14 gavcrimson, 'Deeley-licious: The Brief, Tragic but Memorable Career of Heather Deeley', gavcrimson.blogspot.co.uk (30 August 2008), online: http://gavcrimson.blogspot.co.uk/2008/08/deeley-licious-brief-tragic-but.html?zx=bb16ba40c0380fe2 (accessed 17 November 2015).

15 See, for example, http://www.newstatesman.com/blogs/richard-herring/2007/07/jenny-agutter-love-woman-film; http://www.sabotagetimes.com/tv-film/this-is-jenny-agutter/ (accessed 30 December 2015).

Chapter 7

1   Richard Burt, *Unspeakable ShaXXXspeares: Queer Theory and American Kiddie Culture* (New York: St . Martin's Press, 1998), 122.

2   Published, non-erotic, spoofs include *Harvard Lampoon's Bored of the Rings*, Harvard. Lampoon, *Bored of the Rings: A Parody of J. R. R. R. Tolkien's 'The Lord of the Rings'* (New York: Signet, 1969), written during the hippie Tolkien cult, and, more recently, A. R. R. R. Roberts, *The Soddit Let's Cash in Again* (London: Gollancz, 2003); and A. R. R. R. Roberts, *The Sellamillion*(London: Gollancz, 2004).

3   On hardcore versions, see the documentary, *Shaving Ryan's Privates* (TX. Five 3 November 2003) and http://www.strangethingsarehappening.com/70sadultspoofs.html.

4   Linda Williams, *Hard Core: Power, Pleasure, and the 'Frenzy of the Visible'* (London: Pandora, 1990), 48.

5   See I. Q. Hunter, '*A Clockwork Orgy*: A User's Guide' in *Realities and Remediations: The Limits of Representation*, ed. Elizabeth Wells and Tamar Jeffers McDonald (Newcastle upon Tyne: Cambridge Scholars Publishing, 2007), 101–11; revised and reprinted in *Peep Shows: Cult Film and the Cine-Erotic*, ed. Xavier Mendik (London and New York: Wallflower Press, 2012), 126–34.

6   Constance Penley, 'Crackers and Whackers: The White Trashing of Porn', in *Porn Studies,* ed. Linda Williams (Durham and London: Duke University Press, 2004), 328.

7   Claire Hines, 'Playmates of the Caribbean: Taking Hollywood, Making Hard-core', in *Hard to Swallow: Hard-core Pornography on Screen,* ed. Claire Hines and Darren Kerr (London and New York: Wallflower, 2012), 126–44.

8   Lynn Comella, 'Studying Porn Cultures', *Porn Studies* 1, nos. 1–2 (2014): 65.

9   See I. Q. Hunter, 'Adaptation XXX', in *The Oxford Handbook of Adaptation,* ed. Thomas Leitch (Oxford: Oxford University Press, in press).

10 See, for example, the largely positive reviews at CultureDose.net, online: http://culturedose.net/review.php?rid=10004676 (accessed 19 July 2013), and Modamag. com, online: http://modamag.com/Lord%20of%20the%20G-Strings_DVD.htm (accessed 16 March 2015).

11 Carole Laseur, 'Australian Exploitation Film: The Politics of Bad Taste', *Continuum: The Australian Journal of Media & Culture* 5, no. 2 (1990), online http://wwwmcc. murdoch.edu.au/ReadingRoom/5.2/Laseur.html (accessed 30 July 2004).

12 Mark Jancovich, 'Cult Fictions: Cult Movies, Subcultural Capital and the Production of Cultural Distinctions', *Cultural Studies* 16, no. 2 (2002): 311–12.

13 Craig Fischer, '*Beyond the Valley of the Dolls* and the Exploitation Genre', *The Velvet Light Trap* 30 (Fall): 18–33.

14 Fischer, '*Beyond*', 20.

15 Ibid.

16 Richard Dyer,. 'Idol Thoughts: Orgasm and Self-Reflexivity in Gay Pornography', in *More Dirty Looks: Gender, Pornography and Power,* ed. Pamela Church Gibson (London: British Film Institute, 2004), 109.

17 Graham Fuller 'Kingdom Come', *Film Comment* 40, no. 1 (2004): 24–9.

18 Laura Kipnis, *Bound and Gagged: Pornography and the Politics of Fantasy in America* (Durham: Duke University Press, 1999); Penley, 'Crackers'.

19 Roger Kaufman, '*Lord of the Rings* Taps a Gay Archetype', *The Gay and Lesbian Review Worldwide,* July–August (2003): 32.

20 Kaufman, '*Lord of the Rings*', 32.

21 Ibid., 33.

22 On Tolkien slash fiction, see Anna Smol, 'Oh … Oh … Frodo!: Readings of Male Intimacy in *The Lord of the Rings*', *Modern Fiction Studies* 50, no. 4 (2004): 949–79.

23 Milly Chen, 'When Frodo met Sam', *Sunday Times Style* 18 (July 2004): 16.

24 Sam Littlefoot, 'When the Wizard's Away …', *The Library of Moria: Lord of the Rings Slash and RPS Fanfiction Archive* (2005), online: http://www.libraryofmoria. com/aragornfrodo/whenthewizardsaway.txt (accessed 3 March 2005).

25 Catherine Salmon and Donald Symons, *Warrior Lovers: Erotic Fiction, Evolution and Female Sexuality* (London: Weidenfeld & Nicholson, 2001), 95.

26 Salmon and Symons, *Warrior Lovers*, 92.

27 Burt, *Unspeakable*, 82.

28 Feona Attwood, 'Reading Porn: The Paradigm Shift in Pornography Research', *Sexualities* 5, no. 1 (2002): 102–3.

29 Since this essay was first published, research on pornography and its audiences has expanded considerably, for example: Clarissa Smith, Feona Attwood and Martin Barker, *Pornresearch.org: Preliminary findings* (2012), online: http://www. pornresearch.org/Firstsummaryforwebsite.pdf (accessed 10 July 2015).

30 Jennifer Wicke, 'Through a Gaze Darkly: Pornography's Academic Market', in *More Dirty Looks: Gender, Pornography and Power*, ed. Pamela Church Gibson (London: British Film Institute, 2004), 181.

31 I attempt this in Hunter, '*A Clockwork Orgy*'.

32 Laurence O'Toole, 'The Experience of Pornography', in *Porn 101: Eroticism, Pornography, and the First Amendment*, ed. James E. Elias, Veronica Diehl Elias, Vern L. Bullough, Gwen Brewer, Jeffrey J. Douglas and Will Jarvis (Amherst, NY: Prometheus Books, 1999), 284.

33 Martin Barker, 'Taking the Extreme Case: Understanding a Fascist Fan of Judge Dredd', in *Trash Aesthetics: Popular Culture and Its Audience*, ed. Deborah Cartmell, I. Q. Hunter, Heidi Kaye and Imelda Whelehan (London: Pluto, 1997), 14–30.

34 Susan Backlinie, who plays Chrissie, the shark's first victim, had appeared in *Penthouse* in January 1973 and in 1977, billed as 'The Nude from 'Jaws', would be in the February issue of *Mayfair*.

35 Andrew Yule, *Spielberg: Father of the Man* (London: Warner Books, 1997), 60

36 Peter Benchley, *Jaws* (London: Pan, 1975), 23.

37 Benchley, *Jaws*, 161.

38 On porn versions of horror films, see Thomas J. Watson, 'There's Something Rotten in the State of Texas: Genre, Adaptation and *The Texas Vibrator Massacre*', *Journal of Adaptation in Film & Performance* 6, no. 3 (2013): 387–400; and Steve Jones, '*Porn of the Dead*: Necrophilia, Feminism, and Gendering the Undead', in *Zombies Are Us: Essays on the Humanity of the Walking Dead*, ed. Cory Rushton and Christopher Moreman (Jefferson: McFarland, 2011), 40–60.

39 Benchley, *Jaws*, 9–10.

40 Hines, 'Playmates', 135.

41 http://www.avmaniacs.com/forums/showthread.php?t=34744 (accessed 30 December 2015) posted by Garrett L., 1 February 2008.

42 Linda Williams, *Screening Sex* (Durham and London: Duke University Press, 2008), 316.

43 Iain R Smith, 'When Spiderman became Spiderbabe: Pornographic Appropriation and the Political Economy of the "Soft-Core Spoof" Genre', in *Peep Shows. Cult Film and the Cine-Erotic*, ed. Xavier Mendik (London: Wallflower Press, 2012), 118.

44 For an attempt to interpret British hardcore pornography in terms of theme, style and authorship, see I. Q. Hunter, 'Naughty Realism: The Britishness of British Hardcore R18s', *Journal of British Cinema and Television* 11, nos. 2–3 (2014): 152–71.

45 Clarissa Smith, 'Reel Intercourse: Doing Sex on Camera', in *Hard to Swallow*, 197–8.

Chapter 8

1 For example, the entry for *2001* in the filmography of my *British Science Fiction Cinema* (London and New York: Routledge, 1999), 197; states that it was based on 'The Sentinel. Strictly speaking, this was a mistake, but it merely reiterated common and uncontroversial knowledge'.

2 Arthur C. Clarke, *The Lost Worlds of 2001* (London: Sidgwick and Jackson, 1972), 31–2; and Vincent LoBrutto, *Stanley Kubrick: A Biography* (London: Faber and Faber, 1998), 263.

3 Jerome Abel (ed.), *The Making of Kubrick's 2001* (New York: Signet, 1970), 15–23; Clarke, *Lost Worlds*, 19–28; and Piers Bizony, *2001: Filming the Future* (London: Aurum, 1994), 75.

4 Neil McAleer, *Odyssey: The Authorised Biography of Arthur C. Clarke* (London: Victor Gollancz, 1993), 193.

5 Arthur C. Clarke, *2001: A Space Odyssey* (London: Arrow, 1968), 3. On the cover of both the British Arrow paperback version and the American New English Library edition, the screenplay is credited to Stanley Kubrick and Arthur C. Clarke, giving priority to the director.

6 Thomas Van Parys, 'The Study of Novelisation: A Typology and Secondary Bibliography', *Belphegor* 10, no. 2 (2011), online: http://etc.dal.ca/belphegor/vol10_no2/articles/10_02_paryst_noveli_fr.html (accessed 12 September 2011).

7 Peter Krämer, *2001: A Space Odyssey* (London: BFI/Palgrave Macmillan, 2010), 8.

8 LoBrutto, *Stanley Kubrick*, 268.

9 Krämer, *2001*, 42.

10 Clarke, *Lost Worlds*, 31.

11 Thomas Van Parys, 'The Commercial Novelization: Research, History, Differentiation', *Literature/Film Quarterly* 37, no. 4 (2009): 312.

12 Carrol L. Fry, 'From Technology to Transcendence: Humanity's Evolutionary Journey in *2001: A Space Odyssey*', *Extrapolation* 44, no. 3 (2003): 333.

13 Michel Chion, *Kubrick's Cinema Odyssey*, trans. C. Gorbman (London: BFI, 2001), 7.

14 Clarke, *Lost Worlds*, 30.

15 Van Parys, 'The Commercial Novelization', 307.

16 *Boston Globe*, quoted in Agel, *The Making of 2001*, 256.

17 Clarke, *2001*, 217.

18 Ibid., 223.

19 Krämer, *2001*, 16; see also Clarke, *Lost Worlds*, 239.

20 Peter Nicholls, John Brosnan and N. Lowe, '*2001: A Space Odyssey*', in *SFE: The Encyclopedia of Science Fiction. Third Edition* (2011), ed. John Clute and David Langford, online: http://www.sf-encyclopedia.com/Entry/2001_a_space_odyssey (accessed 11 October 2011).

21 Clarke, *2001*, 39.

22 Joseph Gelmis, 'The Film Director as Superstar: Stanley Kubrick', in *Stanley Kubrick Interviews*, ed. Gene D. Phillips (Jackson: University Press of Mississippi, 2001), 96.

23 Krämer, *2001*, 47–8.

24 Abel, *The Making of 2001*, 299.

25 David Bordwell, 'The Art Cinema as a Mode of Practice', *Film Criticism* 4 (1979): 59.

26 Sara Gwenllian-Jones and Roberta Pearson (eds), *Cult Television* (Minneapolis: University of Minnesota Press, 2004), xvi.

27 Greg Taylor, *Artists in the Audience: Cults, Camp, and American Film Criticism* (Princeton: Princeton University Press, 1999), 133.

28 Mike Kaplan, 'Kubrick: A Marketing Odyssey', *The Guardian* (2 November 2007).

29 McAleer, *Odyssey*, 223.

30 Clarke, *2001*, 201.

31 Robert Castle, 'The Interpretative Odyssey of *2001*: Of Humanity and Hyperspace', *Bright Lights Film Journal* 46 (2005), online: http://www.brightlightsfilm.com/46/2001.php (accessed 10 July 2011).

32 Speaking personally, I am obviously ambivalent and even hostile towards Clarke's novelization (for all its merits) and his sequels to *2001*. That is because I am, like many cineastes, self-evidently a Kubrick cultist, and Clarke, frankly, *gets in the way* of my confident attribution of intention and meaning solely to the director. This is clearly ridiculous. Film is a collaborative industry and, although Kubrick had an exceptional measure of control over his films, he usually co-wrote their scripts from previously published sources and relied upon the skills of numerous technicians to realize them. It is also ridiculous because the novelization offers another route into the *2001* universe, and, as I remark above, a cultist should generally welcome any opportunity to expand his recherché knowledge of a cult film and thereby enhance his cultural capital. I mention this only because, in my case, *caring* about the film for much of my life (and not especially caring for SF literature) leads me to distinguish radically between the film and the novel, which energizes (but hopefully does not determine) my analysis of Kubrick's agonistic style of adaptation. David Church has written about how Kubrick is a kind of gateway auteur for young, especially, male cinephiles – his films have clear signs of authorship, share themes that are attractively grand and pessimistic and combine the thrills of pulp genre cinema with art cinema's stylistic flair and sense of a meticulously controlled authorial universe:

> With a share in both popular and elite culture, the figure of Kubrick-as-auteur proves an especially 'safe' choice of filmmaker for young film buffs to idolize in cultish ways, helping to bridge the gap between those differing economic and cultural strata in the film buff's move from low/mass tastes to the high/elite tastes associated with a higher educational and/or economic level and a wider knowledge of world film. (David Church, 'The 'Cult' of Kubrick, *Offscreen.com* 10, no. 5 (2006), online: http://www.offscreen.com/index.php/phile/essays/ cult_kubrick/P1/ (accessed 11 September 2006)

Moreover, as Thomas Leitch remarks, Kubrick's auteurist persona as it developed in the 1960s of 'the last solitary romantic artist who embraced the technology of cinema only to recoil from its chilling institutional implications' was also 'perfectly calculated to appeal to the emerging academic field of film studies' (Thomas Leitch, *Film Adaptation and Its Discontents: From Gone with the Wind to The Passion of the Christ* (Baltimore, MD: The Johns Hopkins University Press, 2007), 244). In practical terms, as an academic cultist, this makes it difficult for me to frame *2001* as anything else than a Kubrick film, with 'Kubrick' standing for a meta-frame of repetitions, self-references, echoes and thematic elaborations that confers retrospective coherence on his body of work. Clarke, unfortunately, interferes with that meta-frame. My concern for, and even protectiveness of, *2001* may be idiosyncratic, but it is common enough in relation to adaptations generally. Viewers who care deeply about a novel care too about how faithfully and respectfully it is adapted, just as fans and cultists care about how the films they love are treated (or in the case of *Star Wars* mistreated) when they are restored, rereleased and re-edited. As I argued in Chapter 4, adaptation studies could learn a great deal from cult and fan studies about the importance of audiences' emotional investment not only in texts but also in the relationships between them, and how such bonds of caring are structured over time.

33 Barbara Klinger, 'Becoming Cult: *The Big Lebowski*, Replay Culture and Male Fans', *Screen* 51, no. 1 (2010): 3.

34 Matt Hills argues that films, especially blockbusters, are characterized by 'intertextual stretching across culture' so that spectators 'become caught up in intertextual networks determined by marketing concerns' in Matt Hills, '*Star Wars* in Fandom, Film Theory, and the Museum: The Cultural Status of the Cult Blockbuster', in *Movie Blockbusters*, ed. Julian Stringer (London and New York: Routledge, 2003), 180.

35 Jacques Derrida, *The Truth in Painting*, trans. Geoff Bennington and Ian McLeod (Chicago and London: University of Chicago Press, 1987), 54.

36 See Taylor, *Artists in the Audience*, 131–4, for a discussion of the film's reception in those terms by 'younger highbrow critics' such as Annette Michelson, who 'positing the film as *essentially* cinematic … and the cinematic medium as essentially phenomenological' (133) could appropriate it as 'nothing less than the *ultimate* film' (132). Michelson's article, to which Taylor refers, is 'Bodies in Space: Film as "Carnal Knowledge"', *Artforum* 7, no. 6 (1969): 54–63.

37 Fredric Jameson, 'History and the Death Wish: *Zardoz* as Open Form', *Jump Cut*, 3 (1974): 5–8, online: http://www.ejumpcut.org/archive/onlinessays/JC03folder/ZardozJameson.html (accessed 6 June 2011).

38 Leitch, *Film Adaptation*, 240.

39 The sequels, all written solely by Clarke, are *2010: Odyssey Two* (London: Granada, 1982), *Odyssey Three* (London: Grafton, 1988), and *3001: The Final Odyssey* (London: HarperCollins, 1997).

40 Clarke, *2001*, 193.

41 Ibid., 15.

42 Gelmis, 'The Film Director', 90.

43 Peter Nicholls, quoted in Brooks Landon, *The Aesthetics of Ambivalence: Rethinking Science Fiction Film in the Age of Electronic (Re)production* (Westport, CT and London: Greenwood Press, 1992), 4. Landon offers a comprehensive discussion of the inadequacy of this dismissal.

44 Fredric Jameson, 'Afterword: Adaptation as a Philosophical Problem', in *True to the Spirit: Film Adaptation and the Question of Fidelity*, ed. Colin MacCabe, Kathleen Murray and Rick Warner (New York: Oxford University Press, 2011), 232.

Chapter 9

1 Kevin Jackson (ed.), *Schrader on Schrader* (London: Faber and Faber, 1990), 189.

2 Richard Dawkins, *The God Delusion* (London: Bantam, 2006). The book is dedicated to Douglas Adams, who, in the cult radio series, *The Hitchhiker's Guide the Galaxy* (1978), came up with the most succinct and Pythonesque answer to the 'ultimate question of life, the universe and everything': 42. Fans have debated ever since whether Adams's atheistic joke about the futility of searching for answers to insoluble questions has a deeper significance.

3 On the one hand, there is the field of philosophy and film, which explores fundamental questions about the medium; on the other, more popular books that explore philosophical issues through analysing movies. The former is represented

by Paisley Livingstone and Carl Plantiga (eds), *The Routledge Companion to Philosophy and Film* (London and New York: Routledge, 2011); the latter, more relevant to our modest efforts in this chapter, by David Kyle Johnson (ed.), Inception *and Philosophy: Because It's Never Just a Dream* (Chichester: John Wiley & Sons, 2011); Peter S. Fosl (ed.), The Big Lebowski *and Philosophy: Keeping Your Mind Limber with Abiding Philosophy* (Chichester: John Wiley & Sons, 2012); and Timothy Shanahan, *Philosophy and* Blade Runner (London: Palgrave Macmillan, 2014). The books speak to a powerful desire in modern culture for some answers.

4   Laura Mulvey, 'Visual Pleasure and Narrative Cinema', *Screen* 16, no. 3 (1975): 6–18.

5   On the relation between cult and religion, see Ernest Mathijs and Jamie Sexton, *Cult Cinema* (Chichester: Wiley-Blackwell, 2011), 131–41. They conclude that

> Film cults, like other forms of cultism, try to celebrate the breaking free of social restraints by imagining a life unbound, untamed, and untimed that would provide direct knowledge of all existence. ... In that sense, the link between religion and cinema cultism ... pertains to an experience in which co-occur simultaneously the small details of one movie, and an impression of the breeze of the bigger scope of all movies, all of culture, all of human existence. (141)

See also, in relation to the field of cinema and religion, John C. Lyden, *Film as Religion: Myths, Morals, and Rituals* (New York and London: New York University Press, 2003).

6   A more expansive discussion of this is I. Q. Hunter, 'Trash Horror and the Cult of the Bad Film', in *A Companion to the Horror Film*, ed. Harry Benshoff (Chichester: Wiley-Blackwell, 2014), 483–500.

7   One is, however, mindful of Mark Duffett's droll aside that autoethnographies 'tend to be pursued' by 'senior scholars (who, perhaps, have more experience at interpreting their lives in relation to theory, or, more cynically, are too busy to do wider research but still likely to get published)'. *Understanding Fandom: An Introduction to the Study of Media Fan Culture* (New York and London: Bloomsbury, 2013), 309. Point taken.

8   Terry Eagleton, *The Meaning of Life* (Oxford: Oxford University Press, 2007). Eagleton does mention the Python film but is under the peculiar misapprehension that it is four minutes long; perhaps he confused it with the short film, *The Crimson Permanent Assurance* (1983), which preceded it in cinemas (53). Wayne Omura, *Movies and the Meaning of Life: The Most Profound Films in Cinematic History* (Winter Park: Bauu Press, 2011).

9   Fuat Ulus, *Movie Therapy, Moving Therapy! The Healing Power of Film Clips in the Therapeutic Settings* (Victoria, B.C.: Trafford, 2003), n.p.

10 Bernie Wooder, *Movie Therapy: How It Changes Lives* (Ontario: Rideau Lakes Publishing, 2008).

11 Wooder, *Movie Therapy*, xv.

12 Jenny Hartley, *Reading Groups* (Oxford: Oxford University Press, 2001), 135.

13 Jackie Stacey, *Stargazing: Hollywood Cinema and Female Spectatorship* (London: Routledge, 1994), 145.

14 Mark Williams and Danny Penman, *Mindfulness: A Practical Guide to Finding Peace in a Frantic World* (London: Piatkus, 2011), 35.

15 For an exploration, from a Jungian perspective, of the value of mindfulness to understanding the experience, both bodily and intellectual, of cinema, see Luke Hockley, *Somatic Cinema: The Relationship Between Body and Screen – a Jungian Perspective* (London and New York: Routledge, 2013), 70–87. He argues that 'the experience of the cinema can stimulate an affective reaction in the viewer that is personally meaningful ... to the extent that the "intended" meaning of the film is overridden by the new personal meaning that has been found' (70). You don't need to buy into his Jungianism to find useful his idea that 'adopting a mindful approach to the body's emotional responses can help to reveal the unconscious psychological processes which are integral to the cinematic experience' (85). The potential of film as a tool for self-analysis and reinvention in relation to the new science of happiness or 'hedonics' is one of the more stimulating possibilities for expanding film studies and integrating it with mindfulness.

16 Andrei Tarkovsky, quoted in Ian Christie, 'Against Interpretation: An Interview with Andrei Tarkovksy (1981)', in *Andrei Tarkovsky: Interviews*, ed. John Gianvito (Jackson: University of Mississippi Press, 2006), 69.

17 Nancy Peske and Beverly West, *Advanced Cinematherapy: The Girl's Guide to Finding Happiness One Movie at a Time* (New York: Dell, 2002).

18 Peske and West, *Advanced Cinematherapy*, 7.

19 Deborah Yaffe, *Among the Janeites: A Journey Through the World of Jane Austen Fandom* (New York and Boston: Mariner Books, 2013), 150.

20 Ulus, *Movie Therapy*, n.p.

21 Richard Rorty, 'The Pragmatist's Progress', in *Interpretation and Overinterpretation*, ed. Stefan Collini, Umberto Eco with Richard Rorty, Jonathan Culler and Christine Brooke-Rose (Cambridge: Cambridge University Press, 1992), 106.

22 Annette Kuhn, *An Everyday Magic: Cinema and Cultural Memory* (London: I.B. Tauris, 2002), 11.

23 An obvious example is a film like *Gone With the Wind* (1939), where the emotional pull is equal to the repellent politics. Some viewers may need to do some self-searching and ideological acrobatics to rescue the film; as Lyden remarks, it 'is certainly a political apology for the South and an indirect defence of slavery and racism, but it is also often appropriated as a story with a message about how to survive adversity, quite apart from its political agenda' (*Film and Religion*, 5). An example close to my heart is *Taken* (2008), which I adore, but whose racism, which some critics have diagnosed, has to be bracketed off in order fully to enjoy the film's numerous pulpy delights.

24 Mathijs and Sexton, *Cult Cinema*, 140.

25 Hadley Freeman, *Life Moves Pretty Fast: The Lessons We Learned from Eighties Movies and Why We Don't Learn Them from Movies Any More* (London: Fourth Estate, 2015 EBook), loc. 267.

26 Richard Dyer, *Only Entertainment*, 2nd edn (London; New York: Routledge, 2002), 30–1. See also I. Q. Hunter, 'My My, How Did I Resist You?', in *Mamma Mia! Exploring the Movie Phenomenon*, ed. Louise Fitzgerald and Melanie Williams (London and New York: I B Tauris, 2012), 154–70.

27 Ernest Mathijs, 'Television and the Yuletide Cult', *Flow* 11, no. 5 (January 2010), online: http://flowtv.org/2010/01/television-and-the-yuletide-cult-ernest-mathijs-the-university-of-british-columbia/ (accessed 4 January 2014).

28 Soren McCarthy, *Cult Movies in Sixty Seconds* (London: Fusion Press, 2004), 96.

29 Wooder, *Movie Therapy*, 219. On practical Maudism, see http://xsmarkthespot. squarespace.com/blog/2012/12/15/maudism-and-me.html (accessed 12 December 2014). *Harold and Maude* has apparently also spawned the term 'Harolding', meaning 'hanging round cemeteries': Douglas Coupland, 'Harolding in West Vancouver', in *Postcards from the Dead*, ed. Coupland (London: Flamingo Books, 1996), 101–6.

30 Mark Kermode, *The Shawshank Redemption* (London: British Film Institute, 2003), 32. See also the documentary, *Shawshank: The Redeeming Feature* (2001).

31 Kermode, *The Shawshank Redemption*, 36. For a theologically focused discussion of the film's understanding of salvation, see Clive Marsh, *Cinema and Sentiment: Film's Challenge to Theology* (Milton Keynes: Paternoster Press, 2004), 45–59.

32 Margaret Heidenry, 'The Little Known Story of How *The Shawshank Redemption* Became One of the Most Beloved Films of All Time', *Vanity Fair*, 22 September 2014, online: http://www.vanityfair.com/vf-hollywood/2014/09/shawshank-redemption-anniversary-story (accessed 15 December 2014).

33 Nicholas Abercrombie and Brian Longhurst, *Audiences* (London: SAGE, 1998), 94.

34 http://www.telegraph.co.uk/news/celebritynews/12048428/Jedi-church-says-new-Star-Wars-film-leading-to-boom-in-followers.html.

35 Barbara Klinger, 'Becoming Cult: *The Big Lebowski*, Replay Culture and Male Fans', *Screen* 51, no. 1 (2010): 4.

36 Dudeist guides to life include, Oliver Benjamin, *Lebowski 101: Limber-Minded Investigations into the Greatest Story Ever Blathered* (Abide University Press, 2013); Oliver Benjamin and Dwayne Eutsey, *The Abide Guide: Living Like Lebowski* (Berkeley: Ulysses Press, 2011); and The Church of the Latter-Day Dude, *The Dude De Ching: A Dudeist Interpretation of the Tao Te Ching* (Create Space Independent Publishing Platform, 2010). Jeff Bridges and Bernie Glassman, *The Dude and the Zen Master* (New York: Penguin, 2012), is a dialogue between Bridges and a Zen Buddhist *Roshi* that draws parallels between the Dude's easy-going acceptance of life and Buddhist precepts.

37 Klinger, 'Becoming Cult', 18.

38 Matthew K. Douglass and Jerry L. Walls, ' "Takin" "Er Easy for All Us Sinners" ', in *The Philosophy of the Coen Brothers*, ed. Mark T. Conard, Updated Edn (Lexington: University Press of Kentucky, 2012), 149.

39 The Church of the Latter-Day Dude, *The Dude De Ching*, 9.

40 See Nathan Abrams, *The New Jew in Film: Exploring Jewishness and Judaism in Contemporary Cinema* (London: I.B. Tauris, 2012), 149–52.

41 Douglass and Walls, ' "Takin" "Er Easy" ', 157.

42 Ibid., 160.

43 Thomas S. Hibbs, 'The Human Comedy Perpetuates Itself: Nihilism and Comedy in Coen Neo-Noir', in *The Philosophy*, 35.

44 Justin Smith, *Withnail and Us: Cult Films and Film Cults in British Cinema* (London and New York: I.B. Tauris, 2010), 196.

45 Shaft is different, I think. The new assertiveness of the black hero in *Shaft* and the first films of the blaxploitation cycle, like *Sweet Sweetback's Baadasssss Song* and *Superfly* (1972), was part of a representational overhaul of black masculinity in cinema at odds with cult's nostalgic reintegration of fractured white masculinity. The focus on the latter in this chapter should not eclipse the role of cult films in renewing and inventing representations of marginalized groups, whether they are

positive representations or simply unusually complex ones. The emerging cult of
Mad Max: Fury Road (2015), like the cult of *Tank Girl* (1995), *Ginger Snaps* and
Heathers, is inextricable from the sheer exhilarating novelty, for female viewers
especially, of seeing women unbound from conventional depictions of femininity,
even if their legitimacy as 'feminist' is up for endless pleasurable debate. I haven't
said much about this because, first, it is so well covered elsewhere and, second,
my own tastes and circumstances draw me to other kinds of cult films, but it is
important to recognise the 'empowering' impact of these films making such new,
utopian representations visible and ripe for imaginative appropriation. I feel much
the same about Colin Firth's immaculately suited and booted retro-masculinity in
Kingsman: The Secret Service (2014).

46 See Steve Chibnall, *Get Carter* (London: I.B. Tauris, 2003).
47 Stanley Fish, *Surprised by Sin: The Reader in* Paradise Lost, 2nd edn (Princeton:
     Harvard University Press, 1998).
48 Smith, *Withnail and Us*, 205.
49 Patricia Mellencamp in Jon Lewis (ed.), *The End of Cinema As We Know It:
     American Film in the Nineties* (London: Pluto, 2001), 93. *The Matrix* would also
     respond well to Jungian interpretation as an allegory of the journey towards
     individuation. A reading along these lines of *Dark City* (1998), a key precursor
     of *The Matrix*, is provided by Jane Ryan, '*Dark City*', in *Jung & Film: Post-Jungian
     Takes on the Moving Image*, ed. Christopher Hauke and Ian Alister (Hove and
     Philadelphia: Brunner–Routledge, 2001), 95–109.
50 Adam Roberts, *Fredric Jameson* (London and New York: Routledge, 2000), 38.
51 On *The Matrix* as fascist films, see Jonah Goldberg, *Liberal Fascism: The Secret
     History of the Left from Mussolini to the Politics of Meaning* (London: Penguin,
     2009), 389.
52 Sean French, *The Terminator* (London: British Film Institute, 1996), 50.
53 The Wachowskis, quoted at http://www.castlebooks.com/myth.htm (accessed
     30 December 2015).
54 Although as Eve Kossofsky Sedgwick points out, such popular cynicism, 'though
     undoubtedly widespread, is only one among the heterogeneous, competing theories
     that constitute the mental ecology of most people'. Sedgwick, *Touching Feeling:
     Affect, Pedagogy, Performativity* (Durham: Duke University Press, 2003), 141.
55 Hartley, *Reading Groups*, 137.
56 Bret Easton Ellis, *American Psycho* (London: Pan, 1991), 69.
57 See Joan Hawkins, *Cutting Edge: Art-Horror and the Horrific Avant-Garde*
     (Minneapolis: University of Minnesota Press, 2000).
58 Jeffrey Sconce, 'Trashing the Academy: Taste, Excess and an Emerging Politics
     of Cinematic Style', *Screen* 36, no. 4 (1995): 371–93. My conception of the trash
     aesthete is more private, though, and more about the cultivation of individual taste
     than identifying with a subculture.
59 Mikita Brottman, *Offensive Films* (Nashville: Vanderbilt University Press, 2005), 9.
60 Julia Kristeva, *Powers of Horror: An Essay in Abjection*, trans. Leon S. Roudiez
     (New York: Columbia University Press, 1982).
61 Ernest Mathijs and Jamie Sexton, *Cult Cinema* (Chichester: Wiley-Blackwell,
     2011), 106.
62 Amittai F. Aviram, 'Postmodern Gay Dionysus: Dr. Frank N. Furter', *Journal of
     Popular Culture* 26, no. 3 (1992): 183–92.

63 I should emphasize that I am thinking mostly of male fans of trash – this is
    usually seen as a gendered taste. 'Female trash' is conventionally thought more
    likely to connote lowbrow romances and celebrity magazines rather than horror,
    though women are of course avid fans of the genre. The male 'paracinema' fan is
    archetypal, however, and the films he loves are, to put it mildly, often problematic
    in terms of gender representation.

64 The anecdote about Proust and the rats is drawn from Mary Ann Caws, *Marcel
    Proust* (New York, Woodstock and London: Duckworth, 2003), 44.

65 Walter Pater, *The Renaissance: Studies in Art and Poetry*, ed. Adam Phillips (1873;
    Oxford: Oxford University Press, 1986), 152.

66 Richard Rorty, *Contingency, Irony and Solidarity* (Cambridge: Cambridge
    University Press, 1989), xiv.

67 Mathijs and Sexton, *Cult Cinema*, 133.

68 Dean J. DeFino, *Faster, Pussycat! Kill! Kill!* (London and New York: Wallflower,
    2014), 71.

69 http://www.mindbodygreen.com/0-4164/4-Mindfulness-Lessons-From-Ferris-
    Bueller.html (accessed 30 December 2015).

70 Richard Seaford, *Dionysos* (London and New York: Routledge, 2006), 4.

71 Seaford, *Dionysos*, 5.

72 On *The Purple Rose of Cairo*'s 'point about the connection between freedom and
    textual interpretation', see Sam B. Girgus, *The Films of Woody Allen* (Cambridge:
    Cambridge University Press, 1993), 86.

73 This list is close to what Eagleton, as a Marxist, criticizes as a liberal, postmodern
    and highly individualistic approach to addressing the meaning of life: 'A pick-and-
    mix model is accordingly advanced. In designer style, each of us can take what
    we want from these various goods [happiness, pleasure, love, altruism] and blend
    them into a life uniquely appropriate for ourselves' (*The Meaning of Life*, 171).

74 Ulus, n.p.

75 Most of the film is not about Mickey, of course, but rather about the three sisters
    to which his narrative is comic counterpoint as he 'replicates the search for
    completeness and psychic unity that also motivates the other characters' (Girgus,
    The Films of Woody Allen, 101). I've focused here on Mickey's 'journey', a cure for
    hypochondria rather than life, but other viewers will naturally prefer to ponder and
    strike up conversations about the film's representation of how the sisters' changing
    relationship enables them to find solutions through female solidarity and love.

76 Andrei Tarkovsky, *Time Within Time: The Diaries 1970–1986* (1989), journal entry
    1 September 1970.

INDEX